"Dirty Dave" Rudabaugh, Billy the Kid's Most Feared Companion

First Edition

David G. Thomas

Mesilla Valley History Series, Vol 11

Copyright © 2023 by Doc45 Publishing

All Rights Reserved

This book, or parts thereof, may not be reproduced in any form,
including information storage and retrieval systems,
without explicit permission from Doc45 Publishing,
except for brief quotations included in articles and reviews.

Doc45 Publishing, Las Cruces, N. M.
books@doc45.com

To obtain books, visit:
doc45.com

YouTube Channel
youtube.com/c/Doc45Publications

Cover artwork by Dusan Arsenic.
Cover drawing by Kerolos Samy

ISBN 978-1-952580-20-8

00p

DOC45 PUBLISHING

Mesilla Valley History Series

La Posta – From the Founding of Mesilla, to Corn Exchange Hotel, to Billy the Kid Museum, to Famous Landmark – by David G. Thomas

Giovanni Maria de Agostini, Wonder of The Century – The Astonishing World Traveler Who Was A Hermit – by David G. Thomas

Screen with a Voice – A History of Moving Pictures in Las Cruces, New Mexico – by David G. Thomas

Billy the Kid's Grave – A History of the Wild West's Most Famous Death Marker – by David G. Thomas

Killing Garrett, The Wild West's Most Famous Lawman – Murder or Self-Defense? – by David G. Thomas

The Stolen Pinkerton Reports of Colonel Albert J. Fountain Investigation – David G. Thomas, Editor

The Trial of Billy the Kid – by David G. Thomas

The Frank W. Angel Report on the Death of John H. Tunstall – by David G. Thomas

Water in a Thirsty Land – by Ruth R. Ealy, David G. Thomas, Editor

"Dirty Dave" Rudabaugh, Billy the Kid's Most Feared Companion – by David G. Thomas

Mesilla Valley Reprints

When New Mexico Was Young – by Harry H. Bailey

Dave Rudabaugh, Border Ruffian – by F. Stanley, David G. Thomas, Editor

World War II History

Torpedo Squadron Four – A Cockpit View of World War II – by Gerald W. Thomas

Torpedo Squadron Four – Photo Supplement – by Gerald W. Thomas

Incident at Ple Tonan – An Imperial Japanese War Crime and the Fate of U.S. Navy Airmen in French Indochina – by David G. Thomas

Acknowledgments

For generously sharing his research on the gunfights at Coyote Springs and James Greathouse's roadhouse, I thank Josh Slatten of Billy the Kid's Historical Coalition. I also thank Josh for sharing other research and for showing me James Carlyle's long neglected grave location. I thank Doug Siddens for showing me the Coyote Springs gunfight site.

I thank Dan Aranda, Lanty Wylie, and Josh Slatten for proofing the manuscript and making corrections and suggestions.

Special thanks to the many who sought out source materials and provided invaluable help in my research efforts: Dennis Daily, Elizabeth Villa, and Teddie Moreno, Library Archives & Special Collections, NMSU; Evan Davies, Institute of Historical Survey Foundation; Rick Hendricks, New Mexico State Records Administrator; Josh Slatten, Billy the Kid's Historical Coalition; Tomas Jaehn and Portia Vescio, Center for Southwest Research and Special Collections, UNM; Elena Perez-Lizano and Dena Hunt, New Mexico State Records Center and Archives; Hannah Abelbeck and Caitlyn Carl, Palace of the Governors Photo Archives at New Mexico History Museum; Katie Gray, Archives and Cataloging Division, Thomas C. Donnelly Library, NMHU; Jori Johnson and Cassidy Nemick, Stephen H. Hart Research Center at History Colorado; Jonathan Frembling, Amon Carter Museum of American Art.

For permission to use the photograph of the Las Vegas jail placita, I thank Joseph A. Lordi.

Unattributed photos are from the author's collection.

Table of Contents

Acknowledgments iv
List of Images vii
1. Preface 1
2. "Dirty Dave" Rudabaugh 5
    Rudabaugh's Early Life 5
    Kinsley Train Robbery – January 27, 1878 7
    Rudabaugh Moves to Las Vegas – April, 1879 15
    Tecolote Stage Robbery – August 14, 1879 15
    Killing Joe Carson – January 22, 1880 16
    Lynching West, Dorsey, and Henry – February 8, 1880 16
    Killing Michael Kelliher – March 2, 1880 20
    Capturing Hoodoo Brown – March 8, 1880 25
    Webb Appeals Conviction – March 10, 1880 26
    Webb Declines Jail Escape Opportunity – April 2, 1880 26
    Fort Sumner Mail Robbery – October 16, 1880 28
    Webb Escapes Jail – November 11, 1880 29
    Webb and Davis Captured by Deputy Sheriff Garrett – November 25, 1880 35
    Carlyle Killed at Greathouse's Roadhouse – November 27, 1880 36
    Rudabaugh Captured with Billy the Kid – December 23, 1880 46
    Jailing Rudabaugh, Billy, Pickett, and Wilson – December 26, 1880 53
    Rudabaugh Confesses to Stage Robberies – December 28, 1880 56
    Billy, Rudabaugh, and Wilson Almost Escape – February 28, 1881 56
    Webb's Legal Troubles Recommence – January 6, 1881 57
    Rudabaugh Granted Change of Venue – March 19, 1881 59
    Rudabaugh Convicted of Killing Valdez – April 19, 1881 61
    Rudabaugh Given Death Sentence – April 20, 1880 78
    Reconstructing the Crime 81
    Analyzing Rudabaugh's Trial 84
    Rudabaugh Nearly Escapes – September 19, 1881 86
    Rudabaugh, Webb, and Five Others Escape – December 3, 1881 88
    Webb Dies of Smallpox – April 12, 1882 90
    Rudabaugh's Life on the Run – 1881 to 1886 91
    Rudabaugh Meets his Fate – February 18, 1886 94
    Rudabaugh's Obituary - March 23, 1886 95
    Rudabaugh's Death Photos 96
Appendix A – Trial Testimony – Territory vs David Rudabaugh, Murder 99
Appendix B – Billy Wilson's Counterfeiting Case 127
Appendix C – Timeline 135
Appendix D – Cast of Characters 143
Notes 161
Index 173

Doc 45

Buenas noches boys,
A social call no doubt –
Do we talk it over,
Or do we shoot it out?

I'm Doc 45,
Toughest man alive.
Hand over those golden bills
Or I'll dose you up with dirty leaden pills.

List of Images

1. Head of David Rudabaugh viii
2. 1875 Census, Spring Creek Township, Greenwood County, Kansas 6
3. William Barclay 'Bat" Masterson, 1879 photo 10
4. 1882 bird's eye view of Las Vegas, New Mexico 14
5. Layout of the Las Vegas courthouse complex in 1881 18
6. Las Vegas Plaza windmill, circa 1880 19
7. John Joshua Webb, 1881 photo 22
8. San Miguel County Sheriff Hilario Romero, circa 1880 27
9. Ad for Con Cosgrove's "Star" Mail Line, January 18, 1880 29
10. Patrick Floyd Jarvis Garrett, circa 1886 34
11. Coyote Springs Shelter, front view 38
12. Coyote Springs Shelter, back view 38
13. Site of Greathouse's roadhouse 40
14. James "Whiskey Jim" Carlyle's grave site 42
15. John Hurley, undated photo 43
16. Harry A. "Joe" Fowler, 1883 photo 45
17. Fort Sumner, based on the October, 1881, map by Charlie Foor 48
18. Manuel Silvestre Brazil, undated photo 50
19. Tom Pickett, undated photo 51
20. Rock House at Stinking Springs built by Alejandro Perea 52
21. Rock House at Stinking Springs, partially demolished 52
22. Rock House site today, 2020 photo 53
23. Las Vegas train station, photo circa 1880 54
24. Santa Fe jail, Water Street side, undated photo 54
25. John Joshua Webb, 1881 engraving 59
26. LeBaron Bradford Prince, undated photo 60
27. "Exhibit A," drawn by witness Jesus Maria Tafoya 65
28. Ad for Sumner House, March 18, 1881 66
29. Ad for Mendalhall Livery, July 2, 1880 66
30. Las Vegas Plaza, undated photo 68
31. Houghton's Hardware store, undated photo 74
32. Layout of the Las Vegas courthouse complex in 1881 80
33. 1883 Sanborn Fire Insurance map of Las Vegas, Old Town plaza 82
34. 1883 Sanborn Fire Insurance map of Las Vegas, jail complex 82
35. San Miguel County jail, cell doors, 1881 photo 83
36. Parral, Mexico, undated photo 90
37. Head of David Rudabaugh, February 18, 1886, photo by Albert W. Lohn 92
38. Rudabaugh's head on a pole, February 18, 1886, photo by Albert W. Lohn 93
39. Fred Milo Mazzulla, 1981 photo 94
40. Albert W. Lohn, 1919 photo 96
41. "Exhibit A," drawn by witness Jesus Maria Tafoya 106
42. Grave of David L. Anderson (Billy Wilson), 2008 photo 128
43. Manuela Herrera Bowdre, undated photo 144
44. Gravestone of Joseph Samuel Marion Edwards, undated photo 148
45. Gravestone of William Harrison Hudgens, 2013 photo 152

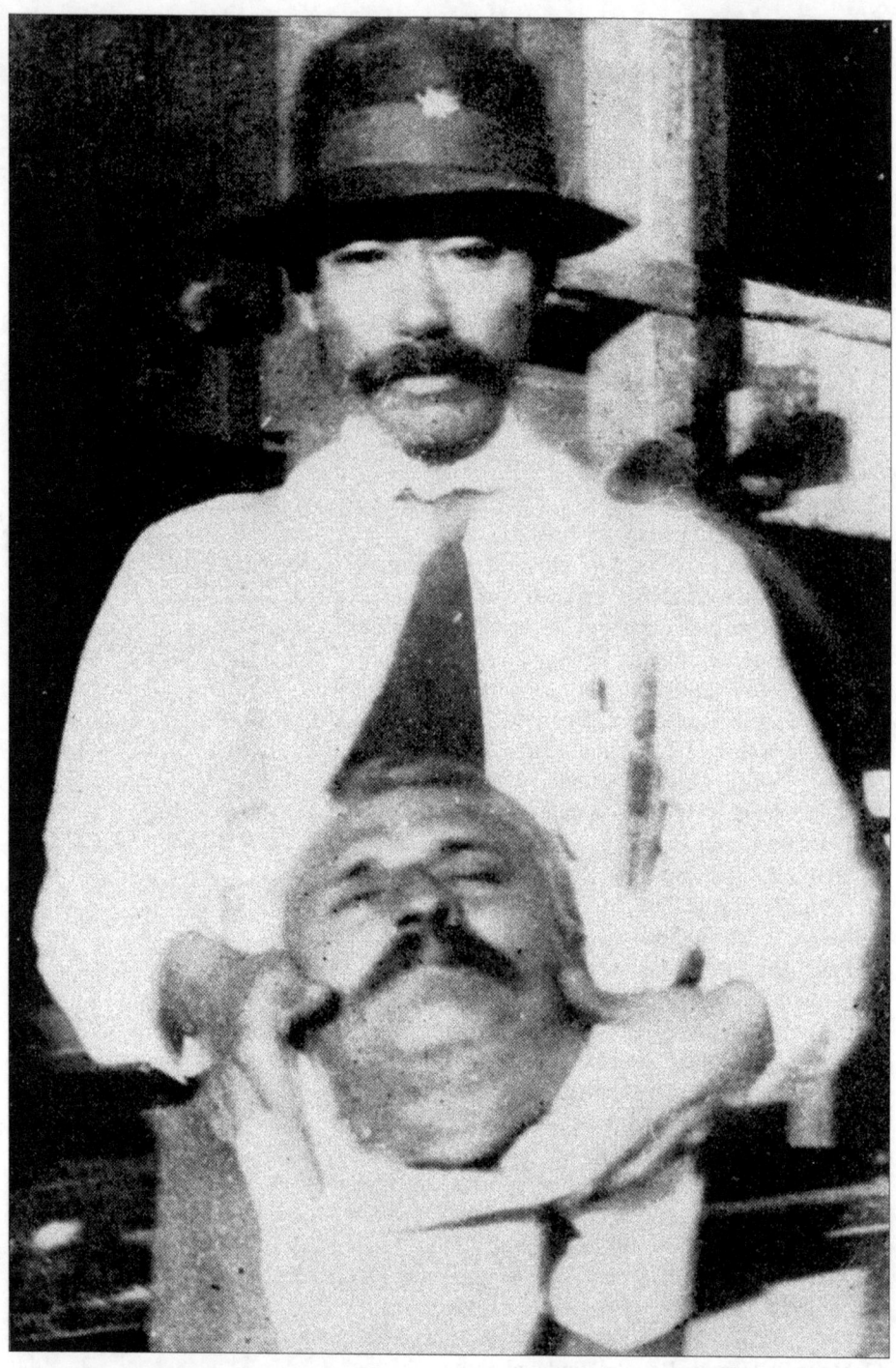

Head of David Rudabaugh, held by a Mexican Rurales (Federal policeman). February 18, 1886, photo by Albert W. Lohn. Courtesy Fred M. Mazzulla Collection, History Colorado-Denver Colorado.

1 | Preface

This book is about David "Dirty Dave" Rudabaugh, a man whose life is both obscure and wildly mythologized.

Rudabaugh's obscurity begins with the spelling of his surname. In the only U.S. census in which he appears, his name is spelled Radenbaugh.[1] His father, in his Civil War service record, spelled his name Rodenbaugh.[2] Rodebaugh is the spelling David uses in his first public document, his confession to an attempted train robbery.[3] Yet, throughout his life, he answered to Rudabaugh, and was usually referred to as such in newspaper accounts and legal documents. That is also how most historians have chosen to spell his name. For these reasons, Rudabaugh is the spelling adopted in this book.

"Dirty Dave," a sobriquet whose original source is unknown, was never applied to Rudabaugh by contemporaries. Its use is relatively recent. The primary source that may have suggested the label is probably this statement in the December 27, 1880, *Las Vegas Daily Optic*:

> *"[Rudabaugh was] dressed about the same as when in Las Vegas [nine months earlier], apparently not having made any raids upon clothing stores."* [4]

Adding to Rudabaugh's obscurity is the small number of articles written about him. The exception to this meager coverage is F. Stanley's *"David Rudabaugh, Border Ruffian,"* a full length book published in 1961. F. Stanley was the pen name of Father Stanley Francis Louis Crocchiola (1908-1996).[5]

Stanley's book provided new information on Rudabaugh, and it is still quoted today by historians. The book, however, with all of its pioneering advantages, is filled with errors, incorrect dates, inaccurate accounts of events, false suppositions and speculations, and even an entire chapter describing valiant adventures Rudabaugh never had.[6]

The mythologizing of Rudabaugh's life, which Stanley does, characterizes almost everything that has been written about Rudabaugh.

One of the oft-repeated myths is that in the early 1870s Rudabaugh was the leader of a gang of cattle rustlers in Texas – and he even killed a man! In fact, as of March 1, 1875, Rudabaugh was living at home on a farm with his 46-year old, single mother and three younger siblings, two brothers and a sister.[7]

The stories continue: that on leaving Texas, he became the boon companion of such famous Dodge-City personalities as Wyatt and Morgan Earp and John Henry "Doc" Holliday. Supposedly, he taught Doc Holliday how to fight with a gun (or knife in some accounts). There is no evidence for any of that, and it is not true.

Another myth is that Rudabaugh was a *"nasty, treacherous bully"* who *"stole and killed and brutalized people.... Dirty Dave would try anything, as long as it was crooked."* [8] Versions of this accusation appear in most writings about Rudabaugh – it is a false characterization. Rudabaugh did turn state's evidence against his fellow train robbers in the Kinsley train robbery, an act that can be called treacherous, but he was making the "best" choice in what in modern gaming theory is known as "the prisoner's dilemma." He was acting in his rational self-interest.

Rudabaugh was an exceptionally smart, well-educated man. His confession to the Kinsley train robbery is a masterpiece of exposition (pages 7-10).

A fictitious accusation leveled against Rudabaugh by virtually all sources is that he cold-bloodedly shot a Las Vegas, New Mexico, jailer during a visit to the city's jail. (Rudabaugh and his friend John J. Allen had gone to the jail to take newspapers and tobacco to their incarcerated friend, John J. Webb.)

The true account of jailer Antonio Lino Valdez's fatal shooting is presented for the first time in this book, based on the never-before-published trial transcript. The trial transcript, which is given in its entirety, contains the sworn testimony of the prosecution and defense witnesses. The unquestionable trial evidence shows that it was John J. Allen who shot the ill-fated jailer, not Rudabaugh.

Rudabaugh was convicted of the murder of Valdez based on the prosecution's argument that he had *"aided and abetted"* the killing, even though zero evidence was presented during the trial that Rudabaugh had in any way aided or abetted Allen's action. Rather, the evidence introduced showed that a drunken Allen impulsively shot Valdez without Rudabaugh having any foreknowledge of Allen's intention.

In the author's opinion, Rudabaugh should have been acquitted (see pages 84-86). Instead, Rudabaugh was convicted of Valdez's murder and sentenced to hang.

A widely accepted belief is that after escaping from jail, following his first degree murder conviction, Rudabaugh went to Arizona and there joined the opposition to the Earps, and even participated in the December 28, 1881, attempted assassination of Virgil Earp in Tombstone. Contemporaneous newspapers are the source for these assertions. The *Ford County Globe* printed a second-hand allegation, quoting a supposed statement by Wyatt Earp, that Rudabaugh was one of Virgil Earp's ambushers.[9] He was not there and he did not participate in that attempted killing.

Other period newspapers report that Rudabaugh was in Arizona after his propitious "jail delivery." Typical is this statement by the *Tombstone Democrat*:

> *"[Rudabaugh] escaped the jail at Las Vegas and fled to Arizona, where he 'rustled' with varying success for nearly two years, when he was driven out of the Apache country and struck for Old Mexico...."* [10]

Rudabaugh did not go to Arizona after escaping. He went directly to Mexico.

On February 18, 1886, Rudabaugh was killed by a Winchester rifle shot to the chest in Parral, Mexico, by a grocery man named José. Following his killing, Rudabaugh was decapitated by José. His head was placed on a pole and paraded around the Parral plaza. Present at Rudabaugh's killing and beheading was Albert W. Lohn, a nineteen-year-old, traveling, professional photographer. Lohn was earning his living by visiting the border towns of Mexico and the United States and peddling family portraits.

The photographs shown on pages vii and 92-93 were taken by Lohn. Lohn originally took four photographs, but he was forced to surrender the only two he printed to the governor of the Mexican State of Durango.[11] The surprising story of how Lohn's two unprinted negatives were acquired by an avid collector of Western memorabilia 57 years after they were taken is given on page 96. This account furnishes the provenance of the photos, showing that they really are photographs of Rudabaugh's severed head. The photos were first published in Stanley's *"David Rudabaugh, Border Ruffian."*

There are several photographs posted on the internet purporting to be photos of Rudabaugh. They are not! The only known, genuine photos of Rudabaugh are the ones of his decapitated head.

Rudabaugh's life story is mesmerizing. It is as adventurous as that of any Wild West figure. The events of his life include being both a wanted man and a lawman. They include a failed train robbery and two successful stage hold-ups. They include the aforementioned accusation of murder. While on the run from that charge, Rudabaugh teamed up with Billy the Kid. Rudabaugh and Billy had never met previously. Rudabaugh participated prominently in Billy's final gun battles with authorities.

Famously, Rudabaugh was captured along with Billy, Thomas Pickett, and Billy Wilson at Stinking Springs by Deputy Sheriff Pat Garrett and his posse. He was jailed with Billy and Wilson in Santa Fe, New Mexico, where they nearly engineered an ingenious escape.

When Billy was convicted in Mesilla, New Mexico, on the charge of murdering Sheriff William Brady in Lincoln, his lawyer, Colonel Albert J. Fountain, refused to appeal his case. (For details on Billy's trial, see *"The Trial of Billy the Kid,"* by the author.) That strikingly unfair, inexcusable decision was not mimicked by Rudabaugh's lawyers. After defending him ably in his murder trial, they immediately appealed his conviction to the New Mexico Territorial Supreme Court. The trial judge approved the appeal and stayed his death by hanging sentence.

Rudabaugh was in jail in Las Vegas waiting on his appeal to be heard by the Supreme Court when he escaped. Whereas Billy's escape from the courthouse jail in Lincoln only gained him 63 days[12] of extra life before he was killed in Pete Maxwell's bedroom at Fort Sumner by Pat Garrett, Rudabaugh's escape gained him 1,538 days of life – until his merciless killing and beheading by José in Parral, Mexico.

Rubabaugh's veritable life story is given in the next chapter. Appendix A gives the entire transcript of Rudabaugh's trial. Appendix B gives the details Billy Wilson's counterfeiting case. That charge is the reason that Wilson was riding with Billy the Kid and Rudabaugh when they were captured by Garrett at Stinking Springs. Appendix C gives the timeline of the events covered in this book. Appendix D gives biographies of 53 men and women who had important roles in Rudabaugh's life. Providing this information in an appendix makes it possible to avoid interrupting the flow of the narrative with repeated biographical asides. Following Appendix D are footnotes and an index. See the publisher's website doc45.com for a bibliography.

All places not otherwise identified are in New Mexico.

2 | "Dirty Dave" Rudabaugh

Rudabaugh's Early Life

David "Dirty Dave" Rudabaugh's early life is lamentably obscure. The only U.S. census in which he or his family appears is the March 1, 1875, Kansas State Census for Spring Creek Township, Greenwood County. That census is extremely sketchy (see page 6). The census lists only the first initial of each person's given name (!), age, sex, race, value of real estate (not filled in), value of personal property, place of birth, and where the person lived before settling in Kansas. Other fields on the form are not completed by the census taker.[1]

The census lists (name, age, sex, birthplace, previous residence):

A. Radenbaugh, 46, Female, Ohio, Iowa, (implied birth date, 1829)
D. Radenbaugh. 21, Male, Illinois, Iowa, (implied birth date, 1854)
Z. Radenbaugh, 19, Male, Ohio, Iowa, (implied birth date, 1856)
I. Radenbaugh, 15, Female, Ohio, Iowa, (implied birth date, 1860)
J. Radenbaugh, 14, Male, Ohio, Iowa, (implied birth date, 1861)

Father Crocchiola in his book *"David Rudabaugh, Border Ruffian"* identifies these persons as Anna, David, Zeth (may have been Zadek), Ida (possibly), and John. Where he obtained these given names is undocumented and thus unknown. They were all born in Ohio, except David, who was born in Illinois. They moved to Kansas from Iowa. A diligent search by the author of census returns, newspapers, and military records produced no further record of Rudabaugh's mother or siblings, with the single exception of an intriguing 1878 newspaper report that Rudabaugh's two brothers were living in Dodge City at the time of Rudabaugh's trial for the Kinsley train robbery.[2]

Father Crocchiola writes that Rudabaugh's father was James Redenbaugh and that he served in Company D, 103rd. Illinois Infantry during the Civil War. The Federal database of Civil War soldiers lists no James Redenbaugh in Company D. It does list a James W. Rodenbaugh in Company G, 103rd Illinois Infantry.[3] That is probably Rudabaugh's father. James Rodenbaugh's brief service record says he joined October 2, 1862, and was discharged January 15, 1863. He served as a musician. Father Crocchiola says he was killed just after his civil war service ended, but the author could find no confirmation of that assertion.[4]

In his sworn confession to the Kinsley train robbery, Rudabaugh gave his surname as Rodebaugh, so that was probably how the family spelled their name.[5] Some of the spellings that have been used by various sources are: Raudenbaugh, Radenbaugh, Radabaugh, Rudebaugh, Rudenbaugh, Radenbaugh, or Redenbaugh. The name means ship or helmbuilder in German. Because he is universally referred to as Rudabaugh by contemporary historians, that is the spelling used in this book.

From the March 1, 1875, Spring Creek Township Census, it is certain that Rudabaugh, his mother, and his three siblings were living in Kansas on that date. Unsourced tradition says that Rudabaugh was living in Dodge City within a year or so after that census and associating with historically-famous Dodge-City personalities such as Wyatt and Morgan Earp and John Henry "Doc" Holliday. Dodge City, Kansas, was founded in June or July of 1872.

6 ~ "Dirty Dave" Rudabaugh

1875 Census, Spring Creek Township, Greenwood County, Kansas, listing A. Radenbaugh and four children. Courtesy ancestry.com.

Kinsley Train Robbery – January 27, 1878

Rudabaugh first came to the attention of the newspaper-reading public – and veritable history – when he was identified as one of the armed men who attempted to rob the westbound train at Kinsley, Kansas, on January 27, 1878.

The six men who perpetrated the train robbery were: Rudabaugh, Michael "Big Mike" Roarke, Dan Dement, Edgar J. West, Thomas Gott, and J. D. Green.[6]

The details of the crime are given in Rudabaugh's confession, which he gave to the court after pleading guilty and turning state's evidence. This is an extraordinary statement and deserves to be reprinted in full. It shows that Rudabaugh possessed a superb memory. He gives moment-by-moment details: locations, distances between locations, times of events, what each robber was wearing, the colors of their horses, what weapons each man carried, which person did what, compass directions, remembered dialog, intentions, and even self-admitted mistakes. This exhaustive, straightforward chronicle suggests that Rudabaugh was unreservedly truthful.

Confession

"My name is David Rodebaugh; age 23; born in July [14], 1854; my home is in Greenwood County, near Eureka, Kansas."

"I met Roark [Roarke] and Thomas Gott in August last, and Dement about the first of October. I was acquainted with Roark and Dement about one year previous to this."

"I met J. D. Green in January, about the first, and West about the same time."

"About Wednesday January 16, 1878, we were all together on Wolf creek – Roark, Dan Dement, Ed. West, Thomas Gott and J. D. Green and myself. I think that Roark and Dement were the two that first broached the subject of attacking the train at Kinsley. It was agreed that the party should consist of the six named. This was the second attempt. The first attempt was to attack the train at Dodge City. This was to have been on or about the first of January, but failed on account of a snow storm. Green was not with us at that time. All the rest were. The first was planned on Beaver creek, about forty-five miles north of Wolf creek. This was planned about the time it was to have been carried into execution. The day after it was planned we started for Dodge. It would take us two days to get there, as it was sixty-five miles from where we planned the attack to Dodge City."

"Roark went west and Gott went to Dodge. I and Dement only went 25 miles. On account of a heavy snow storm, Dement and I went back. Roark and West went into Dodge, but did not stay, as they came right back."

"After this failure we returned and moved over to Wolf creek. We stayed at or near there till the second attempt, which was made on the morning of January 27, 1878. About five days before the attack we started. Mike Roark was leader. He rode an iron gray horse. Dan Dement rode a black horse, Gott rode a sorrel horse, Green rode a roan horse, West rode a bay horse and I rode a sorrel horse. West, Gott and I had rubber shoes. West got his shoes at Jones and Phimmer's ranch. Gott and myself got ours at Dodge City. Roark got Gott's rubber shoes at Dodge, I think at Rath's. These shoes were got a month before the attack, except

West's, which were got at Jones and Phimmers' just before we started. Roark got his gun, a (45) Sharp's, at Rath's sometime before. He got the pistol the time the first robbery was planned of Green; he had only one. Dan Dement had one gun, a Sharp's rifle, and one six-shooter, a Colt's 45. Don't know where he got them. Thomas Gott had a 44 Sharp's and no revolvers. He bought his gun from Roark. Green was armed with one 45 U.S. Springfield patent gun; he had two 45 Colt's pistol's [sic]; he bought one of the pistols at Zimmerman's in Dodge City, between the time of the first plan and before the second robbery; he and I went to Dodge together at this time."

"Ed. West was armed with one United States Springfield gun and one six shooter, Cole's [sic] 45; don't know where he got it. I was armed with one of Sharp's 40 calibre guns and had two Smith and Wesson pistols. We always had a wagon with us and left it on the Beaver and started in the evening. This is about eighty miles from Dodge City. We rode that night about twenty-five miles and camped again on Beaver. The camp is twenty miles about the trail where it crosses the Beaver. The next morning we went across the Cimarron, and that night camped at the head of Sand creek. The next day we went over to Buffalo creek on the Camp Supply road."

"The next day we left at noon. We met the Reynolds stage about five miles north of Bluff creek. We stopped that night on Mulberry, about five miles south of Pat Ryan's ranche. This was Friday, January 25, 1877 [1878]. The next day we went within ten miles of Kinsley. Got there just about dusk. It was in the sand hills, the other side of the river. We carried our food with us. We stayed there about four hours, crossed the river and went over to Kinsley; got to Kinsley about two hours before the western bound train was due. We went to a house near the railroad track and about half way between Kinsley and the water tank. Ed. West asked how far it was to Kinsley, and was told it was abut a mile and a half. We were all close together when the question was asked. He then asked how far it was to the tank, and was answered about the same distance. Two of the party got lost, Dement and West; I think Green fired a pistol when West was lost, and West fired his pistol when Dement was lost. After we left the house we went about half a mile up the railroad. We left the horses at the trestle, half a mile from the tank. Thomas Gott held the horses for the party."

"Ten miles from Kinsley we intended to take the eastbound train, but a snow storm came up and we changed the plan, and decided to take the westbound train, on account of not being able to get to Kinsley in time to take the eastbound train. We just got to the track as the eastbound train passed, and could not have stopped it if we wanted to. After the eastbound train passed we waited about an hour. Gott took charge of the horses and walked down a [on] foot to Kinsley. Roark gave the orders, assigning each man his position. Roark, Dement and I went inside the depot and talked to [Andrew] Kincaid. Roark and I went behind the railing. Dement stayed outside, and I don't think anybody was with him. Green and West was on the platform outside. Roark talked with Kincaid and I talked with him. Roark took Kincaid's pistol away from him and gave it to me and I gave it to Gott. Kincaid intended to shoot me with it. Roark says, 'I'll take that,' and Kincaid gave it to him. When Roark went in he asked Kincaid if he had any money. Kincaid told him he was too late; that the money was all sent on the other train, that had just passed, and pulled open the drawer that was in the counter and showed him there was none there. He offered us a lot of post cards which we did not take. Roark told him to unlock the safe. Kincaid said that Gardner had the key and he was over to the hotel. We all left the office together as the train was approaching. As we stepped outside a man came on the platform and Kincaid told him to go back. Says he, 'Blanchard, go back. These men have all got pistols.' Blanchard not understanding it came to where Kincaid was. By that time the train had got to us."

"West and Dement got on the engine. Roark, Green and me was to get into the express car. When the engine got opposite to us, Kincaid made a sudden jump landing in front of the cowcatcher, barely missing it, and got on the other side of the engine. Then West and Dement started for the engine, and Roark started for the express car. Green and Roark went to the door of the car, and I went to the rear of the baggage car at the front of the coach."

"Roark then tried to get into the express car and the shooting commenced. I took the conductor as he stepped off the coach. There were several men on the platform. I told him and the rest of them to go back. I knew it was the conductor from his lantern and the badge of his hat. The first shot was fired by the express messenger."

"I was to have got into the express car, with the rest. The train running beyond the platform upset our plan completely, as the height from the ground to the car door was so great. Roark could not get in. Roark and Green both ran to the car door to get in quick. Roark spoke to the messenger; don't know what he said. The first shot fired by the messenger came within three inches of hitting Green in the head. I was still on the platform of the depot. I fired four shots, at no one, but merely to keep any one from coming out of the cars. The train then started. Dement told me that he told the engineer to start the train. The object was to rob the train while in motion, and by the time we got to our horses. The signal, in case we got into the express car, was to be two shots. Instead of two there was about a dozen, which scared the men on the engine and let them know there was something wrong. After the train had run past, I walked up the track and overtook Dement and Roark. Green was ahead of us abut half way to the horses. West came in the last. We got to our horses and started for camp."

"We blacked our faces when we stopped ten miles from Kinsley to get supper. We used gunpowder and wet it, as it was easy to wash off. We were all blacked but Gott. We washed it off the next day, twenty miles from Kinsley, south of the river. We crossed the river and was in the Sand Hills by daylight. A party fired at us near where we got our horses, and as we rode off. Sunday night we camped on the prairie near a little lake on the flat. Gott's horse gave out Sunday morning. We left the horse, and hid the saddle in deep grass off of the trail about five miles from the river, in the Sand Hills, about fifty yards to the left of the trail we made. The next day we went to Bluff creek; staid there all night and the next morning separated. Roark and Dement, Green and Gott went towards camp on

William Barclay 'Bat' Masterson, 1879 photo. Wikipedia.

the Beaver. I have not seen any of the rest except West since. Tuesday night West and I staid at the head of Sand creek. Wednesday night we stopped at Lovell's camp and were arrested."

"Mike Roark is a man about six feet tall, sandy complection [sic], blue eyes, thirty years of age, sandy hair; wears a mostache [sic] and imperial; wore an old black, soft felt hat; wore a canvas overcoat, like mine, and canvas overalls; he wore rubbers; I think would weight about 190 pounds."

"Dan Dement is a man about five feet eight inches high, thirty years of age, weight abut 150 pounds, black hair and eyes; wears a black mustache, very heavy; thin face; dressed in canvas overalls and a coat like mine; he wore a black soft hat. He and Mike Roark have been buffalo hunters for the last two years. (Then follows a description of West, Green and Gott [not given])."

"(Signed:) David Rodebaugh"

"Emporia, Kansas, February 26, 1878" [7]

A few hours after the botched holdup, a posse led by ex-sheriff Robert McCause started after the robbers. Because deep snow hid the trail and dense fog limited visibility, they returned empty-handed, *"after riding 115 miles."* [8]. A second posse led by Kinsley Sheriff John Fuller also failed to find any trace of the robbers.[9] The *Kinsley Valley Republican* wrote about these failures:

"There was perhaps a blunder on the part of our officials and posse in not mounting in hot haste and pursuing the disappointed night riders immediately. Yet we cannot censure, for the surroundings offer a broad margin of justification. The attack was unexpected as an earthquake. The excitement ran high. It required time for men of nerve to realize the situation and act intelligently." [10]

On February 29, a third posse led by Ford County Sheriff William Barclay 'Bat' Masterson started out from Dodge City after the robbers. Masterson either had wonderful intuition or inside information, because rather than scour the wintry countryside in *"snow, slush, and sleet"* as the other posses had, he went directly to Harry Lovell's cattle camp, located about 55 miles from Dodge City. Masterson got to Lovell's about 5 pm January 30, in the midst of *"a terrible storm."* There he holed up and waited. The next afternoon, four men rode up to the camp. Two of the men were Rudabaugh and West.

> *"When within a few hundred yards of the camp, they discovered the sheriff's buggy and horses, and asked the other two who were cattlemen, what strange outfit that was. One of the cattlemen recognized a horse from Anderson's stable, and told them so. They hesitated; the boss herder telling them to come on, which they did, when Webb, one of the sheriff's men, went out to meet them, and told them he was on his way to George Anderson's. They came in with Webb, and were decoyed to a dugout where the sheriff and his party were concealed. Bat stood up behind a post, and came out from his concealment, and presenting his pistols, told the two outlaws to throw up their hands."* [11] [John Joshua Webb will later become Rudabaugh's good friend and fellow Las Vegas city constable.]

While escorting Rudabaugh and West back to Dodge City, Masterson encountered and arrested William Tilghman, believing he was one of the train robbers. Tilghman was later cleared of any involvement.[12]

From Dodge City the prisoners were taken to Kinsley by special train. At Kinsley, both Rudabaugh and West waived their right to a preliminary examination. Bail was set at $1,000 each, which neither man could make.[13]

Seventeen days later, on March 16, 1878, two more of the robbers, Gott and Green, were arrested. One of Masterson's deputies, doing his evening rounds, observed Gott at one of Dodge City's dance houses. He reported the sighting to Masterson, who took two deputies and went after the unwary fugitive. At Anderson's stable they learned that:

> *"...two men had just passed by on the south side of the stable and were making their way up the bottom. The officers proceeded in haste and were soon within sight of the robbers, who, observing they were being tracked, put out on a brisk run. The clear moonlight night afforded an easy chase, and the officers soon pounced upon their victims.... The robbers showed some resistance, but one of them found his revolver entangled in his clothing."*

> *"[Gott] stated that they had left three horses hitched to a tree about a mile west of the city. Subsequently the [officers] made a scour of the country and found two horses and a mule, all saddled, and strapped to each was a carbine and a Creedmore rifle."*

> *"There were evidently four in the party, the other two being the notorious characters Mike Roarke and one Lafeu. It is said that all four were in town during the evening... and little fearing a capture they boldly ventured to a less frequented part of the city."* [14]

Prior to their trial, the four captured robbers were jailed in Emporia, Kansas. There, they nearly escaped:

> *"...several inside window bars in the large cell at the jail were found sawed through and were repaired. The prisoners evidently expected to saw the outer bars through and escape the next night. After their plot was discovered, they surrendered the tool, a case knife made into a saw. None would confess as to who did the sawing."* [15]

On June 18, Rudabaugh, West, Gott, and Green were taken to Kinsley in a special train car to stand trial:

> *"The car was kept locked, and was placed at the rear of the train, and admission refused to all who had no business in the coach. But, thanks to Mr. Thatcher, your correspondent got in several times. At every station large crowds assembled to see the prisoners, and excitement ran high all over this portion of the State and along the line of the railroad. At Newton, it was deemed prudent to detach the car from the regular train and send it through on a special. Our train had six picked men with breech-loaders, and the special was likewise guarded, as it was feared an attempt at rescue might be made."* [16]

The trial opened June 19, 1878, in one room of the Cuddy Bank Building, which was serving as the Edwards County Courthouse. The charge against the four men was robbery in the first degree. West, Gott, and Green pleaded "not guilty." Rudabaugh, who had made a deal with the prosecution, pleaded "guilty." The prosecution called eleven witnesses. Rudabaugh was the second. When Rudabaugh took the stand, he testified to the events of the robbery in spectator-pleasing, exhaustive detail – a courtroom performance described as *"sensational"* by the *Kinsley Graphic*.[17] The prosecution rested its case that evening.[18]

When court opened the next morning, the lawyers for West, Gott, and Green negotiated a deal with the prosecution. In exchange for pleading guilty, the prosecution reduced the charge to second degree robbery. The penalty for first degree robbery was ten years in the state penitentiary at hard labor, whereas for second degree it was but five years (still at hard labor).[19] And with second, with good behavior credit, they could shorten their sentences to just fifteen months.[20]

The judge, before sentencing West, Gott, and Green to the prescribed five-year term, told the men that *"the most unpleasant duty he as an officer had to perform was that of passing sentence upon young men."* He added, *"The disposition in our society to encourage crime among our young men who are thrown on their own resources here in the West, and from whom kind word is withheld ofttimes"* is to be *"severely condemned."* He told them *"to despair not but then to resolve to lead different lives and be men...."* [21]

These words are soft, given the violent nature of the crime. One reason for the judge's genial attitude may have been the attendance of West's father at the trial He was described by one reporter as a *"white-haired man, leaning on his cane, standing up with bowed head."* [22] The city newspaper reported that West's father was a prominent politician in Aurora, Illinois, and had a net worth of over one hundred thousand dollars. One of West's sisters was a graduate of Oberlin College, Ohio, and the other of Vassar College, New York.[23] The judge, in his sentencing, asked the three men:

> *"'Had you a pleasant home?' Two answered 'Yes,' one 'no,' two have mothers living, one a father who was present, and all had brothers and sisters."* [24]

The person who answered "no" was Gott. Following their sentencing, the four men were placed on a special train to Leavenworth, Kansas. *"Rudabaugh was taken as far as Newton, where he was released."* [25] The others were delivered to the state penitentiary to begin their prison terms. Newton was the closest train stop to Spring Creek, where Rudabaugh's mother lived, so Rudabaugh was returning "home."

Sympathy for the train robbers apparently extended to Bat Masterson. He applied to the governor of Kansas for a pardon for Green just seven month and two weeks after Green's sentencing.[26]

On March 2, 1879, West wrote Sheriff Fuller.

"John Fuller, Esq"

"Dear Sir:"

"Perhaps you will be somewhat surprised to hear from me. I am doing as well as could be expected under present circumstances. I often think, as I have plenty of time for reflection, why I ever allowed myself to be led into such an undertaking or crime, while I have a home which but few in Kansas possess. Young men don't nowadays appreciate home, friends, etc., but drift from bad to worse as in my case. But when I am released, be it sooner or later, I shall go home and be a man among men, shall conduct myself so every one shall say I am a good citizen and respected by all. I have had enough of the West. Never shall this boy go West, as Greenley directed, again."

"Green works in the paint shop, Gott in the shoe shop, and Ed. is a blacksmith."

"Fuller, I never have received a single letter from anyone west of the Missouri river since I came here, consequently know nothing from your country. Where is or what became of D. Rudebaugh (sic)? Please let me know without fail. Also, do you know of the whereabouts of others, you know whom [Roarke and Dement]. You can rest easy I would help them to a suit of stripes far quicker now than you. How are things in Dodge City? Should you see Thatcher, give him my kindest regards. He has my best wishes – he used me like a gentleman at all times."

"I would like some papers, but no papers printed in Kansas, except the Farmer, allowed here. We are allowed to write once every month. Fuller please answer this letter as soon as convenient; which I hope will be very soon. And wishing you all success in the world, I remain yours respectfully in sorrow and mind of past life. Give respects to the gentlemen who came here with me. Answer sure."

"Edgar J. West" [27]

On August 13, 1878, Roarke and Dement, still uncaptured, and accomplices William Tillman and William Kersey robbed the south-bound train at Winthrop, Missouri, getting $5,100. In response, the Atchison, Topeka & Santa Fe Railroad hired Evander Light as a secret agent to find the robbers. While the four men were on the run, Kersey discovered that Dement was sleeping with his wife. In an act of revenge, he identified Dement and Roarke to the authorities. On October 20, 1878, at Brookville, Kansas, Light attempted to arrest Roarke and Dement. Roarke surrendered peacefully, but Dement, leaving his horse behind, bolted into the woods. Light chased after him. In the protracted encounter that followed, Dement at first pretended to surrender, but then he drew and fired two quick shots at Light. Light returned fire hitting Dement *"squarely in the eye,"* killing him.[28]

Roarke, after a change of venue from Kinsley, was convicted of robbery in the first degree and sentenced to ten years in the state penitentiary.[29] He was given an equal sentence for the Winthrop robbery.[30] Tillman apparently was never caught.

1882 bird's eye view drawing of Las Vegas, New Mexico, by J. J. Stone. The Gallinas River divides the town into West (New Town) and East (Old Town) sections. The insert shows the nearby resort Hot Springs. Courtesy Center for Southwest Research and Special Collections, UNM.

Rudabaugh Moves to Las Vegas - April, 1879

On March 18, 1879, the *Dodge City Globe* reported:

"Dave Rudebaugh (sic), who was arrested as one of the Kinsley train robbers, but turned State's evidence and was discharged, arrived in this city last week from Butler county, where he was a witness against Mike Roarke. Rudebaugh is looking for a job of work and intends to earn his living on the square." [31]

After a few short weeks in Dodge City, at the mandatory insistence of city authorities, Rudabaugh left Kansas for Las Vegas, New Mexico. There, shortly after his arrival, and in spite of his admitted criminal history, he was hired as a city constable by Chief Constable and Justice of the Peace Hoodoo Brown (Hyman Graham Neill). Rudabaugh's fellow constables were Joe W. Carson, John Joshua Webb, Thomas Pickett, and "Mysterious" Dave Mather.

Rudabaugh's public promise to make a living *"squarely"* did not survive the temptations of Las Vegas. (See footnote 32 for details on the founding of Las Vegas.)

Tecolote Stage Robbery – August 14, 1879

On August 14, 1879, three heavily armed men stopped and robbed the National Mail and Transportation Company's stage four miles south of Las Vegas, on the road to Santa Fe:

"The place selected by the gentlemen of the road was the second Puertocito [little port, i.e., little gateway] between Las Vegas and Tecolote. This is a narrow gorge through which the road winds its way. It is extremely rocky and the hills rise up abruptly on either hand. The coach from Santa Fe passes this point near sundown." [33]

The masked robbers:

"...suddenly appeared in the road and covered the driver with their pistols and ordered him to halt. They then ordered the passengers out of the coach and stood the men up in line.... The passengers were at first kept standing but were afterwards allowed to sit on a log.... The chief robber ordered one of his men, a small man, to examine the passengers. This latter rolled up his sleeves and went at it. Each passenger would stand up in turn and take his medicine."

"They allowed each passenger 30 cts. in change to get supper with. One passenger had 15 cts. in change and requested they make up the difference to him. They politely informed him that he might go to h—!" [34]

Rudabaugh and Joseph Martin were accused of the Tecolote robbery and arrested by the county sheriff. At their preliminary examination, the prosecuting attorney inexplicably failed to appear, leading to their charges being dropped.

"This case seems to be involved in a mystery. The prosecution failed to appear, and the evidence was of such a doubtful character that it was uncertain as to whether a case could have been made against them or not." [35]

On August 4, 1880, three innocent men, William Mullen and brothers Joseph and William Stokes, were convicted of this robbery and sentenced to two and a half years in prison.[36]

Sixteen months later Rudabaugh would confess that he, Joseph Martin, and Joe Carson committed the robbery. (See *"Rudabaugh Confesses to Stage Robberies"*) Following Rudabaugh's confession, Mullen, Joseph, and William were released. Less than a year later, Joseph would be lynched by an El Paso, Texas, mob for stealing horses.[37]

Killing Joe Carson – January 22, 1880

On January 22, 1880, four Texas Panhandle cowboys, Tom "Dutch" Henry, James West, William "Tom" Randall, and Jim "Loco" Dorsey, rode into Las Vegas with the intention of settling a score with Las Vegas Constable Joe Carson.[38] A week earlier, Cason had questioned the men about stealing a two-horse, top buggy for which there was an enticing $500 reward. He was driven off with harsh words.[39]

At about 11 pm, the four men entered Close and Patterson's late-night dance hall. They were belligerently drunk and heavily armed.

"[City Constable] Mather requested the men to leave their pistols with the barkeeper, which they refused to do, and commenced to abuse him. They then passed on into the next room, where Carson was reclining on a table, and commenced to abuse him, saying that no man could make them give up their pistols." [40]

Without warning, Henry drew his gun and shot Carson in the left arm, breaking it. In response, Mather pulled on Henry and fired. That led to furious firing between the Texans and the patrons in the dance hall:

"Immediately after firing of the second shot [by] Dave Mather, the lamps in the dance-hall were extinguished by the repeated concussions, and then followed a scene that beggars description. At least thirty shots were fired almost simultaneously, the leaden missiles of death flying as thick as hailstones around the crowded room." [41]

When the firing stopped and the lights were restored, Carson was dead and Randall was mortally wounded. Carson was found with *"eight bullet holes through body and arms and legs"* and Randall with bullet wounds in his *"hip, arm, stomach, and bowels."* [42]

The second cowboy, West, was *"shot through the lower bowels and breast."*

The other two Texans, Dorsey and Henry, escaped, although it was later discovered that Henry had taken a crippling bullet to the leg.

Mather had *"one bullet cut through his clothing, just grazing the flesh."* [43]

Lynching West, Dorsey, and Henry – February 8, 1880

A posse led by Hoodoo Brown consisting of Rudabaugh, Webb, Mather, and John "Dutchy" Schunderberger went after Dorsey and Henry. They were found and arrested at Juan Antonio Dominguez's place in Buena Vista, twenty-seven miles north of Las Vegas, thanks to a cooperating informant. Henry's gravely wounded leg had prevented the men from getting farther away.

The two men were brought to Las Vegas on February 6. In a preliminary examination that day, the presiding judge ruled there was *"plenty"* of evidence to hold Dorsey, Henry, and West for first degree murder. West, although gruesomely wounded, had been in jail since Carson's killing. (44)

During the course of the examination, it was learned that Dorsey's real name was Jim Dawson, Henry's real name was Thomas Jefferson House, and James West's real name was Anthony W. Lowe.

On February 8, a cold, blustery Sunday, at about 3 am, a crowd of as many as 50 men suddenly appeared outside the Las Vegas jail, determined to lynch the surviving killers of Carson. The town had been swirling with rumors of such an action all weekend. Spurred by the rumors, a *Las Vegas Gazette* reporter had visited the jail three hours earlier, at midnight, to see if there was any evidence of lynching preparations:

> *"All was quiet and no more persons on the street than usual at that time of night."* [45]

The lynching was exactly planned. The men, *"who came into town in a body,"* according to the *Gazette*, assembled in front of the jail and demanded the jail door keys from the three jailers inside, Benedito Duran, Dionicio Garcia, and Antonio Lino Valdez (more on Valdez later). When the jailers refused:

> *"[The lynchers] commenced to batter down the doors [marked A on the drawing on page 18].... [One jailer] proposed that he would stand behind the door and when it was opened he would slip out and run away with [the keys]. The other two objected to this for fear they would be killed unless the keys were found."* [46]

So the three jailers took refuge in the kitchen (see jail drawing page 18).

> *"The two outer doors leading to the placita were broken and smashed to splinters [marked B on the drawing]. They were of pine and although bolted and barred on the inside, they offered but slight resistance to the attacks of the lynch party."*

> *"When the crowd came and halioed [helloed] from the outside to open the door, Henry and Dorsey both exclaimed 'there are the lynchers.' They said nothing more, but Dorsey got up and put on his shoes. When the crowd came in and got the keys, they opened the door and three men came in. Henry stood up and asked, 'What do you want?' A man replied, 'We have come for you' and put the rope around his neck. He said 'All right I will go.' They then asked for Dorsey and he got up and said, 'Here I am.' They put the rope around his neck and took him out."*

> *"Two men then opened the cell where West was. They put the rope around his neck and he exclaimed, 'My God! I am suffering enough now, can't you let me alone.' Two more men came in and carried him out. He groaned bodily with pain from his wound."* [47]

The three men were brought to a large windmill in the center of the city plaza (page 19). West, who was unable to walk, was carried on a stretcher. He was quickly strung up. The lynchers were too impatient to go through the process of hanging Dorsey and Henry, so they were just put *"upon the platform [that] surrounded the well, and perforated with bullets."* [48]

> *"The shooting took place at about three o'clock. In five minutes a Gazette reporter was on the ground, but there was not a living soul on the plaza and nothing human but the bodies of James West swinging in the starlight could be*

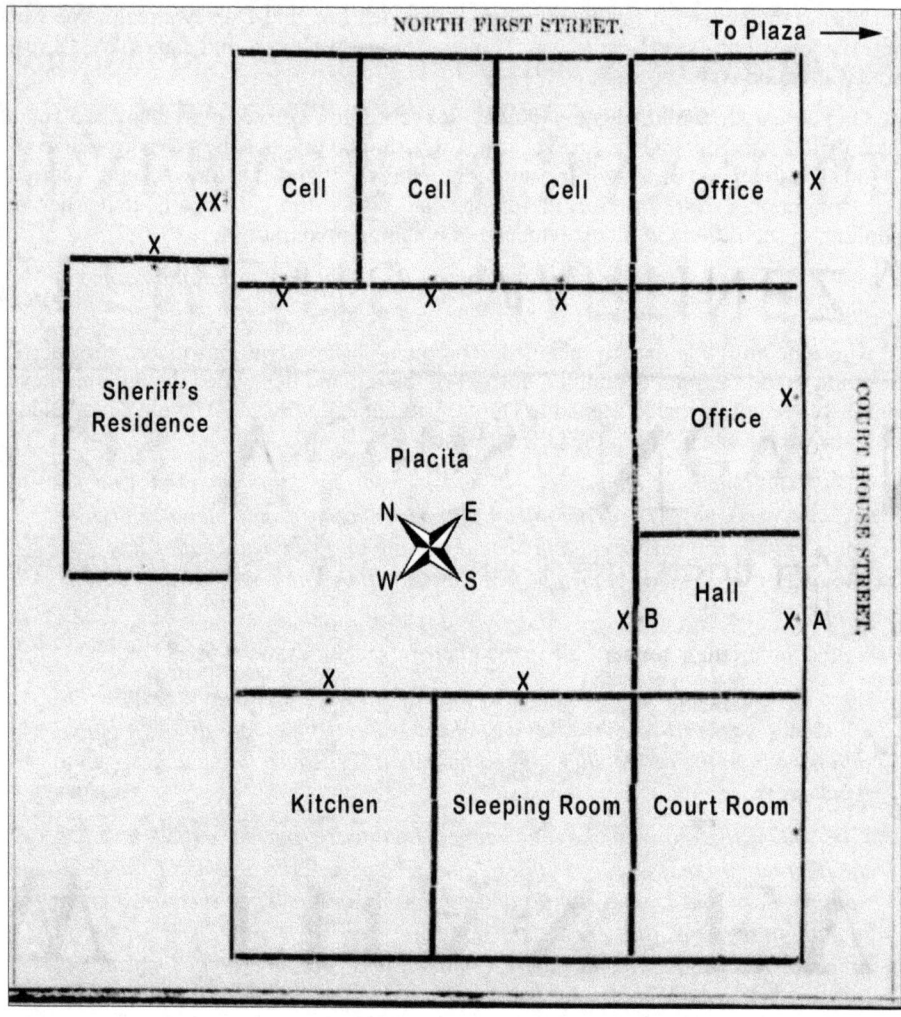

Drawing showing the layout of the Las Vegas courthouse complex in 1880, which contained the Sheriff's residence, jailers' quarters, courthouse, city offices, and the city jail. The complex was located in Old Town (West Las Vegas) one block northeast of the plaza (see also the Sanborn map page 82).

"X" marks doors. "XX" marks an outside exit for the left jail cell. (A) shows where the lynchers entered the complex. (B) shows where the lynchers broke into the placita.

The only entrances into the windowless jail cells were from the placita, with the single exception of the outside exit to the left cell. The cells had no windows.

Las Vegas Daily Gazette, December 4, 1881.

The Las Vegas Plaza windmill where James West was lynched and Jim Dorsey and Tom Henry were *"perforated with bullets,"* February 8, 1880. The well was dug in 1874 by prisoners. The windmill was torn down in 1882. Courtesy Palace of the Governors Photo Archives (NMHM/DCA), 014386.

seen. A latern [lantern] was procured and in company with others called out by the firing, the platform was examined and the bodies of Tom Henry and John Dorsey were found, the warm blood yet oozing from their unclosed wounds." [49]

The tradition in Las Vegas was to leave the bodies of lynched men hanging until noon the next day as an example to future murderers.[50]

The *Gazette*, in reporting the lynching to their readers, wrote that most townspeople agreed with the action, but wished the deed had been done somewhere outside of town. The *Santa Fe Weekly New Mexican* wrote:

"Las Vegas has had another canniballistic feast – cold man for breakfast was served up there last Sunday evening, in three courses." [51]

It is not known for certain if Rudabaugh was among the lynchers, but it is exceedingly likely, because he and Carson were good friends. It is also quite likely that Rudabaugh's fellow constables organized the lynching.

The day after West (Anthony Lowe) was captured, he received a letter from his aunt, Mary E. Lowe, in Leslie, Kansas. She was unaware that he was in jail charged with murder. She wrote, in part:

"What I ask of you is to be a good boy. Don't touch strong drink; don't drink anything stronger than coffee or tea, for the sake of your father and grandfather and mother also.... If you can, write soon." [52]

A reply to his aunt was found in West's pocket by the lynchers as they were taking him out to be hanged. After the deed was done, the letter was mailed to his aunt without being read.[53]

Killing Michael Kelliher – March 2, 1880

On March 2, 1880, Michael Kelliher was killed in the Goodlett and Roberts' Saloon in East Las Vegas (also known as "New Town").

The accounts of the killing conflicted markedly.

William Brickley, who was with Kelliher in the saloon when he was killed, gave this account: Kelliher and Brickley were driving three freighting teams to Las Vegas from Deadwood, South Dakota (Kelliher owned the teams). They arrived at Las Vegas on Sunday, February 29, and camped:

> "...just at the west edge of town. On the evening previous, Saturday evening, they camped this side of Fort Union where Galliher (Kelliher) took out his money and counted it. He carried his money in his pants pocket and it made quite a large roll. He had at that time $2,115.00." [54]

Kelliher intended to deposit some of the $2,115 in a bank in Las Vegas. He planned to use the money to buy cattle. On the day of his killing, their horses strayed off and Kelliher spent most of the day recovering them. As a result, it was sundown before the men could enter town for some much awaited revelry.

After drinking in several dance halls, where it was noted that Kelliher was paying for drinks from a large wad of money, they went to Goodlett and Roberts' Saloon to meet with a never identified acquaintance. Kelliher, according to Brickley:

> "...was leaning on the counter with his elbow when the officer came in from the rear of the saloon, ordered Galliher [sic] to hold up his hands and immediately fired." [55]

Brickley identified the officer who shot Kelliher as city constable John Joshua Webb.

The account of the killing as relayed to the newspaper by Webb's side was:

> "[At about 4 am,] three men, headed by Michael Killiher [Kelliher], entered Goodlett and Roberts' Saloon, all being intoxicated and heavily armed. They soon became very boisterous. Police officer Webb being present and fearing great trouble would arise, ordered them to depart. Killiher refused, exclaiming, 'I wont be disarmed.' He drew his pistol, and was just in the act of leveling the weapon, when Webb, taking in the situation at once, as quick as a wink pulled his pistol and instantly fired a ball into his assailant's breast. Killiher dropped to his side, but still showed fight. The officer fired twice more, balls lodging in the breast and head. Killiher dropped over on the floor and died without speaking." [56]

Most conveniently, the East Las Vegas coroner was Hoodoo Brown, who along with Rudabaugh and Dutchy, was in the saloon when the shooting happened. The coroner's jury, led by Hoodoo, met in the saloon over the bleeding and still-warm body and issued the following finding:

> "We, the jury duly sworn to enquire into the circumstances of the death of Michael Kelliher here lying dead before us, find that deceased came to his

death by pistol shots, fired with a Colt's revolver, loaded with powder and ball, on the morning of March 2nd, 1880 by J. J. Webb, in the town of East Las Vegas and territory of New Mexico. The said J. J. Webb, then and there being a peace officer, and that the said killing was justifiable and absolutely necessary under the circumstances. Signed by the jury." [57]

The killing would probably have ended with the jury's determination of justified killing if the following had not afterwards occurred:

"The next morning after the killing of Mike Kelliher in East Las Vegas, Mr. Neill [Hoodoo Brown] came over and presented himself before Mr. Chas. Blanchard, Probate Judge of this county, and requested that he (Neill) be appointed administrator of the effects of Kelliher. Neill stated that at the coroner's inquest which had just been held, some $1,090 had been found on the body of the deceased. Mr. Blanchard told the officious Justice that he would think about the matter and wanted to know who was to be his bondsman; Neill answered that bondsmen were really not necessary, more than as a mere form, as he himself had property, ample and sufficient to more than cover what the bonds would call for." [58]

Judge Blanchard took Hoodoo at his word and told the Clerk of the Probate Court (Dutchy Schunderberger) *"not to issue any bonds to Neill until further inquiries into the matter had been made,"* letting Hoodoo hold the money for the time being. Those inquiries quickly produced the awkward detail that Kelliher had had $1,950 on his person, not the $1,090 Hoodoo was claiming (evidently Kelliher had spent $165 in his carousing before his killing.) [59]

With this new information, Judge Blanchard ruled that Hoodoo needed to obtain bonds in the amount of $4,000:

"The clerk [Dutchy] was then directed to drop Neill a note, telling him the amount in which he would have to give bonds and that if he desired to be appointed administrator he would have to get good and responsible bonds." [60]

But Justice of the Peace, Chief Constable, and Coroner Hoodoo, accompanied by Clerk Dutchy, had already left Las Vegas by eastbound train – *"for parts unknown."* [61]

Hoodoo's fleeing, with some of Kelliher's money, led to questions about Kelliher's killing. The matter was put before a grand jury on March 4. After listening to witnesses, the grand jury issued a first degree murder indictment for Webb, stating that Webb *"feloniously, wilfully [willfully] and of his malice aforethought without the authority of law"* did shoot and mortally wound Kelliher. The wound was reported to be *"of the depth of three inches and of the breath of half an inch."* [62]

Webb was arrested and jailed by Deputy Sheriff Quinterio Romero.

Webb's murder trial opened March 10 (fast work!). Webb's defense attorney called three witnesses: J. W. Barney, William L. Goodlett, and Dave Mather. (The courthouse was attached to the jail – see drawing page 18.)

Barney testified that he visited nearly all the *"public houses"* every night and did so on the night of the killing. Outside one of the saloons, at about 11 pm, he encountered Kelliher, who was extremely intoxicated. Brickley was with Kelliher and was physically attempting to make Kelliher leave town and return to their camp. Kelliher was resisting, and as Barney passed the two men, Barney heard Kelliher say, *"There goes one of the s-n*

John Joshua Webb sitting in the placita of the Santa Fe jail. His right ankle is ironed. 1881 photo. Courtesy Special Collections and University Archives, NMHU.

of a b--hs now." Kelliher evidently took Barney for a city constable. Barney said he left the men and was already at home when the shooting occurred.[63]

Goodlett testified that he had lived in Las Vegas for three months, and that he operated a saloon facetiously *"known by the name of 'Health office.'"* Goodlett said that when Kelliher came into his saloon, he was boisterously drunk:

> *"[The] deceased called for several drinks; his principal attention seemed to be toward Mr. Webb.... I was watching Killiher [sic]; Webb stepped up to the counter to take a drink, Killiher insisted that the officers drink at his expense; I walked back to the back door and the bar keeper gave me a significant look and put his hand down to where a pistol is usually carried; I knew what he meant; Webb passed [went] out at the back door and soon came back, passed me at the door and said to me, 'Bill, watch them other men, I am going to disarm that man;' I fixed my eyes on Brickley; heard Webb say, 'I want that gun;' I saw Killiher jump back and put his hands on his pistol; Killiher had a large pistol, 41 or 45 caliber, Colt's pattern; Webb was acting as a police officer at the time."* [64]

Fellow City Constable Mather was called as a character witness and testified that he had known Webb for six years and he was a truthful man. He said he did not see the shooting.

Webb then took the stand in his own defense:

> *"I was appointed by H. G. Neill as a police officer for East Las Vegas in January of this year; I continued to act as a police officer until a day or two after the shooting; I was present at the killing of Killiher [and] I saw the two men in the dance hall in the evening; took them for cow men; saw them several times after that; they came into Goodlett & Roberts' Saloon, and treated; deceased eyed me very closely; I got suspicious of them; Goodlett told me that that man was eyeing me very closely; bar tender motioned to me; went to him and he said, 'you want to look out for that fellow.'"*

> *"I then went out at [the] back door, but came back soon and told Goodlett to watch the other man that I was going to disarm that man; I then told him to throw up his hands, that I wanted his gun, he jumped back and put his hand on his pistol and said, 'I won't be disarmed, everything goes.' I then shot him twice, he fell; I then went out and when I came back the coroner's jury had assembled."*

> *"I was acting as a police officer when I demanded his gun; I killed Killiher to save my life; I was told that he was going to kill me and his actions led me to believe that he would; I thought Killiher a dangerous man, [that] is the reason that I wished to disarm him."* [65]

The prosecution called Brickley, who testified that he was with Kelliher all night and that Kelliher never made any threats, especially not the statement that Barney recounted in his testimony. He said Kelliher did not draw his gun on Webb; that Webb shot Kelliher without warning and without provocation. He said he was taken to another room after the killing, so he was not present when Kelliher's money was taken.[66]

The prosecution rested without calling any other witnesses.

Goodlett was recalled by the defense as a rebuttal witness. He testified that he had previously been sheriff of Colfax County, New Mexico, for three years; that he knew Webb well; that Webb kept his saloon for him sometimes when he was busy elsewhere. He said that, although Webb, Hoodoo, Dutchy, and their friends were often in his saloon, they were not *"loafing,"* as there were no chairs in the saloon room. He admitted that he had contributed some money toward Webb's defense.[67]

John Patton was called as a defense rebuttal witness:

"I was standing at the bar when the deceased was killed; Killiher ordered to pay for the drinks of Webb and myself; I don't know what occurred after the first shot was fired as I ran out; when I came back all was confusion; I did not see who fired the shot nor what Killiher done." [68]

W. H. Bennett was called as a defense rebuttal witness and testified that he had known Webb for two years and during the night of the killing he (Webb) was acting as a policeman. He said that he ran into Brickley in Houghton's hardware store the morning after the killing. While the two were there, Webb came in. When Webb left, he (Bennett) got into a conversation with Brickley. During that conversation, he told Brickley that the man who had just left was Webb:

"[Brickley] seemed surprised; I said, 'that's the man that did the killing;' He said, 'Is it? I thought the man that did it had black whiskers all over his face." [69]

Charles Jones was called as a defense rebuttal witness:

"I know Mr. Webb; I first met him at Las Vegas on August 27th, 1879; I have always seen him here when I visited this place; he was a deputy United States Marshall; since that time I have known him as exercising the functions of police officer at East Las Vegas." [70]

The defense then called Detwiler, Willard, and Sebben. Each testified that as long as they had known Webb, he had been an East Las Vegas policeman.

However:

"Hoodoo's official books were then produced [by the prosecution] in court and examined, but no trace of a record could be found indicating that J. J. Webb had ever been appointed as an officer." [71]

The case went to the jury, which returned a verdict of murder in the first degree. The obligatory punishment under New Mexico Territorial Law for first degree murder was hanging.[72] Consequently, Webb was sentenced by the judge to be *"hanged by the neck until he be dead."* The date of the hanging was set for Friday, April 9, 1880.

"Great excitement [prevailed] in town over the sentence; many approving of it, and as many thinking it cruel and unjust. Webb appears haggard and ten years older than he was a week ago." [73]

The jury apparently made its decision primarily on the fact that Webb appeared to not be an official policeman, even though he had been recognized as such by the public for three months. If he was not legitimately a policeman, he did not have the legal right to disarm Kelliher, much less shoot him. If Hoodoo had been in town, he would have testified that he had appointed Webb a policeman, but had neglected to record it in his book. (The court would later accept that Webb was a legally-appointed policeman at the time of the killing.) If it was not for the introduction of this completely false "fact," and the appearance of a conspiracty to kill Kelliher suggested by Hoodoo's fleeing, Webb would almost certainly have been acquitted.

A defense fund was quickly raised for Webb, with contributions from as far away as Dodge City, where Webb lived before he moved to Las Vegas. Forty-two people from Dodge City added $191.50 to the defense fund. Bat Masterson was one of the three top contributors, giving twenty dollars.[74]

Capturing Hoodoo Brown – March 8, 1880

Two days before Webb was tried and convicted, news reached Las Vegas that Hoodoo had been captured at Parsons, Kansas (630 miles due west by train). He was found registered at the Belmont House under the name Henry Graham. The sheriff of Parsons had received a telegram notifying him that there was a $300 reward for arresting Hoodoo. A malevolent desire to collect that reward is the explanation for the very strange actions that followed Hoodoo's arrest:

> "The prisoner was taken to the city jail and searched, after which he was taken to the Abbott house and placed in irons.... An attempt was made to convince our citizens that the prisoner was taken away on the 2 p.m. train... remarkable maneuvers were executed for that purpose but to no effect."

> "Long after the train had departed [this reporter] saw the officers conducting the prisoner, who was hand cuffed, through the back alleys to the hotel. We made great efforts to obtain an interview, but were repulsed and the Marshal refused to converse with us on the plea of earnest business. Despite all of these peculiar efforts to smuggle the facts the man let his condition be known to some of our prominent attorneys, and about 11 o'clock last night officers Mason and Abbott were served with a writ of Habeas Corpus ['show me the body']."[75]

Habeas Corpus required the authorities to show legal cause as to why they were holding Hoodoo, which evidently they were unable to do, so Hoodoo was released the next day.

In another peculiar twist, shortly after Hoodoo was arrested, he was joined by a woman who turned out to be Mrs. Joe Carson, the not-so-grieving widow of murdered Las Vegas Constable Joe Carson. Mrs. Carson had Joe's body with her – she was taking it to be buried in Carson's home town of Houston, Texas.

> "The meeting between the pair, after [Hoodoo] was arrested, is said to have been affecting in the extreme and rather more affectionate than would be expected under the circumstances."

> "His female companion went south on the M. K. & T [Missouri, Kansas & Texas railroad]. Tuesday noon, he starting several hours ahead on horseback [probably bought with some of Kelliher's money]. They will doubtless meet again further south."[76]

Whether Hoodoo later joined Mrs. Carson is unknown, although several sources speculate that he did, and that she became his common law wife. What is known, is that Hoodoo went to Mexico and began living under the name Henry Graham, and later, "Santiago" Graham. He died November 13, 1910, in Torreón, Mexico, where he had gone for his health. In an obituary, published in the *Lexington Intelligencer*, it is stated that:

> *"For the past twenty years he has filled many positions of trust and responsibility in the employ of Mr. Chas. Thornton of Pitsburg [sic], Pa., and Mr. Jno. McDonald of New York in the building of railroads in Mexico, Guatamola [sic] and Ecuador. His intimate knowledge of the language and habits of Mexico made him many admirers."* [77]

Hoodoo's body was returned to and buried in Machpelah Cemetery in Lexington, Missouri, by his brother.

Webb Appeals Conviction – March 10, 1880

Immediately after Webb's conviction, his lawyers filed a request for a new trial. They offered a number of perfunctory grounds, such as that Webb's arrest warrant was flawed and the judge improperly denied Webb's change of venue request, but two appeal grounds had determinative weight.

In the prosecution's closing argument, the judge permitted the prosecutor to tell the jury that Webb had participated in the illegal hanging of three men some weeks earlier. This was a reference to the lynching of James West, Tom Henry, and Jim Dorsey – a statement that certainly created a severe prejudice against Webb in the minds of the jury and one that was not supported by trial witness testimony.

Second, immediately before the jury was to retire for its deliberations, the county sheriff entered the courtroom and loudly announced to the court and the jury that:

> *"...a party of armed men were at the door of the Court house for the purpose of and intending to rescue the defendant."* [78]

The jury members and everyone present in the courtroom scrambled back to their seats and waited there until the so-called threat was declared eased. That the sheriff made such a nocuous statement was supported by a *Gazette* news article and by sworn affidavits by several men who were in the courthouse, including Dave Mather.[79]

Webb Declines Jail Escape Opportunity – April 2, 1880

On April 2, Rudabaugh and John J. Allen[80] took a horse-drawn taxi to the Las Vegas jail. They arrived at the jail at about 2 pm. Their stated intention was to take Webb tobacco and newspapers, which Rudabaugh, at least, had done as a courtesy many times since Webb was jailed. Rudabuagh clearly retained no hard feelings against Webb for being one of the possemen who arrested him for the Kinsley train robbery. The jailers let the two men into the jail, because Rudabaugh was well-known and a city constable.

What happened inside the jail is given in detail in the later section *"Rudabaugh Convicted of Killing Valdez,"* based on the trial testimony of Rudabaugh and other witnesses. To sum it up here, jailer Antonio Lino Valdez was shot and mortally wounded by John J. Allen, who then removed the keys from Valdez's body and threw them to Webb. Allen's plan was to break Webb out of the jail.

Webb refused to leave his cell, because he believed that he was unjustly convicted, and because he had an appeal before the Territorial Supreme Court, which he expected would reverse his conviction. Following the killing of Valdez, Rudabaugh and Allen fled the jail, stole the taxi that had delivered them to the jail, and hightailed it out of Las Vegas, going east.[81]

San Miguel County Sheriff Hilario Romero immediately organized a posse, but failed to find the men after searching all day. An individual, Ignacio Sena, who took after them on horseback:

> "...caught up near enough to shoot. He fired several shots at the hack, one ball going through the upper part. The hack stopped and one of the men got out and returned the fire. Sena not having much ammunition then returned for a new supply." [82]

Rudabaugh and John J. Allen had gotten away clean.

The movements of the two men for the next few weeks are unknown. A hint of where the men went is given by two newspaper accounts of Allen's death. Both accounts allege that Allen was killed by Rudabaugh. One says that he was killed on the Jornada del Muerto ("Route of the Dead Man"), a stretch of dry, flat, desert land between Socorro and Las Cruces.

San Miguel County Sheriff Hilario Romero. Photo circa 1880. J. Paul Taylor Papers. Courtesy Archives and Special Collections, NMSU.

The second and probably the most reliable account reports that:

> "Allen met his death a few weeks after the memorable break from Las Vegas. Sick and crippled with rheumatism, life became a burden to him, especially as he could get no medical attention.... He frequently besought Rudebaugh [sic] to kill him and the latter, as they were riding along one day, put his pistol to Allen's head, blew out his brains, and buried him by the roadside, in the sand near Alkali Wells." [83]

The fact that Allen was dead was recognized by the Las Vegas District Court, which dropped its case against Allen for killing Valdez:

> "Territory of New Mexico vs John [J.] Allen"

> "Now comes the said plaintiff by T. B. Catron Esquire who represents and acts in place of an Attorney General, and suggests to the Court here the death of the said defendant. It is therefore considered by the Court that this cause be, and the same hereby is, abated." [84]

It would be expected that Rudabaugh would head as fast as he could for the sanctuary of Mexico after Allen's death, but he did not. By October 16, 1880, he was demonstratively in Fort Sumner hanging out with Billy the Kid (William Henry McCarty). When Rudabaugh met Billy and when Billy added him to his group (or "gang" as the New Mexico newspapers usually called it), is entirely unknown.

Billy and Rudabaugh had never met previously, so that first meeting between the two must have been a very curious affair. Billy would have known that Rudabaugh was an escaped prisoner and a wanted man. Why would Billy welcome Rudabaugh and give him his assistance and, later, his trust and friendship? The answer to that question is unknown, but the saying, "birds of a feather flock together" probably gives a strong clue.

Fort Sumner Mail Robbery – October 16, 1880

On October 16, 1880, three men held up the "Star" mail and passenger line four miles north of Fort Sumner (the line was owned by Cornelius "Con" Cosgrove and managed by his brother Michael "Mike" Cosgrove). The line's mule-drawn buckboard had just left Fort Sumner and was heading for Las Vegas. (The line ran weekly both directions between Las Vegas and Las Cruces.)

The driver and U.S. Mail carrier was Fred Weston:

"Three men stopped the buckboard and robbed [Weston] and Mrs. Deolatere, who was the only passenger he had, of all the money they had and also cut open and rifled [riffled] two mail bags.... Only one man approached the buck board. He was on horseback, and two other men who remained a little off from the road were backing him. All three men were masked and the two who staid back wore only their underclothes."

"The man on horseback rode up to the buckboard and presenting his pistol, ordered Weston to stop. The mule that Weston was driving started to run and the man rode by the side of the buckboard and told Weston that if he didn't stop, he would kill him." [85]

At the time, everyone believed that Billy was one of the robbers, his reason supposedly being to read the mail being sent to Las Vegas to learn what, if any, plans were being made to capture him.[86] This assertion has been repeated by every author since. However, Billy was not one of the robbers. As Rudabaugh later confessed, he, Billy Wilson, and Thomas Pickett were the three robbers.[87]

Taking one's clothes off for a disguise is bizarre. The reason two of them did it, even though they wore masks, was because their clothes were easily recognizable, especially those of Rudabaugh, who had a reputation for wearing the same clothes for months, even years.

Besides riffling the mail, the robbers stole $22 from Weston and $15 from Mrs. Deolatere:

"Weston was also made to surrender his pistol, which the robbers made him throw out on the sand. Mrs. Deolatere told the man that she would not be able to get to Las Vegas without her money and he condescended to give her back five dollars 'to see her through' as he said."

"The morning after the robbery Mr. [Michael] Cosgrove, the superintendent of the line visited the spot designated by Weston as being the scene of the robbery and found fragments of letters lying on the ground. [Postal] Detective [J. F.] Morley took charge of the matter, and after investigating it arrested Weston and Mrs. Deolatere upon suspicion that they had robbed the mail themselves and had made up this story to conceal their guilt." [88]

The arrest of Weston had a bizarre aspect:

"The prisoners were arrested in Las Vegas and brought to Santa Fe [by train] to be locked up. Before being put into jail they were searched and a small

> **Las Vegas & Las Cruces**
> **U. S. MAIL LINE**
>
> *Via Anton Chico, Gallinas Springs, Santa Rosa, Puerto de Luna, ort umnery, Roswell, Lincoln, Fort Stanton, South Fork and Tularosa.*
>
> Carries Passengers and Express on Reasonable Terms.
>
> ## C. COSGROVE.
> Proprietor.

Ad for Con Cosgrove's "Star" Mail Line, January 18, 1880.
Las Vegas Daily Gazette.

piece of paper, a leaf from a memorandum book was handed by Weston to the detective, which bore the words, 'if your wife don't squeal, you're all right. She told the marshal she'd tell all she knew before she'd be locked up.'"

"*The prisoner said at the time that the paper was handed him on the train by one of Morley's friends, and that he had kept it just to see what would become of it. Morley testified, however, that he had never seen or heard of the paper before the prisoner had given it to him.*" [89]

In spite of that unexplainable note and Morley's firm conviction of their guilt, Weston and Mrs. Deolatere had their case dismissed.

Webb Escapes Jail – November 11, 1880

"*Jail Jugglery – Midnight Court Held by Six Prisoners who Discharged Themselves*" (90)

That was the *Las Vegas Gazette* headline Monday morning, November 11, 1880.

"*The discovery was made by old Pablo Dominguez, chief of the guards, who rising about day break found the door at the end of the passageway connecting with the placita standing ajar. Upon inspection of the cells he found that in one, instead of seven prisoners whom he had locked up Tuesday night, only one was visible.*" [91]

Later that day, an investigation by Judge Morrison, furious at the break out, determined that no posse was immediately dispatched after the escapees. It was also determined that the jailers were seriously derelict in their duties. The jailers had been complaining of the overwhelming cold as there were no stoves in the jail, so a few days before the escape, a new heating stove was installed *"in the passageway [hallway] leading to the entrance and everything made comfortable for them."* Nevertheless, the jailers had all retired to warmth of the large cooking stove in the kitchen and had gone to sleep.

(The winter of 1880 was a record-breaking cold year throughout the entire country. On November 19, 1880, Las Vegas recorded an all-time low temperature of 12 degrees below zero. The unheated jail cells must have been nearly unbearable.) [92]

The seventh person in the cell with the six men who escaped, Pablo Montes de Ochoa, did not grab his opportunity for freedom. He was in jail waiting trial for the *"murder of a freighter"* some months earlier:

"Sometime before midnight... his fellow prisoners began the work of picking the locks on the cell door, there being a padlock at the top and bottom [see photo page 83]. The door is constructed of iron bars placed at right angles, and through the square apertures, the men were able to squeeze their hands and work away at picking the locks.... Pieces of wire about the size of telegraph wire was used for this purpose."

"In order to deaden all sounds within the cells, blankets were tucked through the bars of the door, and after awhile one lock gave way.... Outside the iron door was a wooden door which should have been kept locked, but was pushed open without any difficulty."

"The next thing to be done was to relieve themselves of their shackles and bracelets. Several were able to slip the latter over their hands.... A file was produced and before long their shackles were filed off, at the second link at one end, the rest of chain being concealed about their persons." [93]

The six men who escaped were: Webb, James Allen, George Davidson, John Murray, William Mullen, and George Davis.

James Allen (not to be confused with John J. Allen) was in jail waiting on the Territorial Supreme Court to review his conviction for murdering James Morehead at the St. Nicholas Hotel in Las Vegas. On March 2, 1880, the same day Kelliher was killed, Morehead asked Allen, a waiter, to bring him some fried eggs. Allen replied, *"that the cook did not have time to fry eggs."* The matter was dropped.

"The next day, Morehead jokingly referred to the matter and remarked that it would not be long until the cook would not have time to fry steak. This remark rather incensed Allen and hard words ensued." [94]

They began fighting. Morehead, the bigger man, threw Allen to the floor. Allen got up, went into an adjacent room, returned with a pistol, and called Morehead a *"s– of a b—-h, and ordered him to get on his knees.... Morehead refused and made an attempt to knock the pistol away."* Allen then shot and mortally wounded Morehead, who was unarmed. *"The ball entered the [man's] left side, passed through the stomach and liver, and came out on the right side."* [95]

Morehead was taken to an upstairs room and placed in a bed. It was obvious to his visitors that he was dying. He was advised to make a death-bed statement, so that his killer would not go unpunished. In his statement, Morehead described the origin of the fight – the fried-egg insult – and the physical encounter that followed the next day. He said that when Allen returned with *"a cocked pistol in his hand,"* he jumped for him, but failed to block the shot. *"After shooting me, he [Allen] turned and went back into the dining room and closed the door."* [96]

Allen was immediately arrested. As word of Morehead's shooting and later death spread through town, people began to talk of lynching Allen:

> *"By early evening, public opinion had decided upon a meeting at 11 o'clock in a vacant building on Railroad Avenue and the sequel was rather clearly forecast."* [97]

Allen's lynching was only prevented when word was sent to the mob that the jail would be defended with all necessary force.[98]

James Allen's preliminary hearing was held the day after his arrest. The court ordered him held on a charge of first degree murder. Afterwards, he was interviewed by a *Gazette* reporter. He told the reporter he was 23 years old and *"respectably connected."* He would not state where he was born or where his parents and siblings lived, *"as he did not wish his family to know anything of his present situation."*

> *"He stated that he is quick tempered and often says things for which he is afterwards sorry. He desires a show, as he expressed it, and a fair trial, and that he is willing to abide by the result.... He alleged that he had no intention of killing Morehead, but that it was done in self defense. He complained that the cells of the jail were in a filthy condition.... He looks worked up to a high state of nervous excitement over the crime and has a generally distressed appearance."* [99]

Allen was tried for the killing on August 3, 1880, in Santa Fe, on a change of venue from Las Vegas. The jury deliberated all night before it returned a verdict of murder in the first degree:

> *"[Allen received the verdict] with apparent indifference and outwardly unmoved, not a muscle of his face moving. The same stolid expressionless look remained on his face that he had possessed throughout the trial; and a casual spectator would never have imagined that he was the man most directly affected by the verdict."* [100]

On October 17, 1880, *Las Vegas Gazette* published the following letter by James Allen:

> *"Gentlemen: You were very kind to me when I was a free man, and that is the reason I write this letter asking you to do an act of charity, and send me something to protect me from the cold, if it is nothing but a pair of socks. I have no friends or money, and have appealed to them in charge, but have received nothing from them."*
>
> *"I may not have long to live, but would like to be protected from the cold blast of winter while alive. To be imprisoned and chained is hard, but with proper clothing I could bear it very well; if you see fit to send me anything, any of the hack drivers will bring it to the jail. Hoping gentlemen, that you will help me, I remain very truly, Yours, James Allen."* [101]

The *Gazette* had noted earlier that:

"*[James] Allen is chained hand and foot, to the extent of making even the slightest movement of his body attended with much difficulty.*" [102]

Escapee George Davidson was in jail awaiting trial for the senseless killing of Las Vegas hack driver Charles Nelson W. Starbird on April 8, 1880. At about 2 o'clock the morning of the killing, Davidson exited an East Las Vegas dance hall and hailed a hack. He asked to be taken to Mackley's Stable. He *"was rather full, but not drunk."* When the hack passed another hack containing a pretty woman, Davidson drew his pistol yelling he *"wanted to hunt a woman."* He was blocked from firing by his driver. At Mackley's Stable, Davidson climbed out. To his raving frustration, the stable was closed for the night. When Starbird's hack passed by, Davidson opened up on it and killed Starbird.[103]

The *Gazette* reported:

"*Davidson was just boiling over, going to utter ruin in order to kill somebody. He wanted to kill a woman in a hack they met coming over.... The poor hardworking young man shot down without cause... was killed because he was innocent and his young wife is left heart-broken.*" [104] [Starbird had married Josie Nellie Heard just ten months earlier.]

As in the case of James Allen, a vigilante committee was organized to lynch Davidson. And, again, as in Allen's case, Davidson's lynching was only prevented by word that the jail would be guarded by all of the city constables. The lynchers satisfied themselves by posting this notice around town:

"*A TIMELY WARNING*"

"*To Murderers, Confidence Men, Thieves*"

"*The citizens of Las Vegas have tired of robbery, murder, and other crimes that have made this town a byword in every civilized community. They have resolved to put a stop to crime even if in attaining that end they have to forget the law, and resort to a speedier justice than it will afford. All such characters are, therefore, notified that they must either leave this town or conform themselves to the requirement of law, or they will be summarily dealt with. The flow of blood MUST and SHALL be stopped in this community, and the good citizens of both the old and new towns have determined to stop it, if they have to HANG by the strong arm of FORCE every violator of the law in this country.*"

"*VIGALENTES*" [105]

Escapee John Murray was in jail awaiting trial for the murder of a railroad grader near Tecolote. There appears to be no other information on Murray and his crime. (The first train pulled into Las Vegas on July 4, 1879. It was greeted by a blaring brass band and an ecstatic, city-wide celebration.) [106]

Escapee William Mullen was one of the men falsely convicted of the Tecolote stage robbery, carried out by Rudabaugh, Martin, and Carson. He was awaiting transfer to the state penitentiary to serve out his two-and-a-half-year sentence. William Stokes, falsely convicted along with Mullen of that robbery, was locked up in the cell next to Mullen. He probably would have happily jumped at freedom if his cell door had been picked open or unlocked.[107]

Escapee George Davis was in jail waiting trial for stealing a span of mules. (This is not the "George Davis" who was in the posse that chased after and killed John Henry Tunstall. That person's real name was Jesse Graham and he was killed by Texas Rangers July 3, 1880, at Fort Davis, Texas. See *"The Trial of Billy the Kid"* by David G. Thomas.)

Following the escape, several men tried to duplicate the trick of picking the cell locks and were unable to, leading many to believe that Ochoa's account was false, that the men had used smuggled keys. However, Mullen and Webb later confirmed that they had indeed picked the locks with telegraph wires.[108]

Commenting on the jail break, the *Santa Fe New Mexican* wrote:

> *"It needed no further proof or evidence than has already been furnished to prove that the jails of New Mexico are little more than so many farces but the Las Vegas jail authorities have just come forward with another one of these proofs which is more conclusive perhaps than any of those which have preceded it."* [109]

After a fiery judicial scolding by Judge Morrison, Sheriff Hilario Romero dispatched a posse of six men with orders to find the escapees and bring them back *"dead or alive."* Late that evening, the posse came upon James Allen, Davidson, Mullen, and Murray lying around a campfire seven miles east of Chaperito. After yelling a warning in Spanish, posse leader Desidero Apodaca:

> *"...snapped his revolver at Mullen who was lying nearest him, but it missed fire, and the latter snatched at it but missed it. [Apodaca] quickly wheeled about firing into the crowd and this was seconded by his companions, the firing being kept up till [James] Allen and Davidson were killed."* [110]

Mullen and Murray fled and hid. The next morning:

> *"[Mullen] started out on foot for Las Vegas, having the raw winds in his shirt sleeves. He reached town last evening and gave himself up and is now safely locked up in jail... He declares that he has nothing to fear by standing trial... and only took advantage of his liberty when it was offered him without stopping to consider the risks he was running."* [111]

Murray was never caught as far as the author can determine.

A coroner's jury ruled that the killings of Allen and Davidson were fully justified. Mullen testified before the jury that because the warning shouted out by the posse before the firing was in Spanish, he and the other men did not understand it. They would have immediately surrendered if they had known it was the law ambushing them.[112]

When Miguel Antonio Otero published his memoirs in 1935, he claimed that there was a secret, Machiavellian side to the escape of Webb, Allen, Davidson, Murray, Mullen, and Davis. He wrote that certain Las Vegas residents were afraid that Allen (especially), Davidson, and Murray would not be convicted. They decided to engineer their jail-house escape, so that they could be killed resisting arrest when recaptured:

> *"They bribed one of the jailers to go to the four prisoners and offer to help them escape provided they would pay him a certain amount of money, which they were to secure from their friends and confederates in East Las Vegas. This they were able to do, and thus their escape was brought about."* [113]

Patrick Floyd Jarvis Garrett, photo circa 1886. Courtesy IHSF.org.

Otero added:

> *"This explains why the posse when it surrounded the four fugitives sitting about their campfire did not go through the usual formality of demanding their surrender. The posse was instructed fully as to its part in the grim business."* [114]

Otero was living in Las Vegas at the time of the escape, and he was a good friend of Morehead. Nevertheless, the author does not believe Otero's escape-conspiracy tale, dramatic as it is. Both Mullen and Webb – who had no reason to lie – confirmed that they had picked the locks, which later testing proved to be quite difficult. If you wanted to ensure that certain prisoners would escape, you would not leave it up to them to pick difficult locks. In addition, there was no evidence of an intentional jail break or a plot to murder the escaped prisoners discovered in the rather thorough investigation by Judge Morrison that followed.

Webb and Davis Captured by Deputy Sheriff Garrett – November 25, 1880

On November 19, "Star" line driver Michael Cosgrove reported that he had met Webb at Bell's ranch[115] on the Pecos River, below Puerto de Luna. He took supper and spent the night at Bell's, as did the unidentified man. The next morning he left for Fort Sumner, the stranger trailing along with him. He stopped at John Gerhardt's ranch for breakfast – so did the stranger.[116]

They rode into Fort Sumner together:

"Mr. Cosgrove did not recognize the man until an acquaintance in Sumner informed him that the man who had been travelling on horse back with him was none other than Webb. When he made this discovery, he talked with the man, and is satisfied that it was indeed him."

"Webb related to him full particulars of the jail break and protested that he effected his escape by means of the piece of wire as was first related. According to Webb's story, he hung around new town the day following his escape and in the evening rode out of town and struck the Pecos route. He said that he was on his way to Texas.... He was clad in a good suit of clothes, warm overcoat, wore two six shooters and appeared to be well supplied with money." [117]

Webb clearly had had bounteous help from someone in Las Vegas.

After spilling his identity to Cosgrove, Webb continued to blab. The *Dodge City Times* quotes Webb telling an unidentified source:

"Hoodoo appointed me police and told me to shoot Kelliher if he made any bad break, as Kelliher was going to kill the first officer he saw. Hoodoo lied to me, got me into trouble, deserted me and now I propose to hunt him up and kill him." [118]

At Fort Sumner, Cosgrove met George Davis. Davis told him that:

"...he was out in the timber 'rustling' round for wood when he heard the pursuing party come up and when the firing commenced, he started to run and never looked behind but once and that to see Davidson and Allen fall. Still he was not fleet enough to get out of harm's way and received a shot, though not of a very serious nature." [119]

On November 25, 1880, Webb and Davis were captured by Deputy Sheriff Pat Garrett.

The capture of the two men was a surprise to Garrett. Garrett had been elected Lincoln County Sheriff November 2, 1880, based on a promise to voters that he would devote his first efforts to capturing Billy the Kid and his "gang." His official term, however, did not start until January 1, 1881. So that he could begin hunting Billy immediately, he was appointed Deputy Sheriff by the man he would replace, Lincoln County Sheriff George Kimbrell.

In recounting the capture of Webb and Davis, Garrett wrote:

"I had heard that they [Billy and his companions] and were afoot, and guessing they would go to Dan Dedrick, at Bosque Grande, for horses." [120] [Garrett knew that Billy and Wilson had had their horses killed in the shootout at Coyote Springs – see next section for details.]

Garrett, who was living *"five miles"* from Roswell, collected twelve of his neighbors for a posse and set out for Dedrick's place. On the evening of November 24, about 9 o'clock, they struck the Pecos River and turned north:

"At day-break we surrounded Dedrick's ranch, at Bosque Grande, twenty-eight miles north of Roswell." (121)

They demanded the surrender of the men inside. Webb and Davis came out, not the expected Billy and his companions – one of whom was known to be Rudabaugh.[122]

Webb and Davis were ironed and taken to Fort Sumner. So as not to be diverted from his sworn purpose, Garrett left them there shackled together while he continued to scour the countryside for Billy. (It is not known where they were jailed, there being no jail in Fort Sumner.) On December 12, Garrett brought Webb and Davis into Las Vegas:

"The cavalcade approached the city quietly, and their presence was not known until after the prison bars had closed upon the captives. A reporter for the Optic was successful in obtaining a short conference with Webb. He stated that he regretted his return to Las Vegas, but that it cannot be helped and must be born with fortitude. He would have gone direct to Mexico as he had calculated upon, but his horse was taken lame and it was while he was trying to rest up that he was re-captured." [123]

Carlyle Killed at Greathouse's Roadhouse – November 27, 1880

On November 22, an *"unknown"* party attempted to steal horses from Jason B. Bell's place, *"who lived in the southwestern portion of the town of White Oaks."* [124] The following day, news reached White Oaks that Billy the Kid and some companions were camped at Fletcher A. Blake's saw mill, located in Canon del Ojo, *"three miles from town."* [125] Garrett, who reports the incidents, does not say that Billy was behind the horse-stealing raid at Bell's, but the townspeople were certain he was. With Billy were Rudabaugh, Billy Wilson, Joseph "Bob" M. Edwards, and Joseph "Joe" Cook.[126]

Wilson was riding with Billy because he was wanted for passing counterfeit $100 notes (see Appendix B for details on Wilson's situation). Edwards had participated in the theft of eight horses from Alexander Grzelachowski's place at Puerto de Luna a week earlier, and Cook was wanted for horse stealing in Texas.[127] When these three men joined up with Billy and Rudabaugh is unknown, but it probably happened at Fort Sumner in early September, 1880.

Lincoln County Deputy Sheriff William H. Hudgens, who, with his brother John, owned the Pioneer Saloon in White Oaks, put together a posse of eight citizens to go after Billy.[128] The posse members were: John Hudgens, James W. Bell, John P. Eaker, George C. Neil, John Longworth, James Carlyle, William Stone, and James S. Redman (alias of S. J. Woodland).[129] They faced snow-covered ground and daunting low temperatures.[130]

The posse did not find Billy and his companions at Blake's saw mill as had been reported, but tracks in the snow from there led toward Coyote Springs. On the way to Coyote Springs, the posse encountered two men riding toward White Oaks, Mose Dedrick and William J. Lamper. The two men were arrested as possible suspects.[131] (Mose and his two brothers Dan and Sam were well-known allies of Billy's.)

At Coyote Springs, the posse:

"...rode up to within 125 steps of 'the Kid's' party when the latter opened fire. They [the Kid's party] had a most excellent position, and the advantages were two to one in favor the outlaws, but they soon made themselves scarce, Billy Wilson mounting his horse and riding off through the brushes, one having had his horse captured, the other's [horse] being shot from under him." [132]

The person who had his horse shot out from under him was Billy. The quote above implies that Wilson got away on his horse, but, although Wilson did escape, his horse was killed. The person who had his horse captured was Rudabaugh.[133] Posse member John Hudgens' horse was killed at the beginning of the firefight:

"John Hudgins (sic) was the leader of the posse and was in front on a fine horse, owned by him. Coming to a straight stretch of the canyon, a shot rang out from below, and Hudgins's horse fell dead, shot through the brain. If the horse had not raised his head just when he did, the shot would have killed John Hudgins." [134]

It was learned later that Billy had been warned of the posse's approach by Mose and Lamper.

At the abandoned Coyote Springs camp, the posse:

"...found a fine saddle, said to be the property of 'the Kid' beside the dead body of the horse. They also found an overcoat, known to have been worn in White Oaks that morning by Mose Dedrick, and another known to have been the property of Sam Dedrick...."

"'The Kid' was known to be without an overcoat, and his friend Sam had, doubtless supplied the 'much felt want.' ...besides the spoils above named, the sheriff's posse found a considerable quantity of canned goods and other provisions together with a pair of saddle-bags containing useful dry goods, all of which were known to have been purchased at White Oaks that morning [by Mose and Lamper]." [135]

Newspaper reports at the time said that *"the outlaws"* outnumbered the sheriff's posse *"two to one."* Not true. It was only Billy, Rudabaugh, Wilson, Edwards, and Cook at the Springs.[136]

Although the five *"outlaws"* got away from the posse, they were forced to split up. Billy, Rudabaugh, and Wilson, now horseless, fled the scene on foot. Cook and Edwards escaped on their horses. According to Garrett, Cook got away with an extra horse.[137] (Edwards and Cook never rode with Billy again. Cook was captured and jailed by Garrett on November 25, 1880. Edwards was killed by Garrett's deputy Thomas "Kip" McKinney at Hank Harrison's ranch near Black River on May 8, 1881. Unusual for an "outlaw," Edwards was married and had four young kids when he was killed.)[138]

With no alternative, Rudabaugh, Billy, and Wilson walked the six miles to White Oaks, probably arriving before daybreak. After sneaking into town undiscovered, they went to Dedrick and West's livery stable and obtained replacement horses. (There are

Strong circumstantial evidence suggests that this previously undiscovered, well-hidden shelter at Coyote Springs is where Billy, Rudabaugh, Wilson, Edwards, and Cook were camping when attacked by Hudgens' posse. Artifacts of the appropriate time period have been located at the site. August 27, 2022, photos by the author.

no primary sources confirming that the three men walked to White Oaks, but as they no longer had horses, how else could they have gotten there?) [139]

The stable was owned by Sam Dedrick and William H. West. Wilson had owned the stable until he sold it to West four months earlier (August 3, 1880).[140] West paid Wilson with four counterfeit $100 bills. The spending of those bills was what made Wilson a wanted man (see Appendix B). By this date, William West had left Lincoln County for Topeka, Kansas, as it was known that he was the distributor of the counterfeit bills.[141]

On their way out of White Oaks, one of the three men, now supplied with horses from Dedrick's stable, *"seeing Jim Redmond [Redman] standing in front of Will Hudgens' saloon, fired on him."* [142] This last statement, by Garrett, does not attribute the shooting to Billy, but other sources do, including several by early residents of White Oaks, who report that bad blood existed between Billy and Redman.[143] Redman was in Hudgens' posse when the two sides got into it at Coyote Springs.

On November 26, a second posse led by White Oaks constable Thomas "Pinto Tom" Longworth and James Carlyle (deputized for the purpose) went after Billy. They had no need to search hard for their prey, as they had intelligence that Billy's party was holed up at James "Whisky Jim" Greathouse's roadhouse.[144]

Greathouse's roadhouse was located on the road between Las Vegas and Anton Chico, near the Red Cloud crossroads (about seven miles southwest of present day Corona). He and his partner Fred W. Kuch had built the house a year earlier.[145] The roadhouse was constructed like a *"little fortress,"* according to one account. There were two horse corrals, one 100 yards west of the roadhouse and one 200 yards east of the roadhouse.[146]

The posse arrived at Greathouse's before sun break and stationed themselves around the house. Joe Steck, who was freighting for Greathouse, gave the following account of what happened next:

"[Just] after daylight, I got up and went out to where my team was picketed. When about 300 yards from the house, somebody hollered, 'Halt.' I naturally turned around to see what was up, when to my great surprise two men had their guns pointed at me. They ordered me to approach them, all the time keep[ing] their guns at me. I went like a little man!"

"When I got to them, they got behind me and ordered me to march toward what I supposed was a bunch of fallen timber – and so it was, but there were men behind it, two bold, ferocious looking men, with plenty of guns and ammunition. When I got amongst them, one of my captors said: 'Captain. We've got one of the s of b's,' and I did not resent it a little bit."

"They ordered me to lie down with them, and I did so. They wanted to know if Billy the Kid, Billy Wilson, or Dave Rudabaugh were in the house. I told them that I did not know. They doubted my word and I did not allow myself to get mad. They gave me a description of the man they were after and I told that three such men were in the house." [147]

After being sworn to return, Steck was sent into the house with a note telling the occupants that they were surrounded *"on all sides"* and their only option was to surrender, because there was zero chance of escape. Further, they were told that *"large parties from Lincoln were enroute with provisions and everything necessary for [a long] siege."* [148]

Site of Greathouse's roadhouse. All that can be be seen today are a few foundation stones and a man-made depression. August 5, 2022, photo by the author.

"I took the note in and delivered it to the one I knew to be Billy the Kid. He read the paper to his compadres who all laughed at the idea surrender. They told me also to rest easy and not to be alarmed as no harm would come to me from them. They sent me out with a note demanding to know [who] the leader of the party was, and invited him into the house to talk the matter over." [149]

Carlyle agreed to enter the house *"to talk,"* and in exchange, Greathouse agreed to surrender himself to the posse outside as a good-faith hostage. Both men left their arms with their own parties.

"Getting hungry about 11 o'clock, I [Steck] went into the house to rustle up a dinner. I found Carlisle getting under the influence of liquor and insisting on going out, while the others insisted on his staying. While I was getting diner Mr. Cook [Kuch], Greathouse's partner, carried dispatches between the camps. For some reason the White Oaks boys became suspicious; things were not as they should be with their leader, and they decided to storm the fort, therefore sent me word by Mr. Cook to come out as war would commence in earnest." [150]

In an account that Billy later provided to Governor Wallace in a letter, Billy wrote:

"When I got up next morning the house was Surrounded by an outfit led by one Carlyle, who came into the house and Demanded a Surrender. I asked for their Papers and they had none. So I Concluded it amounted to nothing more than a mob and told Carlyle that he would have to Stay in the house *and lead the way out that night. Soon after a note was brought in Stating that if Carlyle did not come out inside of five minutes they would kill the Station Keeper Greathouse who had left the house with them. In a short time a shot was fired on the outside and Carlyle thinking Greathouse was Killed jumped through the window, breaking the Sash as he went and was killed by his own Party they thinking it was me trying to make my Escape* [presented as written]." [151]

Billy also explained to Governor Wallace why he had gone to White Oaks:

"My business at the White Oaks the time I was waylaid and my horse killed was to see Judge Leonard who has my case in hand. He had written to me to Come up, that he thought he could get Everything Straightened up. I did not find him at the Oaks & should have gone to Lincoln if I had met with no accident." [152]

The shot that spooked Carlyle and caused him to bolt through the closed window was an accidental misfiring by posse member John P. Eaker.[153] Deputy Sheriff James W. Bell, a member of the posse, gave this account of events to the *Daily Gazette*, claiming Carlyle was killed on purpose by someone in the house:

"Carlyle, after trying to make his escape through one of the doors, all of which were barricaded by sacks of flour, leaped through the top sash of a window and started for his men. He was evidently dazed, for he ran in the wrong direction, and had he taken an opposite course would have succeeded in getting out of range of the outlaw's guns. As it was he was shot down in cold blood. A rattling fire on both sides was kept up and then the Oak boys retreated as they could not endure the siege longer in their condition [meaning the brutally cold weather]." [154]

Almost two months later, Bell supported his assertion that Carlyle was killed deliberately by telling the *Las Vegas Optic* that he spoke with Wilson and Rudabaugh shortly after they were captured by Pat Garrett and jailed in Las Vegas:

"The first words of Wilson were: 'Bell, help me out of this scrape!' Bell replied: 'That is a hard thing to ask of me after you killed Carlyle in cold blood, as you did.' Wilson hung his head and replied: 'I didn't shoot at him and tried to keep the others from doing so.'

"Radabaugh [sic] overhearing this last remark of Wilson's, put in with, 'You are a damned liar. We all three shot at him. You and I fired one shot a piece and Kid twice.'" [155]

The *Optic* went on to editorialize:

"The worst thing Kid ever did was to kill poor Carlyle, after pledging his word that he should not be harmed. If he is such a noble fellow, why should he resort to stratagem in order to murder in cold blood, the poor fellow who trusted in his word?" [156]

There is no evidence other than hearsay that Billy killed Carlyle, or even that he wanted to.

When Billy, Rudabaugh, and Wilson fled the shootout at Greathouse's, they did so, as at Coyote Springs, without horses. Perhaps the posse had driven off all the horses in Greathouse's corral, or maybe they just had no opportunity to retrieve their horses.

James Carlyle's grave site. A gravestone to mark the site – identified previously only by rocks – was installed August 5, 2022, by members of Billy the Kid's Historical Coalition (BTKHC). The gravestone was paid for by donations solicited by the BTKHC. August 5, 2022, photo by the author.

In any case, they walked *"in deep snow"* first to Lon Spencer's place, about four miles away, where they obtained breakfast and presumably some provisions – but no horses. From Spencer's, they walked to Fort Sumner, a distance of about 90 miles due east. Billy, in his letter to Governor Wallace explaining his actions at White Oaks, already partially quoted, says:

> *"I made my way to this Place [Fort Sumner] afoot...."* [157]

He added:

> *"I had been at Sumner Since I left Lincoln making my living Gambling.... There is no Doubt by what there is a great deal Stealing going on in the Territory. and a great deal of the Property is taken across the Plains as it is a good outlet but so far as my being at the head of a Band there is nothing of it in Several Instances I have recovered Stolen Property when there was no chance to get an Officer to do it."* [158]

John Hurley. Undated photo. Courtesy Maurice G. Fulton Papers, Special Collections, UA.

That the three men had no horses after escaping Greathouse's is confirmed by Garrett and by newspaper accounts.[159] Garrett, however, says that they walked to Anton Chico, which was 90 miles northeast. To walk first to Anton Chico and then to Fort Sumner would have almost doubled the distance. There is no reason not to believe Billy's statement, that they walked to Fort Sumner, where, as Billy wrote in his letter, he was *"living."* He felt safe in Fort Sumner. That would not have been true in Anton Chico.

Steck reports that following the shootout, he and Kuch took shelter at a nearby ranch (possibly Spencer's also). When they returned to Greathouse's the next morning:

> *"We found poor Carlisle (sic) frozen stiff where he fell, tied a blanket around him and made a hole a little toward the east from where he fell, and buried him the best we could. He was afterwards taken up and put in a box by a sheriff's posse* [and reburied at a different location]." [160]

Later that day, November 28, a party, under the *"command of a government official,"* returned to Greathouse's and burned down the roadhouse and surrounding buildings.[161] The unidentified official was Deputy Sheriff John Hurley, who was leading a posse out of Lincoln.[162] Greathouse told the *Daily Gazette* that the posse had burned him out in retaliation for Carlyle's death. He claimed *"he lost $2000 by the conflagration, including ranch property and general merchandise."* [163]

After burning Greathouse's, Hurley's men went to Spencer's Ranch. Spencer, an older man who lived alone, had built his roadhouse in an effort *"to establish a shorter route from 'Vegas' to the 'Oaks' by turning the road by his place."* When questioned,

Spencer readily admitted that Billy the Kid, Rudabaugh, and Wilson had come to his place the morning after the fight at Greathouse's, and he had fed them breakfast at their request.[164]

Enraged by this admission of aiding the enemy, they burned his place, just as they had Greathouse's. Further, according to one account, they put a rope around Spencer's neck and were only stopped from hanging him by the vehement objection of one of their party.[165]

All of the actions of the posses – besieging Greathouse's roadhouse and burning it and Spencer's – were without legal justification, as Billy pointed out in his letter.

When Garrett was later asked by the *Las Vegas Gazette* if he considered the burning of Greathouse's roadhouse to be *"perfectly justifiable,"* he replied:

"Of course I do. If the other boys hadn't burned it, I would." [166]

Garrett made this statement because of Greathouse's well-known, law-breaking past. Greathouse earned the sobriquet "Whiskey Jim" in 1874 at Fort Griffin, bootlegging huge amounts of drinking alcohol to Native Americans. His illicit liquor peddling was so aggravating that the commander of the Fort, Colonel Ranald S. Mackenzie, ordered his arrest – dead or alive. Greathouse quickly moved on to stealing horses and cattle in West Texas. When that became too hot after several rustlers were lynched, he moved north to the Texas Panhandle. There he hunted buffalo and dealt in stolen livestock on the side. He moved from there to New Mexico shortly before building his roadhouse.[167]

Secret Service Agent Azariah F. Wild, who was in Lincoln County secretly tracking currency counterfeiters (his primary target was Billy Wilson), visited Greathouse's Roadhouse and wrote the following about his undercover visit:

"I will respectfully state that the man (Greathouse) referred to by Mr. [John S.] Chisum is a hard character and a 'Pal' of Wilson and Co. He keeps a small store in company with a man named Kuck [Kuch] and has a ranch near by the store where he received stolen stock.... Fred W. Kuck who keeps this store with Greathouse is a bad man. He has been connected with several Post Office transactions of a very doubtful character, and is regarded as a bad man."

"When at his store I claimed I was purchasing sheep and made myself as agreeable as I could. He told me he was engaged in smuggling goods in from Mexico and other foreign countries. He showed me two Panama Hats which would retail in New Orleans at $45 each. He said he smuggled in four dozen and that this two were from that lot." [168]

Rudabaugh and Wilson were indicted for Carlyle's death. The indictment stated that Carlyle was shot three times, once each in the *"head, breast and body."* Greathouse was indicted as an accomplice in Carlyle's death, even though he was outside the house without arms when Carlyle was shot. Greathouse's charges were eventually dropped.[169]

Greathouse was killed December 15, 1881, by a double-barreled shotgun blast at the Point of the Rocks[170] in the foothills of the San Mateo Mountains by Harry A. "Joe" Fowler.[171] (Many sources say Fowler was known as "Joel" Fowler, but the newspaper reports about him almost all use "Joe.")

A day earlier, Fowler and his foreman Jim Ike had encountered Greathouse, Jim Finley and Jim Kay, who Fowler suspected of having stolen 40 head of his cattle. The

Harry A. "Joe" Fowler, 1883 photo. Courtesy Geronimo Springs Museum.

two parties confronted each other with drawn weapons. In the parley that followed, Fowler did not tell Greathouse that the cattle they had stolen were his. Rather, he said he was interested in acquiring "rustled" cattle. Greathouse, Finley, and Kay agreed to accompany Fowler to his ranch.[172]

When they got to the Point of the Rocks, they stopped for lunch. At some point during that stop, *"Finley became suspicious that all was not right and opened fire."* Fowler replied with his shotgun, killing Greathouse and Finley. Ike killed Kay.[173]

Believing that his ranching neighbor, C. F. Blackington, was the mastermind behind the rustling, Fowler left the bodies of Greathouse, Finley, and Kay were they fell and rode to Blackington's. There he *"arrested"* Blackington and an employee. Blackington escaped before he could be delivered to the sheriff and eventually satisfied authorities that he was not involved.[174]

Although Fowler and Ike claimed they killed the three men in self-defense, many believed they were cold-bloodedly murdered. A coroner's jury, meeting over the bodies, however, ruled the killings justified.

The *Santa Fe New Mexican*, in it report on the killings, gave the following description of Greathouse:

> *"Greathouse was rather a tall man, with a heartless, staring countenance and always wore a white hat, clown fashion."* [175]

Fowler met his own end twenty-five months later. On November 7, 1883, Fowler killed James E. Cale with a knife in the Grand Central Hotel in Socorro (some accounts say it happened in the street). On January 22, 1884, while awaiting trial for Cale's killing, Fowler was taken from jail by a mob of 200 men and hanged from a nearby tree: [176]

> "Fowler had been asleep and was wholly unprepared for the entertainment gotten up by the vigilantes. When the cell door swung open he awoke with a start, took in the situation at a glance, and began begging for mercy.... The prisoner was unshackled from the bull-ring in the floor and taken out into the night.... as they headed toward 'death alley,' the poor criminal broke down completely.... calling upon his Maker for mercy and imploring leniency from the infinite power."

> "As is customary in such cases, Fowler was granted the privilege of making a final request, which was to the effect that his remains be sent to Fort Worth for interment." [177]

By the time of his lynching, Fowler was a widely hated man, as reflected by the news reports of his lynching:

> "More Room in Hell than Socorro for F O W L E R!" [178]

> "Presented With a Real Hempen Necktie at Socorro. But it Fit So Closely that it Strangeled Him to Death."

> "Yesterday the glad news of the lynching of the notorious Joe Fowler at Socorro was reported in this city, and on every hand and from every moth came open thankfulness that the boasting murderer had at last met his just fate." [179]

Rudabaugh Captured with Billy the Kid – December 23, 1880

On December 14, 1880, about one o'clock in the afternoon, Garrett left Las Vegas to resume his quest for Billy.[180] He had with him Frank Stewart and Barney Mason. Stewart, real name John W. Green, was a range detective who had been hired by the Texas Panhandle Cattleman's Association for the purpose of combating cattle stealing.[181] He had been in New Mexico since mid-November hunting Billy and other rustlers. Mason was a good friend who Garrett had hired as a deputy and a spy.[182] (The two had married their wives on the same day in the Anton Chico Catholic Church.[183]) Mason lived in Fort Sumner, knew Billy well, and knew his habits and likely movements.[184]

Garrett met a group of other Texans at Anton Chico who had come to New Mexico independent of Stewart, at the instigation of LX Ranch foreman Bill Moore. The LX Ranch, located in the Texas Panhandle, had for several years suffered serious cattle depredations, much of it blamed on Billy and his companions.[185] Seven of the Texans at Anton Chico agreed to join Garrett's posse, bringing it to ten with Garrett. (The seven joiners were: Lon Chambers, Thomas "Poker Tom" Emory, Jim East, Philip "The Animal" Bousman, Cal Polk, Lee Hall, and Robert "Tenderfoot Bob" Williams.[186])

From Anton Chico, they rode 45 miles to a campsite located fifteen miles north of Puerto de Luna, arriving there in the evening. They stayed the night and then made for Puerto de Luna, arriving there in the morning.

> "To rest and save our horses we determined to lay over until the next morning. We spent the day infusing warmth into our chilled bodies through the

medium of mesquite-root fires and internal applications of liquid fuel, and in eating apples and drawing corks." [187]

The weather was tortuously cold; the record breaking polar cold wave which had hit the country in November had abated for a few weeks, but it was now back in restored force.

About 3 pm the next day, Garrett and his posse left Puerto de Luna. They reached John Gerhardt's ranch at about 9 pm, *"in a terrible snow storm from the northwest."* [188]

On December 18, they reached Fort Sumner just before dawn. Garrett now led a party of 13, having gained three possemen at Gerhardt's: Juan Roibal, Charles Rudolph, and George Wilson.[189] (See footnote 190 for details on the founding of Fort Sumner.)

At Fort Sumner, Garrett went first to Henry A. "Beaver" Smith's Saloon. (The well-known tintype of Billy is said to have been taken in Smith's saloon by an itinerant photographer in late 1879 or early 1880.[191]) Smith and Garrett had been business partners in Fort Sumner until just a few months earlier.[192] Interrogated, Beaver Smith said he thought Billy and friends were in an abandoned building across the plaza. The posse approached the building and observed a fire burning in the fireplace:

"Garrett pushed the door open and we all jumped in [in] unison. We found that it was the mail carrier. He said, 'Very good. Don't shoot boys.' We came mighty near shooting him, not knowing who he was and not having much light." [193]

The mail carrier was Michael Cosgrove, who over-nighted at Fort Sumner on his stage runs. Leaving Cosgrove to his refuge, the posse took shelter in the Fort's old hospital building, a U-shaped adobe structure partitioned into numerous small rooms. Charles and Manuela Bowdre lived in one room of the building. The posse spent the night in the building.[194] (See drawing page 48.)

The next morning, from a man he met in the plaza, Iginio Garcia, Garrett learned that Billy and his companions were at the Brazil-Wilcox Ranch, about 10 miles east of Fort Sumner.[195] Garrett forced another man that he met, José Valdez – a friend of Billy's – to write a note to Billy saying Garrett and his posse had left for Roswell.[196]

Billy was fooled by José Valdez's note. That evening, December 19, Billy, Rudabaugh, Tom O'Folliard, Charles Bowdre, Tom Pickett, and Billy Wilson galloped into Fort Sumner. Garrett was prepared, having posted a guard to watch the road.

When Billy and the others rode into shooting range:

"Garrett hollered at the bunch to throw up their hands. They jirked [sic] their six-shooters, and the fight commenced." [197]

"They was about 40 shots fired." [198]

Everyone in Billy's party *"whirled"* their horses and fled – with the exception of the person riding the lead horse –Tom O'Folliard. His horse *"ran in a circle and came back."* [199]

Posse member James East described the events that followed:

"Garrett said, 'Throw up your hands, or we'll shoot you down.' [O'Folliard] said, 'Don't shoot any more, Pat, I'm dying....' He was shot through the heart. We took him inside and laid him down on my blanket. The boys went back to playing poker and I sat down by the fire."

48 ~ "Dirty Dave" Rudabaugh

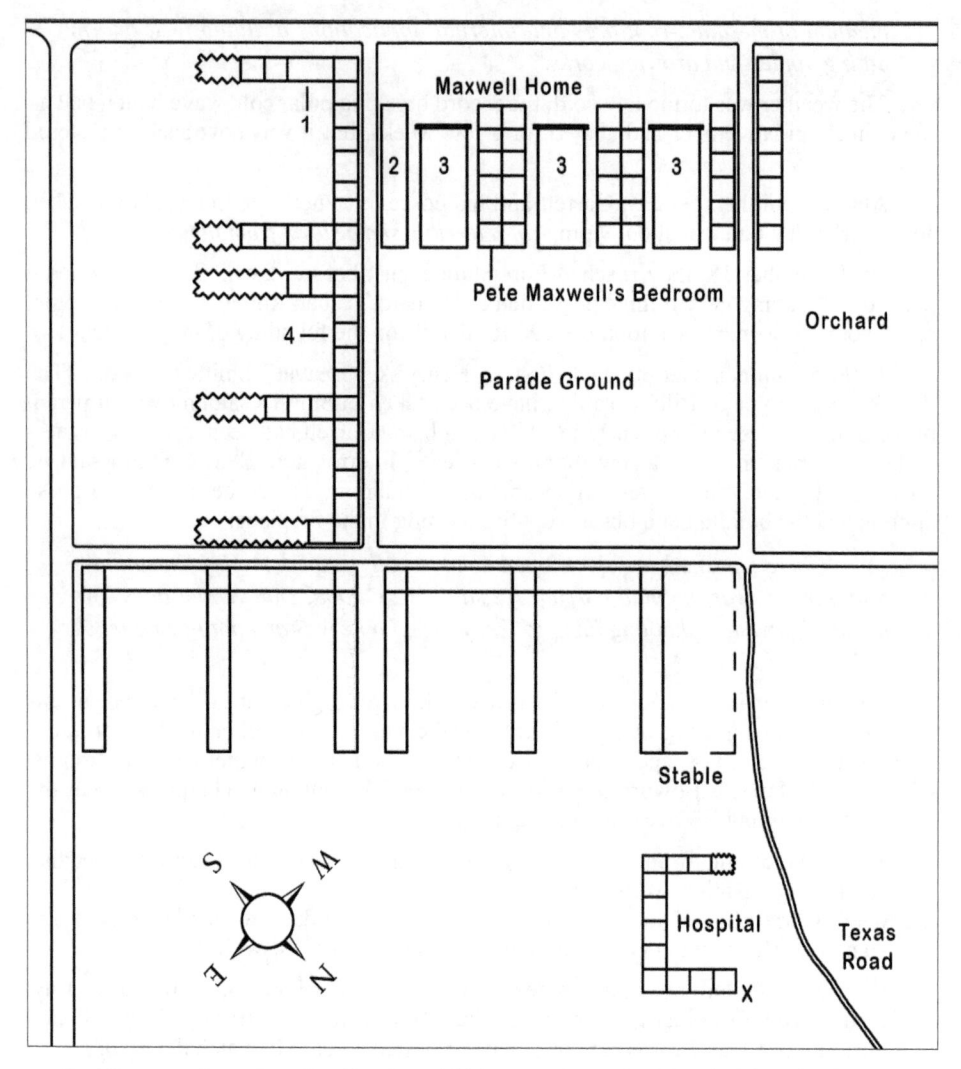

Fort Sumner, based on the October, 1881, map drawn by Charlie Foor. (1) Beaver Smith's saloon/store, (2) Dance hall and (3) flower gardens. (x) Spot where Tom O;'Folliard was shot. Pete Maxwell's bedroom was located in the southeast corner of the Maxwell home. The June, 1880, census shows Billy, Charles and Manuela Bowdre, A. B. Bennet, and Wilis Pruitt living in one room of the Hospital Building. Also living at Fort Sumner at the time according to the 1880 census are Barney Mason and his 17-year-old wife Juana María.

> *"Tom, in a low voice, cussed Garrett, saying 'God damn you Pat, I hope to meet you in hell.' Pat said, 'I wouldn't talk that way Tom, you're going to die in a few minutes,' and then [Tom] said, 'and go to Hell, you longlegged S—of B–.'"*
>
> *"The game went on and blood began running inside Tom, gurgling. He asked me to get him a drink of water. I did and he drank a little, laid back, shuddered, and was dead. The poker-playing went on. It was a thing to get their mind off the fight, and to keep the men from growing weary."* [200] [Intense thirst is a symptom of heavy bleeding – satisfying it invariably quickens death.]

In the exchange of gunfire, a bullet hit Rudabaugh's horse. Rudabaugh was able to ride the horse for miles before it died; he then doubled up behind Wilson.[201]

O'Folliard was buried the next morning in the frigid, snow-covered Fort Sumner cemetery. He was 22 years old. A resident was paid to build a wooden box for his body. [202]

The day of O'Folliard's burial, Manuel Brazil came to Fort Sumner. He was dispatched by Billy to determine if Garrett remained at Fort Sumner.[203]

Billy's trust in Brazil was fatal. On arriving in Fort Sumner, Brazil immediately sought out Garrett. Brazil agreed to return to his ranch and tell Billy that Garrett was *"considerably scared"* and intended to leave for Roswell. Garrett instructed Brazil that if Billy was at his ranch, he was to remain there; if Billy was not at his ranch, Brazil was to return to Fort Sumner.[204]

At his ranch, Brazil found Billy, Rudabaugh, and their companions gone. Brazil promptly turned around and made the hard trek back to Fort Sumner, reaching Fort Sumner about midnight:

> *"There was snow on the ground, it was desperately cold, and Brazil's beard was full of icicles."* [205]

Garrett ordered his men to saddle up. It was snowing heavily. Garrett planned to take a *"circuitous route"* to the ranch. Brazil was ordered to ride directly to his ranch and determine whether Billy had returned. A few miles from the Fort, the posse spotted *"a dead horse, the one Dave Rudabaugh had ridden to death."* The corpse was frozen and was shot *"through the entrails."* [206]

Three miles from the Wilcox-Brazil ranch, the posse met Brazil. Brazil had been to his ranch already, determined Billy was not there, and learned where he was. Billy and his companions had left for an abandoned – and now infamous – "Rock House" at Stinking Springs.[207]

Brazil pointed to a line of horse tracks in the snow – it was Billy's trail, he told Garrett. That act was a treacherous betrayal of Billy by Brazil. Garrett emphasized in his book that Brazil had always been Billy's *"faithful friend"* before this duplicitous double-cross.[208] Although Garrett does not say it, it is certain that Brazil was paid something for his "help."

Garrett and his men arrived at the Rock House about 2 in the morning:

> *"When we come in sight of there horses tide in front of a little house that had been a ranch, but was vacant. We got down tide our horses and left too men with them. The balance of us sliped up to a little spring branch which ran along in front about 20 steps from the door.... We crauld up and went all around the*

Manuel Silvestre Brazil, undated photo.

little house to see if they was any port holes in it." [Polk account, spelling uncorrected.] [209]

Garrett continued the story:

"Shivering with cold, we awaited daylight or a movement from the inmates of the house. I had a perfect description of the Kid's dress, especially his hat. I had told all the posse that, should the Kid make his appearance, it was my intention to kill him, and the rest would surrender.... [I] told my men when I brought up my gun, to all raise and fire." [210]

As the sun broke over the snow on that December 23, a man carrying a moral (nosebag) stepped out of the house to feed his horse. Garrett, thinking it was the Billy:

"...gave the signal by bringing my gun up to my shoulder, my men raised, and seven bullets sped on their errand of death." [211]

The man was hit by three bullets, *"one in the leg and too (sic) in the body."* [212]

But the mortally wounded man wasn't Billy – it was Charles Bowdre. Garrett, so certain he could recognize Billy by his clothes and hat, had made an appalling mistake.

It was discovered later *"that [Bowdre] had been shot through the right breast, the ball coming out in the neck."* [213]

Bowdre fell back *"with his head back in the house."* [214] The men inside dragged him out of gunfire range:

"[Inside] we could hear them talk. Kid said, 'Charles, you're going to die anyway, so go on out to see if you can't get more of them.' He came out but we could see he was staggering along. He had a six-shooter in his hand, but was not able to cock it. The bank was about 2 1/2 feet high. Lee Hall and I [East] were lying together, and he fell over on Lee. We took his six-shooter which was useless to him, as he was dead." [215]

Garrett saw that someone inside was trying to lead one of the horses tethered outside into the house. Seeing that the tether to the horse was *"shaking"* too much to shoot it, he shot the horse dead, *"just as the horse was fairly in the opening."*

"To prevent another attempt of this kind, I shot the ropes in two which held the other two horses, and they walked away." [216]

The felled horse obstructed the entrance, forestalling any attempt to make a wild break for freedom on Billy's bay racing mare, *"celebrated for speed, bottom, and beauty,"* one of the two horses confined inside the house. [217]

(In 1884, Lon Reed visited the rock house and saw the *"bleached skeleton" of the horse Garrett shot still lying in the doorway."* [218]

Garrett shouted for Billy to surrender; Billy refused. In the banter that followed, Garrett made it clear to Billy – *"to drop on the fact"* – that he was betrayed by Brazil.

After about six hours, debating their situation, recognizing the inevitable, and – as they later admitted – impelled by the enticing aroma of sizzling bacon, the "gang" resolved to surrender. Rudabaugh thrust out a stick with a white rag tied to it.

"We asked what he wanted and he said Billy said he wanted to surrender. He wanted to surrender under the conditions that we would give thim (sic) safe conduct to Santa Fe. Garrett promised the Kid safe conduct through Las Vegas."

Tom Pickett, undated photo. Courtesy Palace of the Governors Photo Archives (NMHM/DCA), 089720.

"Kid and his men came out with their hands up. Barney Mason said, 'Kill him, he's [slippery] and may get away....' He leveled his gun and Lee Hall and I [East] threw our guns down on Mason and said, 'If you fire a shot, we'll kill you.'" [219]

Surrendering with Billy were Rudabaugh, Thomas Pickett, and Billy Wilson.

Following their decision to surrender:

"...the boys came on out and left the arms in the house. When they got to us they all shuck (sic) hands with every man then sat down and [ate] supper. After supper we all mounted our horses. I took Billy the Kid up behind me while the other boys doubled up on ther horses and we started to Wilcoxes ranch...." [220]

"The Kid and Rudabaugh were cheerful and gay during the trip. Wilson seemed dejected, and Pickett was frightened." [221]

On arrival at the Wilcox-Brazil ranch, Garrett dispatched Brazil, Mason, and Rudolph back to the rock house with a wagon to recover the arms abandoned in the house and to retrieve Bowdre's now-frozen corpse.

"Billy made me [Polk] a present of his Winchester and Frank Stewart took his fine Bay mare." [222]

"Stewart now has the pleasure of owning the fleetest horse in the territory." [223]

Garrett took a *"Winchester 1873 saddle ring carbine and a Colt Frontier six-shooter"* from Billy Wilson. Both weapons fired a .44 Winchester cartridge, a huge advantage as both weapons could be carried without requiring two kinds of ammunition. Garrett would use that pistol to kill Billy 203 days later. (For more details on these two weapons,

52 ~ "Dirty Dave" Rudabaugh

Rock House at Stinking Springs built by Alejandro Perea. To the left of the building you can see the remains of a "summer porch," an outdoor workspace. In 1884, Lon Reed visited the rock house and saw the *"bleached skeleton"* of the horse Garrett shot still lying in the doorway. Undated photo. Courtesy Bosque Redondo Memorial Monument

Partially demolished Rock House at Stinking Springs. Undated photo. Courtesy Donald Cline Collection, image 74337, box 10422, f. 157, New Mexico State Records Center and Archives.

Rock House site today. 2020 photo by the author.

and the lawsuit that Garrett's widow filed to recover the weapons in 1933, see *"Killing Pat Garrett, The Wild West's Most Famous Lawman – Murder or Self-Defense?"*) [224]

At the Wilcox-Brazil ranch, *"Wilcox's wife fixed some supper and we took turns guarding [the prisoners], two of us at time."* [225] Next morning, the posse and prisoners left for Fort Sumner. They *"had a wagon and put the prisoners in it while the other boys rode horse back."* [226]

Garrett left Fort Sumner that evening with the prisoners, taking only Mason, Stewart, East, and Emory as guards. After a short layover at Gerhardt's ranch, the party reached Puerto de Luna at 2 pm. They put up at Alexander Grzelachowski's residence/store. It was December 25, 1880 – Christmas Day.[227]

All but East enjoyed a celebratory Christmas dinner with the Grzelachowski family. East spent the time uneasily guarding the prisoners. After supper, not wanting to take any chance of the prisoners being rescued or escaping, Garrett ordered that they leave immediately for Las Vegas. They travelled all night and reached the city late in afternoon of December 26 (75 miles).[228]

Jailing Rudabaugh, Billy, Pickett, and Wilson – December 26, 1880

"The greatest excitement prevailed yesterday afternoon when the news was noised abroad that Pat Garrett and Frank Stewart had arrived in town [Las Vegas] bringing with them Billy 'the Kid,' the notorious outlaw and three of his gang. People stood on the muddy street corners and in hotel offices and saloons talking of the great event...."

"Groups of people flocked to the jail and hung around the corners straining their necks to catch a glimpse of... the brave fellows who had brought in the

54 ~ "Dirty Dave" Rudabaugh

Las Vegas train station, photo circa 1880. Courtesy Palace of the Governors Photo Archives (NMHM/DCA), 114893.

Santa Fe jail, Water Street side. Undated photo. Courtesy Palace of the Governors Photo Archives (NMHM/DCA), 163219.

outlaws. But they went quietly from the jail to the corral and from there to the National House where the half-starved, tired men sought to escape the scrutinizing gaze of the scores of hero worshippers." [229]

Many in the boisterous crowd lauding the capture of the four outlaws wanted to immediately *"mete out justice"* to Rudabaugh for his presumed role in Valdez's death.[230]

It was because of their fears of this "justice" that Billy and Rudabaugh – especially Rudabaugh – had surrendered only on the terms that Garrett would jail them in Santa Fe, not Las Vegas. Stewart affirmed this agreement in a later newspaper interview: *"we gave all four our word that we would take them to Santa Fe."* [231]

The outlaws' arrival was rousing news. The men were interviewed by both Las Vegas newspapers.

The *Las Vegas Daily Gazette* noted that just prior to their reporter's interview:

> *"Mike Cosgrove... had just gone in with four large bundles.... One by one the bundles were unpacked disclosing a good suit of clothes for each man. Mr. Cosgrove remarked that he wanted 'to see the boys go away in style.'"*

> *"'Billy, the Kid' and Billy Wilson who were shackled together stood patiently up while a blacksmith took off their shackles and bracelets to allow them an opportunity to make a change of clothing."* [232]

The other local newspaper, the *Las Vegas Daily Optic*, reported:

> *"[Rudabaugh was] dressed about the same as when in Las Vegas [nine months earlier], apparently not having made any raids upon clothing stores.... He inquired anxiously in regard to the feeling in the community, and was told it was very strong against him."* [233]

Evidently the *Daily Optic* interview happened before Rudabaugh was gifted his new clothes.

Garrett recognized the menacing threat of the townspeople's spreading anti-Rudabaugh sentiment. He decided to leave Pickett in jail in Las Vegas, as the charges against him were minor. Billy, Rudabaugh, and Wilson he would take to Santa Fe, as promised. He had with him Stewart, East, Emory, and Mason as fellow guards. He asked Michael Cosgrove to join them. For extra help, he wired J. F. Morley in Santa Fe, asking him to rush to Las Vegas. Morley was the U.S. Postal Inspector that had filed robbery charges against Weston and Mrs. Deolatere for the Fort Sumner stage robbery.[234]

> *"After breakfast we went to the jail for our prisoners. They turned out the Kid and Wilson to us, who were handcuffed together. We demanded Rudabaugh. They refused to yield him up, saying... they wanted him for murder. I told them my right to the prisoner ranked theirs...."* [235]

Garrett hauled his prisoners by mule wagon to the train depot and loaded them into the smoking car of the Santa Fe train.[236]

While Billy was leaning out of one of the car's windows, a *Daily Gazette* reporter got another chance to question him:

> *"'If it hadn't been for the dead horse in the doorway, I wouldn't be here. I would have ridden out on my bay mare and taken my chances of escaping,' said he. 'But I couldn't ride out over that, for she would have jumped back,*

and I would have got it in the head. We could have staid in the house but there wouldn't have been anything gained by that for they would have starved us out. I thought it was better to come out and get a good square meal – don't you?'" [237]

Just after the prisoners were loaded, the train was surrounded by a *"posse"* of thirty well-armed men led by Sheriff Hilario Romero meaning to seize the prisoners by force and lynch Rudabaugh.[238]

Morley gives this account of the events:

"...when I arrived at Vegas the mob had the train captured... I at once went on the train where Pat had the Prisoners, Pat told me he was going to cut the Irons off the Boys and let them make a fight for there (sic) lives.... I went up to the residence of A. A. Robinson the Chief Engineer for the Santa Fe RR, and asked him for a train crew to take the train out. Robinson told me I could have all the rolling stock of the Company but would have to man it myself." [239]

Morley, an ex-train engineer, stoked the steam engine and piloted the train to Santa Fe. By 7:30 that evening, the prisoners were securely locked in the Santa Fe jail.[240]

Rudabaugh Confesses to Stage Robberies – December 28, 1880

On December 28, the morning after his jailing in Santa Fe, Rudabaugh was taken before U.S. Commissioner Samuel Ellison for a preliminary examination. He pleaded guilty to two charges of robbing the U.S. Mail, thereby adopting the "confession" strategy that worked so successfully for him in the Kinsley train robbery. Rudabaugh told the court that:

"...he has nothing to gain by keeping silent longer and resolved to make a clean breast of it. His confession establishes the innocence of the Stokes boys." [241]

His confession to the Tecolote stage robbery cleared Mullen and William and Joseph Stokes. His confession to the Fort Sumner robbery established that he, Wilson, and Pickett were the robbers. Circumstantial evidence of Wilson's guilt was found in his pocket when he was captured at the Rock House – a crumpled $20 dollar bill that was identified as the one taken in the Fort Sumner stage robbery.[242]

On February 26, 1881, Rudabaugh was sentenced to life in prison for his part in the two stage robberies. (Because his robberies included stealing from the U.S. Mail, he was sentenced under Federal law.) Mullen and William and Joseph Stokes were released. The *Las Vegas Optic* in reporting their liberation noted:

"The men have been closely confined in filthy quarters fit only for dumb brutes, and now with ruined health and damaged character step forth to begin life anew. There remains no doubt that they were the victims of a conspiracy and have been suffering for crimes committed by others." [243]

(As noted earlier, Joseph Stokes would later be lynched in El Paso.)

Billy, Rudabaugh, and Wilson Almost Escape – February 28, 1881

"[On the afternoon of February 28], it was discovered that the Kid and his gang had concocted and were stealthily carrying out a plan by which they hoped to gain their freedom and escape the fate that awaits them. And very

fortunate it was that the discovery was made just when it was, for a night or two more would have sufficed for the completion of the well laid scheme."

"It appears that [Deputy] Sheriff Romulo Martinez fearing that the four desperate men, the Kid, Rudabaugh, Billy Wilson and ["Choctaw"] Kelly, would ere long make a desperate effort to get out had promised to pay one of the prisoners if he would assist the guard in keeping watch and yesterday the fellow informed him that the men were trying to dig out. Sheriff Martinez, accompanied by Deputy Marshal [Tony] Neis, at once proceeded to the jail, and entering the cell, found the men at supper. They examined the room and found that the bed ticking was filled with stones and earth, and removing the mattress discovered a deep hole."

"Further investigation showed that the men had dug themselves nearly out, and by concealing the loose earth in the bed and covering the hole up with it had almost reached the street without awakening the suspicion of the guard." [244]

Webb's Legal Troubles Recommence - January 6, 1881

Now that Webb was back in custody, he was again facing his pending legal charges.

On January 6, 1881, the Territorial Supreme Court considered Webb's appeal for his conviction for killing Kelliher in the Goodlett and Roberts' Saloon. (The consideration of the appeal had been deferred by Webb's jail escape.) The Supreme Court upheld the murder decision of the trial court and ordered that Webb be executed.[245] On January 29, Acting Governor William Ritch signed Webb's death warrant ordering his hanging February 25, 1881, in Las Vegas (Governor Wallace was traveling and unreachable).[246]

On February 12, Webb was tried for being an accomplice in the Tecolote stage robbery. Rudabaugh testified in Webb's defense. He told the jury that he led the men that robbed the stage and Webb was *"not at all concerned in the affair."* [247]

"No amount of persuasion or threats would induce him to give the names of those who were connected with him in the robbery, and inasmuch as he is already in jail awaiting trial for his delinquencies and it was not in the power of the court to punish him farther for his contumacy, the advantage remained with him and his secret was safe. Rudabaugh preserved a composed and resolute manner during the whole affair...." [248]

Rudabaugh would later admit that the other two holdup men were Joseph Martin and Joe Carson.[249]

The jury acquitted Webb of the robbery charge after deliberating for an hour and twenty minutes.[250]

Immediately after Webb's acquittal in the Tecolote robbery, his lawyer for that case, Eugene A. Fiske, started a petition to commute Webb's death sentence for killing Kelliher to life in prison. Numerous influential persons joined the effort, including Las Vegas Judge John F. Bostwick and F. D. Locke, owner of the *"finest billiard hall in Las Vegas."* L. Johnson, a resident of Dodge City, Kansas, started a petition there and obtained a large number of signatures, including those of several Kansas legislators.[251]

Bostwick, Locke, and Johnson travelled to Santa Fe at their own expense to meet with Governor Wallace (Bostwick and Locke from Las Vegas, Johnson from Dodge City). The *Las Vegas Gazette* noted:

"There is one thing certain, no man ever had such determined men at work to save his life as J. J. Webb.... All three of the gentlemen... carry letters to the governor asking, at least, that there be a stay of proceedings." [252]

On February 22, Governor Wallace granted Webb a 20-day stay of execution:

"...to permit an investigation of the petitions for a commutation of sentence to imprisonment for life. The petitions in the case are very strong...." [253]

On February 25, the *Las Vegas Daily Optic* published Webb's life story. The article was based on an extensive interview with Webb and was surprisingly sympathetic. It strongly suggests the orchestrating hand of Webb's lawyers, the purpose of the article being to help Webb gain a commutation of his death sentence. Accompanying the article was an engraving of Webb made from a specially commissioned photograph taken by Las Vegas photographer Frank Evans (shown on page 58).

The article opens with the headline *"Will Hang on Saturday, March 12, Unless Gov. Wallace Intercedes."* The original date for Webb's hanging was February 25. With the 20-day extension, the new hanging date was March 12. The article continued:

"[The] Governor has granted a reprieve until the 12th day of March and will perhaps commute the death sentence to imprisonment for life, thus preventing a ghastly spectacle that all would shudder to witness.... John Joshua Webb, the doomed, policeman whose life is a dark and dreary one at best, for solitary confinement during one's natural life is to be dreaded nearly as much as grim death itself, was born of hard-working, respectable parents in Keokuk county, Iowa, on the 13th day of February, 1847, being now 34 years of age."

"His parents, from whom he has been estranged many years, are now living a quiet secluded life on a farm near Oskaloosa, Kansas, and, besides, he had eleven brothers and sisters living in different parts of the county." [254]

The article revealed that Webb could not read or write, having had no childhood education. At 17 he left home for Colorado. For the next six years he worked jobs in Colorado, Kansas, Indian Territory (Oklahoma), and New Mexico.

In 1871, he acquired a ranch outside of Caldwell, Kansas. Being in *"unusually poor health and not in a condition to endure the exposure incident to a frontier life,"* he sold the ranch a year later. He next tried his hand at saloon keeping. He sold that, tried buffalo hunting, ox team freighting (in Texas), and hauling supplies from Dodge City to Canton, Texas, for the U.S. Army:

"Becoming tired of making these long, lonely trips and enduring untold dangers and hardships, he returned to Dodge City in 1875 and was given a position as wagon master in the army." [255]

Webb continued to work as a freighter until early 1879 when he opened the Lady Gay Saloon in Dodge City. During the "Railroad War" between the Rio Grande and the Atchison, Topeka & Santa Fe Railroads at Royal Gorge, Colorado, he was the chief of guards for the AT&SF Railroad.

"Here it was that Webb conducted himself in a most praiseworthy manner, making many friends who have not forsaken him in the present trouble. At one time, according to his own statement, he refused a bribe of $8000 offered by enemies of the [AT&SF]. Before leaving the employ of the company, they

presented him with $500 as a partial reward for his faithfulness and unflinching courage." [256]

Asked if he and Hoodoo Brown had planned the killing of Kelliher in order to steal his money, he emphatically denied it, *"Hoodoo never approached him in [any] endeavor to put up a job on anybody."*

The article ended with:

"Webb's life is a horrible one and in it there is a world of warning to the young man, who has a fondness for liquors and loud company." [257]

On March 4, Governor Wallace commuted Webb's death sentence to life in prison. His stated reasons were:

John Joshua Webb. Engraving published with his life story, February 25, 1881. *Las Vegas Daily Optic.*

"That John J. Webb was at the time of the killing acting as police guard; ...that the deceased was a stranger in the city, drunk and armed; that the prisoner [Webb] came to him in a saloon and ordered him to throw up his hands, but without giving him time for compliance with the order, or waiting to see if such extreme measures were necessary, fired upon and killed the man. There is no evidence showing any intent to rob the deceased. Under the circumstances and considering that the prisoner was an officer charged with duties similar to those of a policeman, always difficult of performance, but in Las Vegas at the time of the killing both difficult and dangerous; ...in consideration of the very large petition forwarded to the executive office by intelligent and respectable citizens of East and West Las Vegas; ...the undersigned does grant and direct that the sentence of death for said killing [be] commuted to imprisonment at labor for life." [258]

Rudabaugh Granted Change of Venue – March 19, 1881

On February 26, District Court Judge L. Bradford Prince suspended Rudabaugh's Federal life sentence for robbing the U.S. Mail so that he could be returned to Las Vegas and be tried for killing Valdez. The decision:

"...created no little talk on the streets. Many persons claim that the judge was in error and among these were several prominent lawyers, who assert that inasmuch as the offenses against the United States laws, of which the prisoner was accused and of which he plead guilty, were committed before the offense which made him amenable to the laws of the Territory and that inasmuch as he was arrested and found guilty at the expense of the United States, he should have been made to serve out his sentence of imprisonment for life." [259]

Following this decision, the *Santa Fe New Mexican* reported that public opinion against Rudabaugh in Las Vegas was *"venomous"* and he was almost certain to be hung from *"the nearest tree."*

"Rudabaugh, himself, thinks with the people of Santa Fe, and gives up his case as hopeless. He says that he had made up his mind that he must go to the penitentiary for life and had resigned himself to that fate. 'But now,' he said, 'I am gone. When I leave here for Las Vegas I tell you all good-bye for good. They will murder me just as sure as I go to Las Vegas.'"

"He remembers the demonstration at the Las Vegas depot when he, 'The Kid,' and Billy Wilson were brought through to Santa Fe, and looks upon his death at the hands of the mob there as inevitable." [260]

On March 7, Rudabaugh was transported to Las Vegas by Sheriff Hilario Romero.

LeBaron Bradford Prince, undated photo. *Old Santa Fe*.

"Radabaugh was brought up in irons and showed a restless, uneasy condition of mind when he was taken from the [train] cars. He retained a stolid, hangdog demeanor, and showed no disposition to recognize any of his old acquaintances. He is poor in flesh, and does not weigh by twenty pounds as much as he did a year ago, while prancing up and down the streets of Las Vegas. What a chance a year has brought forth! Then the free man – now the chained culprit, doomed to the decree of justice or possible Judge Lynch's mandate, for we hear the grumblings of men who have revenge in their hearts." [261]

Rudabaugh's trial for killing Valdez opened March 18, 1881, in the First District Court, Judge Prince presiding. Rudabaugh pled destitution and the court appointed W. M. Whitelaw and Edgar Caypless as his legal representatives. They immediately asked the court for a continuance so they could prepare a motion for change of venue, which Judge Prince granted.[262]

That afternoon, his lawyers presented the court with five arguments as to why Rudabaugh could not get a fair and impartial trial in Las Vegas. Summarized, their arguments were:

- The people in the county subject to jury duty are very greatly prejudiced against Rudabaugh.
- A large number of citizens of this county have threatened to unite in forcibly taking this defendant from the jail and hanging him.
- That Valdez, who Rudabaugh is charged with killing, is very largely connected in this community by blood and marriage and the wide influences of these persons will prevent the defendant from receiving a fair and impartial trial.

- That articles published in the *Las Vegas Gazette* and *Las Vegas Optic* have made allegations very injurious to the defendant that were calculated to prejudice the people of this and other counties.
- That when the defendant was moved from Las Vegas to Santa Fe a few weeks ago, a large number of armed citizens went to the train depot to forcibly take the defendant from the custody of the sheriff and kill him. [263]

To further support their argument, Rudabaugh's attorneys submitted a sworn affidavit by Postal Inspector J. F. Morley, affirming:

"That for most of the time for the last six months he [Morley] has been in official duties which caused him to be a good deal in the Counties of San Miguel and Mora, that during that time he has heard many prominent men of both communities express their opinions with reference to the guilt of said Rudabaugh... and affiant does not believe that [Rudabaugh] could have a fair and impartial trial in either of said Counties." [264]

Judge Prince was persuaded by these arguments and ordered Rudabaugh's trial moved to Santa Fe.

On March 21, Rudabaugh was taken by train to Santa Fe. Las Vegas authorities tried to keep the departure time of the trip secret, but failed. When Rudabaugh arrived at the train depot accompanied Sheriff Hilario Romero and his deputies, they had to make their way through a large, menacing crowd. In spite of repeated, loud calls to seize Rudabaugh, no serious attempt was made by the mob to take him by force. A man who was on the same train as Rudabaugh told the *Santa Fe New Mexican*:

"[The man] emphatically contradicts the assertion of one of the Las Vegas papers to the effect that Rudabaugh was badly frightened by the crowd which had assembled at the depot.... [He says] that he could not detect the slightest uneasiness on [Rudabaugh's] part throughout the whole affair.... He says the prisoner is as cool and brave a customer in danger as he ever saw." [265]

Rudabaugh Convicted of Killing Valdez – April 19, 1881

Rudabaugh's trial for killing Valdez opened April 19 in the First District Court in Santa Fe, Judge Prince presiding. The charge was murder in the first degree, the penalty death by hanging.

Rudabaugh's defense attorneys were George G. Posey and Marshal A. Breeden (the lawyers that had handled his change of venue motion were sick). The attorney for the Territory (the prosecution) was William Breeden. Rather oddly, especially for a criminal trial, Prosecutor William Breeden was the older brother of Defense Attorney Marshal Breeden.[266]

One of the visitors at Rudabaugh's trial with a personal interest in his fate was Frank Stewart, who, with Pat Garrett and others, had captured him at Stinking Springs. Stewart made the trip to Santa Fe from Las Vegas by train, for just that reason. Garrett did not attend the trial.[267]

The complete transcript of the testimony in the trial is given in Appendix A.

The prosecution opened its case against Rudabaugh by calling San Miguel County Sheriff Hilario Romero.[268] After being sworn, Romero testified that he knew Valdez, a jailer in the Las Vegas jail. Asked if he knew how Valdez died, Romero replied that he died of a gunshot wound in the *"right or the left side"* in one of the guard rooms of the jail. He said he did not see the actual shooting. Romero was asked about Rudabaugh:

> ***Wm Breeden:*** *Did you see the defendant that day?*
> ***Romero:*** *I did.*
>
> ***Wm Breeden:*** *Where was it you saw him?*
> ***Romero:*** *I saw him running from the hall of the Court House to the corner, as he turned around.*
>
> ***Wm Breeden:*** *Was he running.*
> ***Romero:*** *Yes sir.*
>
> ***Wm Breeden:*** *Any one with him?*
> ***Romero:*** *Yes sir.*
>
> ***Wm Breeden:*** *Who was with him?*
> ***Romero:*** *Another man whose name I did not know at the time.*
>
> ***Wm Breeden:*** *Did he have anything with him?*
> ***Romero:*** *They had pistols in their hands.*
>
> ***Wm Breeden:*** *Did the defendant have pistols?*
> ***Romero:*** *Yes sir.*
>
> ***Wm Breeden:*** *You saw them running out of the hall of the Court House?*
> ***Romero:*** *I saw them running until they turned the corner.*

Romero testified that it was a sudden sound that called his attention to the events in the jail:

> ***Wm Breeden:*** *Had you at the time shortly before seeing the defendant, or had you seen or heard anything that attracted your attention?*
> ***Romero:*** *Yes sir.*
>
> ***Wm Breeden:*** *What?*
> ***Romero:*** *I heard a shot.*
>
> ***Wm Breeden:*** *Where did the sound of the shot come from?*
> ***Romero:*** *From inside the enclosure [placita].*
>
> ***Wm Breeden:*** *The enclosure where the man was shot?*
> ***Romero:*** *Yes sir.*
>
> ***Wm Breeden:*** *How long after you heard the shot did the defendant run out?*
> ***Romero:*** *About six or seven minutes.*

Defense Attorney Posey in his cross examination extracted more details from Romero about hearing the shot and seeing Rudabaugh and another man sprint from the jail, but none of this elicited testimony discredited or contradicted Romero's prior testimony.

After Romero was excused, the prosecution called County Clerk Jesus Maria Tafoya:

> ***Wm Breeden:*** *Do you know how he [Valdez] came to his death?*
> ***Tafoya:*** *I don't know any more but what he told me before he died.*

Wm Breeden: *Did he make a statement before he died?*
Tafoya: *Yes sir.*

Wm Breeden: *What was his condition?*
Tafoya: *He could understand everything I asked him.*

Wm Breeden: *What condition was he in regard to heath?*
Tafoya: *He was badly wounded.*

Wm Breeden: *How was he wounded?*
Tafoya: *By means of a shot.*

Wm Breeden: *Did he understand his condition?*
Tafoya: *Yes sir.*

Wm Breeden: *You say he was badly wounded. In what part of the person?*
Tafoya: *On the breast. Somewhere on the breast.*

Wm Breeden: *Did he say anything about his condition?*
Tafoya: *Yes sir.*

Wm Breeden: *What did he say as to his condition?*
Tafoya: *He said he was very ill or sick.*

Wm Breeden: *Did he say anything more?*
Tafoya: *He answered to the questions I asked him.*

Wm Breeden: *Do you know how he felt or whether he knew he was very ill or not?*
Tafoya: *He told me he expected to die.*

Wm Breeden: *How long after did he die?*
Tafoya: *He died about nine or ten o'clock at night of the same day.*

Wm Breeden: *When did he make the statement as to how he received the wounds?*
Tafoya: *About two o'clock in the afternoon.*

Wm Breeden: *What statement did he make?*
Tafoya: *I believe I am going to die. I am very sick.*

Wm Breeden: *What did he say about it?*
Tafoya: *When I saw him he was wounded. I asked him who gave him that shot and the said that it was the smallest man of the two, who went inside the jail. He fired the shot at me, and the other man took the keys which I had tied at my belt and threw them into Webb's cell. That is all he told me.*

Tafoya was asked about Rudabaugh:

Wm Breeden: *Did you see the defendant about there that day?*
Tafoya: *Yes sir.*

Wm Breeden: *State where and under what circumstances you saw him.*
Tafoya: *I was at that time at the office of the Probate Court. One of the jailers, Benito [Benedito] Duran, was with me. A few moments after he had been there we heard a shot. I heard that the shot thundered very much. I*

told the jailer [Duran] I thought that shot was inside the jail and he went out and I heard a noise at the door of the hallway to the jail [he means the outside door into the hall]. He rapped it for the second time. When I heard him rap the door the second time I came out and looked towards the door. Then I went towards the door myself. I stood there until he turned around. He told me the prisoners were going out on the other side.

Few minutes after I rapped two times and no one responded. I heard the grunts or complaints of someone inside the jail, I did not know who. A few minutes afterwards Rudabaugh opened the door with his left hand. He opened the door and with his right he had a pistol which he pointed at me and said 'Look out Jesus.' Then I turned to one side of the door and he kept pointed the pistol at me and Allen came out of the hallway and went under his arm and then they went away together.

After they went away, I went inside the jail. There I met Ramirez, one of the witnesses in this case, with a sharp shooter in his hand. I went on further in and saw the pool of blood where the deceased first fell [in the placita]. I tracked the blood or spots of blood to the kitchen where he was lying down. I found him lying down on a bed there.

Tafoya was asked to draw a map of the jail, which he did (shown on page 65).

In his cross examination, Defense Attorney Posey elicited additional details from Tafoya, but nothing that discredited his testimony.

The prosecution next called José Ramirez, one of the jailers.

Wm. Breeden: Do you remember the day Antonio Lino Valdez was shot?
Ramirez: Yes.

Wm. Breeden: Where were you at that time?
Ramirez: I was a jailer in Las Vegas.

Wm. Breeden: Were abouts in Las Vegas were you at the time of that occurrence?
Ramirez: I was in a room [kitchen] inside the jail.

Wm. Breeden: State what you heard and saw then?
Ramirez: I heard a shot and then I saw the defendant and another one running out of the jail.

Wm. Breeden: Immediately after hearing the shot?
Ramirez: Yes.

Wm. Breeden: What were they doing?
Ramirez: When I heard the shot, I stepped out of the door of the kitchen and went out [into the placita]. I saw two men, they had pistols.

Wm. Breeden: Did this man have a pistol? (indicating defendant)
Ramirez: Yes sir.

In his cross examination, Posey, as with previous witnesses, elicited more details about what Ramirez saw, but, again, nothing to discredit Ramirez's testimony.

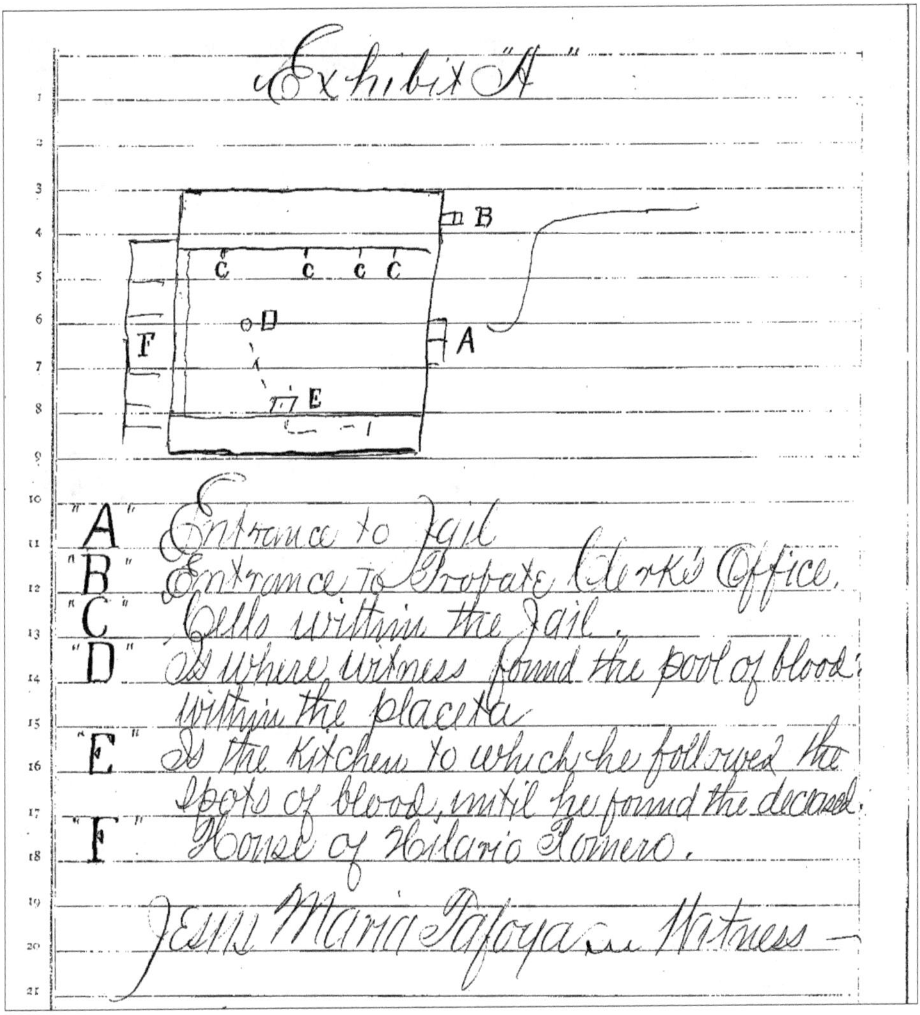
Exhibit "A"
B
C C C C
D
F
A
E
"A" Entrance to Jail
"B" Entrance to Probate Clerk's Office.
"C" Cells within the Jail.
"D" Is where witness found the pool of blood: within the placeta
"E" Is the Kitchen to which he followed the spots of blood, until he found the deceased.
"F" House of Hilario Romero.
Jesus Maria Tafoya — Witness —

"Exhibit A" drawn by witness Jesus Maria Tafoya. Note that the map mistakenly shows four jail cells. Territory of New Mexico vs David Rudabaugh, Case No. 128.

Posey did elicit one detail that would contradict part of Rudabaugh's later testimony:

> ***Posey:*** *When you came out of the room after you heard the shot, what did you do?*
> ***Ramirez:*** *I stood at the door.*
>
> ***Posey:*** *Did you pull your pistol?*
> ***Ramirez:*** *No.*
>
> ***Posey:*** *Didn't you have a pistol?*
> ***Ramirez:*** *I did not.*

SUMNER HOUSE
EAST LAS VEGAS, NEW MEXICO,
Geo. Sumner, Prop'r

This house is bran-new and has been elegantly furnished throughout. The Sumner is a first class house in every respect, and guests will be entertained in the best possible manner and at reasonable rates.

MENDENHALL & CO
Livery, Feed, and Sale
STABLE.

Dealers in Horses and Mules, also Fine Buggies and Carriages for Sale. Rigs for the Hot Springs and other Points of Interest. The Finest Livery Outfits in the Territory.

Top: Sumner House advertisement. *Las Vegas Gazette*, March 18, 1881.
Bottom: Mendalhall Livery advertisement, *Las Vegas Gazette*, July 2, 1880.

So far, none of the witnesses called by the prosecution had seen the shooting, only the events afterward. That deficiency would not be rectified by the next witness, the prosecution's last.

The prosecution called J. C. Cauldwell, a Las Vegas taxi driver.

Wm. Breeden: Where do you live?
Cauldwell: In Las Vegas

Wm. Breeden: Do you know this defendant?
Cauldwell: Yes sir.

Wm. Breeden: Where were you in the early part of April 1880?
Cauldwell: In Vegas.

Wm. Breeden: Do you know this man here? (indicating defendant)
Cauldwell: Yes sir.

Wm. Breeden: Do you remember the time a jailer was killed Las Vegas?
Cauldwell: Yes sir....

Wm. Breeden: What was your occupation?
Cauldwell: I was a hack driver.

Wm. Breeden: Did you see the defendant that day?
Cauldwell: Yes sir.

> ***Wm. Breeden:*** *Now state all you know about the circumstances connected with this case that you know of.*
> ***Cauldwell:*** *I don't know as I can call the day of the month. Somewhere between the third and the fifth. I have been driving a hack ever since Las Vegas had a new town. I was driving a hack at that time. It was between one and two o'clock. It was might have been after two in the afternoon that I saw this man Rudabaugh and John Allen. I came from the new town with a load of passengers and drove them to the Sumner House [in East Las Vegas]. Rudabaugh and Allen told me to wait. And they would go to the new town.*
>
> *And I waited and they told me to drive around by the jail, as they wanted to see Webb. After they got in, I drove around to the jail and stopped and Allen spoke to Rudabaugh and said something to Rudabaugh about he is not here and told me to drive up on the hill to the house of Tom Pickett. And I drove up there and they got down out of the hack and went in and had a conversation for half an hour. And then Rudabaugh and Allen and Pickett and another man, I never learned his name, came out of Pickett's house and got into the hack. They then told me to go on and I came down the back street to Mendenhall's [Livary] and from there I intended to drive into the stable but they said 'hold on we want to see Webb.'*
>
> *Then Pickett and the other man got out of the hack and went out into the Plaza and I went down to the jail with Rudabaugh and Allen. Then they got out of the hack and told me to wait. They went and rapped on the jail door and the man who was killed let them in. In a few minutes I heard a pistol shot and got a little frightened, and as I had an idea that something was the matter, I drove my team around to the Plaza. I did not know whether they had done anything, and I was kind of anxious to find out, so I stopped my team as soon as I got in the plaza. I thought I would tie my team and go back on foot and see what they had done. Just as I was in the act of getting out of the hack they came running around the corner and jumped into my hack and Allen said 'drive to the new town.' And I drove them over to the new town.*

Cauldwell was asked about the arms that Rudabaugh and Allen carried:

> ***Wm. Breeden:*** *Did they have arms when they went through the jail?*
> ***Cauldwell:*** *They had revolvers in their belts and before we got to the jail, I saw Allen's revolver.*
>
> ***Wm. Breeden:*** *You drove them to the new town [East Las Vegas]?*
> ***Cauldwell:*** *Yes sir.*
>
> ***Wm. Breeden:*** *Any thing occur on the road?*
> ***Cauldwell:*** *They each held their pistol in their hands from the old to the new town. Where we crossed the creek, Allen was pointing his revolver at me and I turned around to push it away. As I turned around Rudabaugh is the man who loaded his revolver at that time.*

Las Vegas, New Mexico, plaza. Undated photo by James Furlong. Courtesy Palace of the Governors Photo Archives (NMHM/DCA), 037187.

Wm. Breeden: *Was it a cartridge pistol or what?*
Cauldwell: *Yes sir.*

Wm. Breeden: *How many loads did he put in?*
Cauldwell: *One load.*

Wm. Breeden: *Did he remove anything?*
Cauldwell: *He took out a shell.*

Wm. Breeden: *You saw him remove a shell from the pistol and afterwards put in a new cartridge?*
Cauldwell: *Yes sir.*

Wm. Breeden: *You afterwards found an empty shell in the carriage?*
Cauldwell: *Yes sir.*

Wm. Breeden: *What was done with the cartridge?*
Cauldwell: *He put [it] into the pistol.*

This testimony was potentially damaging to Rudabaugh. Prior testimony established circumstantially that it was the *"smallest man,"* Allen, who apparently had shot Valdez. With Cauldwell's testimony, the prosecution was presenting indirect evidence that Rudabaugh had shot Valdez, because his pistol contained a spent cartridge. Reloading in the hack implied that the pistol had just been fired.

Asked what happened next, Cauldwell said:

Wm. Breeden: *Well? [What happened next?]*
Cauldwell: *When we got to the new town Rudabaugh jumped out and went into Goodlett's [Saloon] and I wanted Allen to get out and let me go. He wouldn't do that and then I wanted him to take the hack and let me go. Then Rudabaugh came out with a double barrel shot gun and laid it in the back*

and I started to get out. Allen said, 'you son of a bitch, if you make a move I will blow your brains out.' Then I said to Rudabaugh, you can take the team and go as far as you please, and he did not make any reply. So I jumped out of the hack and Allen was going to shoot and Rudabaugh said, 'don't make a fool of yourself, I will drive.' Then Rudabaugh took the lines and drove across to Houghton's Hardware store. They went in and Rudabaugh got some guns, I don't know how many, and put them in the hack and drove off [stealing the hack].

Wm. Breeden: *When they rode in the hack after leaving the jail and between there and the new town, did they say what they had done?*
Cauldwell: *I asked Allen what he had done and he said, 'that Greaser wouldn't give us the keys and we killed the son of a bitch.'*

Posey, in his cross, shredded Cauldwell's testimony that Rudabaugh had reloaded his pistol:

Posey: *Where did Rudabaugh sit?*
Cauldwell: *He sat in the back seat....*

Posey: *How did you happen to see Rudabaugh loading the pistol?*
Cauldwell: *He might have put all of the loads in at that time.*

Posey: *He might have had his pistol empty for all you know?*
Cauldwell: *Yes sir....*

Posey: *You did not notice whether all the chambers of Allen's pistol was full or not?*
Cauldwell: *No, he had them in his hand.*

Posey: *He might have had some empty?*
Cauldwell: *Yes sir.*

Posey: *Might not that have been Allen's pistol that Rudabaugh loaded?*
Cauldwell: *They must have changed.*

Posey: *Might not Allen have passed his pistol back to Rudabaugh while you were driving?*
Cauldwell: *It might have been done.*

With this exchange, Posey cast persuasive doubt on Cauldwell's testimony that Rudabaugh replaced a spent cartridge in his pistol. Posey also attacked Allen's supposed confession:

Posey: *Where did this conversation between you and Allen about killing the son of a bitch occur?*
Cauldwell: *While crossing the creek.*

Posey: *That was in the rocky part of the road?*
Cauldwell: *I had just crossed the rocky part.*

Posey: *You were going pretty fast?*
Cauldwell: *Yes sir....*

> **Posey:** *You say Rudabaugh made no reply when Allen said, we have killed this man?*
> **Cauldwell:** *I did not hear him.*

William Breeden in his redirect examination concentrated on bringing out the details of Rudabaugh and Allen's stealing of Cauldwell's hack after running from the jail. Breeden had failed to address this theft in his direct examination:

> **Wm. Breeden:** *You say Rudabaugh and Allen went off with your hack after coming out of Houghton's Hardware store?*
> **Cauldwell:** *Yes sir.*
>
> **Wm. Breeden:** *Did you see where they went?*
> **Cauldwell:** *I was in sight of them for about twelve or fourteen miles.*
>
> **Wm. Breeden:** *You kept in sight for about fourteen miles?*
> **Cauldwell:** *From twelve to fourteen.*
>
> **Wm. Breeden:** *Which way did they go?*
> **Cauldwell:** *They went East.*
>
> **Wm. Breeden:** *At what rate did they go?*
> **Cauldwell:** *I don't know. They went pretty fast.*
>
> **Wm. Breeden:** *When did you again see your hack?*
> **Cauldwell:** *After I lost sight of it I did not see it again until after sundown.*
>
> **Wm. Breeden:** *Where did you see it then?*
> **Cauldwell:** *It was then about twenty four miles East of Vegas.*

With Cauldwell's testimony, the prosecution rested. Breeden had shown that Valdez was mortally wounded by a gunshot and the perpetrator was either Rudabaugh or Allen. But he had not presented any direct evidence showing who fired the fatal shot.

The defense opened its case by calling William Mullen. Mullen was in the cell next to Webb's when Valdez was killed (he was serving his sentence for his false conviction of the Tecolote stage robbery). Mullen was an eye witness to the shooting. What an irony! Mullen was now testifying in defense of the man who had actually committed the crime for which Mullen was serving time!

Why had the prosecution not called Mullen? Because Breeden did not want any evidence before the jury that Allen had shot the jailer, not Rudabaugh. They wanted an encircling cloud of unfocused suspicion to enclose both men.

> **Posey:** *What is your name?*
> **Mullen:** *William Mullen*
>
> **Posey:** *Where do you live?*
> **Mullen:** *I live in Santa Fe now [by the time of this trial, he had been cleared and released].*
>
> **Posey:** *Where were you on the second day of April 1880?*
> **Mullen:** *In Las Vegas.*
>
> **Posey:** *Where in Las Vegas?*
> **Mullen:** *In jail.*

Posey: You say you were in jail?
Mullen: Yes sir.

Posey: Will you state to the jury whether you saw Rudabaugh that day?
Mullen: Yes sir.

Posey: Were you there when the jailer was killed?
Mullen: Yes sir.

Posey: Was Rudabaugh there?
Mullen: Yes sir.

Posey: State all you know about the circumstances connected with the killing.
Mullen: Rudabaugh and Allen came in there one afternoon abut two o'clock and had some tobacco and newspapers. They came in and Rudabaugh had his hand on the door of the cell. The first thing I heard was Allen saying 'Give me those keys you son of a bitch.' I don't know what the jailer said in Mexican. Then Allen shot him and ran behind and took the keys. And Rudabaugh ran out of the door.

Posey: Did Allen give the jailer any time to give up the keys?
Mullen: No sir. The pistol went off immediately.

Posey: What was Rudabaugh doing at that time?
Mullen: He had his hands up on the door talking to me and Webb.

That could not be more straightforward: Allen shot Valdez without warning and without Rudabaugh's advance knowledge.

Mullen was asked what happened next:

Posey: What happened after the shot was fired and Rudabaugh ran out?
Mullen: Allen threw the keys down to Webb, and said 'take these and unlock the door, I have to go.'

Posey: Were there any of the jailers in sight?
Mullen: No sir. I believe there was one [Ramirez] in the kitchen.

Posey: Did any of them come on the firing of the shot?
Mullen: Yes in two or three minutes.

Posey: Was Rudabaugh there when they came out?
Mullen: Yes sir.

Posey: How far were these men from you when the shooting took place?
Mullen: Not over two feet. Allen might have been four feet.

Posey clarified Rudabaugh's non-involvement in the shooting:

Posey: Did Rudabaugh say anything when the shot was fired?
Mullen: I didn't hear him.

Posey: He ran out immediately?
Mullen: Yes sir.

> *Posey:* Did Rudabaugh have a pistol in his hand.
> *Mullen:* I didn't see any.
>
> *Posey:* Could you have seen one?
> *Mullen:* Yes sir.
>
> *Posey:* When that shot was fired what was the position of his hand when the shot was fired?
> *Mullen:* He had them on the cell door.
>
> *Posey:* He was talking to you and Webb through the grating?
> *Mullen:* He was asking us how we got along.

In his cross examination, William Breeden tried to show that Mullen was an unreliable, untrustworthy witness:

> *Wm. Breeden:* What were you in jail for?
> *Mullen:* Train [stage] robbery.
>
> *Wm. Breeden:* What was Webb in for?
> *Mullen:* Murder.
>
> *Wm. Breeden:* You say Rudabaugh was in the habit of visiting you frequently?
> *Mullen:* Yes sir, nearly every day.
>
> *Wm. Breeden:* How long have you known Rudabaugh?
> *Mullen:* I had known Rudabaugh four months.
>
> *Wm. Breeden:* How long had you been in there?
> *Mullen:* Somewhere between eight and ten months.
>
> *Wm. Breeden:* He visited you all that time?
> *Mullen:* Not every day.
>
> *Wm. Breeden:* He is a friend of yours?
> *Mullen:* Yes sir.

Interestingly, Mullen only knew Rudabaugh through jail house visits, but, even so, he considered Rudabaugh a friend. Rudabaugh's actions reveal his considerate nature: having spent time in jail himself, he was moved to bring Mullen presents such tobacco, thereby earning Mullen's gratitude. Or was it guilt, since Mullen was convicted of a crime that Rudabaugh had committed?

Next, Breeden, incompetently, brought out information that helped Rudabaugh.

> *Wm. Breeden:* As soon as the shot was fired Rudabaugh ran off?
> *Mullen:* Yes sir.
>
> *Wm. Breeden:* Turned and ran did he?
> *Mullen:* Yes sir.
>
> *Wm. Breeden:* How long did Allen remain there after Rudabaugh left?
> *Mullen:* Two or three minutes, just long enough to –
>
> *Wm. Breeden:* Never mind what he did, you answer my questions.

> **Wm. Breeden:** *Where did you say he got the keys?*
> **Mullen:** *Out of the jailer's pocket.*
>
> **Wm. Breeden:** *After he fell?*
> **Mullen:** *Yes sir.*
>
> **Wm. Breeden:** *How do you know he got them out of the jailer's pocket?*
> **Mullen:** *I saw him come back with them.*
>
> **Wm. Breeden:** *You did not see him take them out of the pocket?*
> **Mullen:** *No sir.*
>
> **Wm. Breeden:** *Can you swear positively that Rudabaugh did not take them?*
> **Mullen:** *Yes sir.*
>
> **Wm. Breeden:** *How can you swear?*
> **Mullen:** *Because Rudabaugh was standing at the door when the shot was fired and turned and ran out.*
>
> **Wm. Breeden:** *Rudabaugh was not at the door where the keys were taken out of the dead man's pocket?*
> **Mullen:** *No sir.*

This testimony provided further evidence that Allen shot Valdez without Rudabaugh having advance knowledge of Allen's intention. It also further supported the impression that Allen had an impulsive, uncontrollable character.

Breeden continued to damage his own case:

> **Wm. Breeden:** *You just swore that Rudabaugh did not do it and now you undertake to swear he did not do it when you did not see him.*
> **Mullen:** *I saw Allen fire the shot.*
>
> **Wm. Breeden:** *You said you could not see the dead man. Now how can you swear positively that Allen was the man who took the keys and not Rudabaugh?*
> **Mullen:** *Allen jumped on top of he jailer and took the keys.*
>
> **Wm. Breeden:** *How do you know he jumped on top of him when you couldn't see? You can swear positively to what you did not see? How do you manage to do that?*
> **Mullen:** *The jailer fell on that side and Rudabaugh ran out on that side....*
>
> **Wm. Breeden:** *Did Rudabaugh draw a pistol when he ran?*
> **Mullen:** *No sir.*
>
> **Wm. Breeden:** *Did you see that he had a pistol?*
> **Mullen:** *I did not see any pistol about him.*

Breeden tried to show that Mullen was lying and had been prepped to do so by the defense:

> **Wm. Breeden:** *Have you talked about his case before today?*
> **Mullen:** *No sir.*

74 ~ "Dirty Dave" Rudabaugh

Houghton's Hardware store. Undated photo. Courtesy Palace of the Governors Photo Archives (NMHM/DCA), 132734.

Wm. Breeden: Tell anybody what you could testify?
Mullen: Yes sir.

Wm. Breeden: Tell Rudabaugh?
Mullen: No.

Wm. Breeden: When were you subpoenaed?
Mullen: This morning.

Wm. Breeden: You talked to these lawyers about it?
Mullen: I believe this gentleman called me outside and talked to me about it.

Wm. Breeden: Didn't you talk to Rudabaugh?
Mullen: No. I spoke to Mr. [Marshal] Breeden. The first time I spoke of it, I told them what I said here.

Posey, in his redirect examination, countered Breeden's attempt to discredit Mullen:

Posey: Were these last charges against you dismissed at the last term of court?
Mullen: Yes sir.

Posey: You are not under indictment now?
Mullen: No sir.

Mullen was dismissed and the defense called their "big gun" to testify, Rudabaugh himself.

Posey: What is your name?
Rudabaugh: David Rudabaugh [the spelling in the transcript].

Posey: You are the defendant in this cause?
Rudabaugh: Yes sir.

Posey: You were in Las Vegas in April 1880?
Rudabaugh: Yes sir.

Posey: You were present in the killing referred to?
Rudabaugh: Yes sir.

Posey: State to the jury how you came to be there?
Rudabaugh: I had been a police officer in Las Vegas prior to the killing of the jailer and was a personal friend of Webb who had got into a difficulty there and I used to go and see him and take him tobacco and newspapers and see how he was getting along. I was well acquainted with this jailer as well as the rest and was never refused admittance. I went over this day to the Sumner House in East Las Vegas. Allen went with me. We went to see a man who owed me some money. Mr. Allen wanted to go to the jail to see Webb, and I said I was going too.

The man I wanted to see was not at the Sumner House. This man was Tom Pickett. I went up where he lived. He was sick in bed and I went up to see him. I was there fifteen or twenty minutes and he said he was going

> down town and got into the hack and went with us to Menden Hall's [Mendenhall's] stable. There he got out.
>
> I told the hack driver to drive us to the jail. I wanted to see Webb. When we got there I got out and knocked at the door. The jailer [Valdez] admitted us. He asked me if I wanted to see Webb. I said I did. He showed us the cell he was in. I had some newspapers which I gave them and asked them how they were getting along, and stood there talking to them. I was standing there with my hands crossed on the door and Allen shot the jailer. I turned around and said, 'what did you do that for?' I looked round and saw the jailer fall. I started to go out when a jailer [Ramirez] drew a pistol on me. I jumped out of range and pulled my pistol. By that time men [Benedito Duran and Tafoya] were knocking at the front door. I opened the door and ran out. The hack I left at the door was gone. I ran down and overtook it in the Plaza, and asked him why he didn't wait. I never looked back.
>
> By the time I got into the hack Allen was there. He got in the hack and told the driver to drive as fast as he could drive. On the way to the new town he tried to load his pistol but could not as he was under the influence of liquor. He gave me the pistol and asked me to load it and I loaded it. We drove over to the new town and I went into Goodlett's Saloon, where he [Allen] told me there was a double-barrel shot gun belonging to him. Then we drove to Houghton's Hardware store and got these other guns. He [Allen] brought them out, got into the hack and we left the town going in an Easterly direction. We drove about ten miles and gave the hack to two Mexican herders.

Just as he had when testifying in the Kinsley train robbery case, Rudabaugh gave a detailed account of events. He explained why he was at the jail. He described what he was doing at the time of the shot: *"I was standing there with my hands crossed on the door."*

Rudabaugh makes it clear that he had no idea that Allen intended to shoot the jailer. He reveals Allen's condition: dunk, so drunk he could not load a pistol. And with that detail, he also explains why he loaded the pistol, not Allen.

Posey asked him about Allen's alleged confession to the hack driver:

> **Posey:** It is testified that on your way to the new town, Allen said to the driver of the hack, 'I killed the son of a bitch' or words to that effect. Did you hear such a remark?
> **Rudabaugh:** No sir.
>
> **Posey:** How do you account for such a remark?
> **Rudabaugh:** I think if he had said it, I should have heard it.
>
> **Posey:** Did you [know] anything about it?
> **Rudabaugh:** No sir.
>
> **Posey:** Did you make any threats to any body?
> **Rudabaugh:** None whatever.

> **Posey:** And you only pulled your pistol when you were threatened by another jailer?
> **Rudabaugh:** Yes sir.
>
> **Posey:** Were you in the habit of carrying pistols?
> **Rudabaugh:** Yes sir.

Why did Posey not ask him if it was part of his duty as a city constable to carry a weapon?

Breeden's cross examination was brief and concentrated on claims Tafoya made in his testimony. Breeden asked Rudabaugh if he pointed a pistol at Tafoya (Tafoya testified that as he was entering the jail, he ran into Rudabaugh leaving, and Rudabaugh pointed a pistol at him and said, *"Look out Jesus"*). He asked Rudabaugh if he went to the jail with the intention of freeing Webb. Rudabaugh denied both contentions.

The presentation of the witness testimony portion of the trial ended at 6 pm. Judge Prince then ordered a one-hour recess. The *Santa Fe Daily New Mexican* made the following comment about Rudabaugh's testimony:

> *"The story was very consistent with the facts as they appeared in evidence, except that it threw the blame upon Allen. All the statements made by witnesses except as to the actual killing and who fired the fatal shot were dove tailed in very cleverly and if the account had come from a man of better character than Rudabaugh's and under different circumstances it would possibly have carried conviction with it."* [269]

The *Daily New Mexican* in the quote above says, *"All the statements made by witnesses except as to the actual killing... dove tailed in very cleverly..."* with Rudabaugh's account. This is implying that there was evidence introduced that Rudabaugh did the *"actual killing."* There was no such evidence.

About 7 pm, court resumed. The two sides made their closing arguments, finishing about 8 pm. The Judge then issued his instructions to jury. The full text of his instructions is given in Appendix A. The key passages are:

> *"Certain facts are undisputed and this simplifies your labors. It is undisputed that the deceased Valdez died from a wound received in the placita of the Las Vegas jail, on the day alleged in the indictment and that at the time of the firing of the pistol shot, the defendant and Allen were in such placita and soon after went out rapidly from the gateway thereof."*
>
> *"Here the indisputable evidence may be said to cease and you are to judge from all the evidence before you as to the other facts connected with the killing. You are first to decide whether the deceased was killed, and if you agree as to that, then as to who it was who killed him."*
>
> *"There is no evidence at all tending to show that the killing in any case was justifiable or excusable or that the circumstances existed to make such killing any degree of murder less than first."*
>
> *"The statuary definition of Murder in the First Degree is the unlawful killing of a human being perpetrated from a <u>premeditated</u> design to effect the death of the person killed and the penalty death."* [Emphasis added by author.]

"It is a principle of law founded on reason, that if a felony is committed by one man and another is present, aiding and abetting such person in the commission thereof, the abettor is as guilty as the first. The act in such case is the act of both, and both are equally guilty."

"If then, from all the evidence you are satisfied beyond a reasonable doubt that the defendant killed the deceased in such a manner as to constitute murder in the first degree, or that that crime was committed by Allen, the defendant now on trial, being present aiding and abetting in the commission of such murder, it is your duty to find a verdict of Guilty of Murder in the First Degree."

"If you do not so believe beyond a reasonable doubt, then it is your duty to acquit."

"In this as in all criminal cases you are to remember that the law presumes every man to be innocent until he is found to be guilty. That the defendant is entitled to the benefit of every reasonable doubt and that unless you are satisfied of the guilt of the accused beyond such reasonable doubt, he is entitled to an acquittal."

"A reasonable doubt, however, in the view of the law is a substantial doubt founded on the evidence, and not a mere fancy or the possibility of a doubt."

"From various requests to charge, I give you the following, asked by the defendant's counsel:"

"If the jury believes that at the moment of the shooting the defendant was engaged in conversation with Mullen and Webb and was uninformed of any intent on the part of Allen to commit murder, then they must find for the defendant." [270]

The case was given to the jury at 8:30 pm. The jury, which consisted of six Anglos and six Hispanics, took an hour and a half to return a verdict of guilty of murder in the first degree (see footnote for jury members).[271] The *Daily New Mexican* noted:

"Rudabaugh appeared perfectly calm throughout the trial, giving no evidence of excitement or agitation of any kind. His manner was serious and impressed one with the fact that the fully realized his situation, but had no occasion to resort to an assumption of that stolid indifference behind which prisoners frequently strive to hide their feelings in such cases." [272]

Rudabaugh Given Death Sentence – April 20, 1880

The next day, a shackled Rudabaugh was brought into court to receive his sentence. Judge Prince preceded his sentencing with a long statement. Here it is in its entirety:

"DAVID RUDABAUGH – You were indicted by the grand jury of San Miguel county at the term of August, 1880, for the highest crime known to the law, that of a willful murder of a fellow being. In this case the crime as alleged is made, if possible, even more grave by the person killed being a public officer engaged in the performance of his duties. A change of venue was taken on your application to this county in order that an absolutely impartial jury might be impaneled to try your case; and such a jury was obtained, all of its members

being acceptable to your counsel. Although the counsel originally assigned for the defense were prevented by sickness from attending, yet others of marked zeal and intelligence conducted the defense, and labored with ability and earnestness to secure for you every right and privilege which the law provides."

"The jury in the performance of their duty as judges of the facts have found you guilty of murder in the first degree, the punishment for which is the penalty of death."

"Nothing which I can say would add to the solemnity of this verdict or of the circumstances which now surround you, as its subject. Certainly I am far from desiring to add a single word which would increase the profound sense of sorrow which must now fill your heart."

"For some years your life seems to have been peculiarly one of lawlessness. By your own admission in open court, you were a prominent actor in two outrages against society and the laws, in the stage robberies between Las Vegas and this city which attracted so much attention a year or two since, and after the commission of this murder you were found in the company of notorious breakers of the law in the southeast part of this Territory."

"Let us all hope that this awful example of the result of such a course of life in one whose natural abilities might have led him to success and honor, this evidence the law is strong to punish as well as to protect, and that in the long run it is sure to overtake even those who are most successful in avoiding its power and penalties, this will be the means of restraining others from a similar course of violence and crime, which might lead to the same fate."

"And let me here admonish you to use well and profitably the time which under the laws of the Territory still remain to you in this life, that so you may be prepared as fully as possible for the other life in another world so soon to come."

"It now only remains for me to perform the sad and impressive rite of pronouncing the death sentence which the law imposes in your case, which is, that you be conveyed hence to the county of San Miguel, and delivered to the custody of the Sheriff of that county, and there safely kept until Friday the 30th day of May 1881, and that on that day you be taken by the sheriff of that county to some suitable place within said county of San Miguel, and be there, between the hours of 10 A. M. and 3 P. M., hung by the neck until you are dead, and may God have mercy on your soul." [273]

Rudabaugh's lawyers immediately filed an appeal to the Territorial Supreme Court. They listed the following trial errors as grounds for the appeal:

- The court admitted illegal and improper evidence
- The court refused to include in the instructions to the jury wording requested by the defendant
- The court gave improper and illegal instructions to the jury

80 ~ "Dirty Dave" Rudabaugh

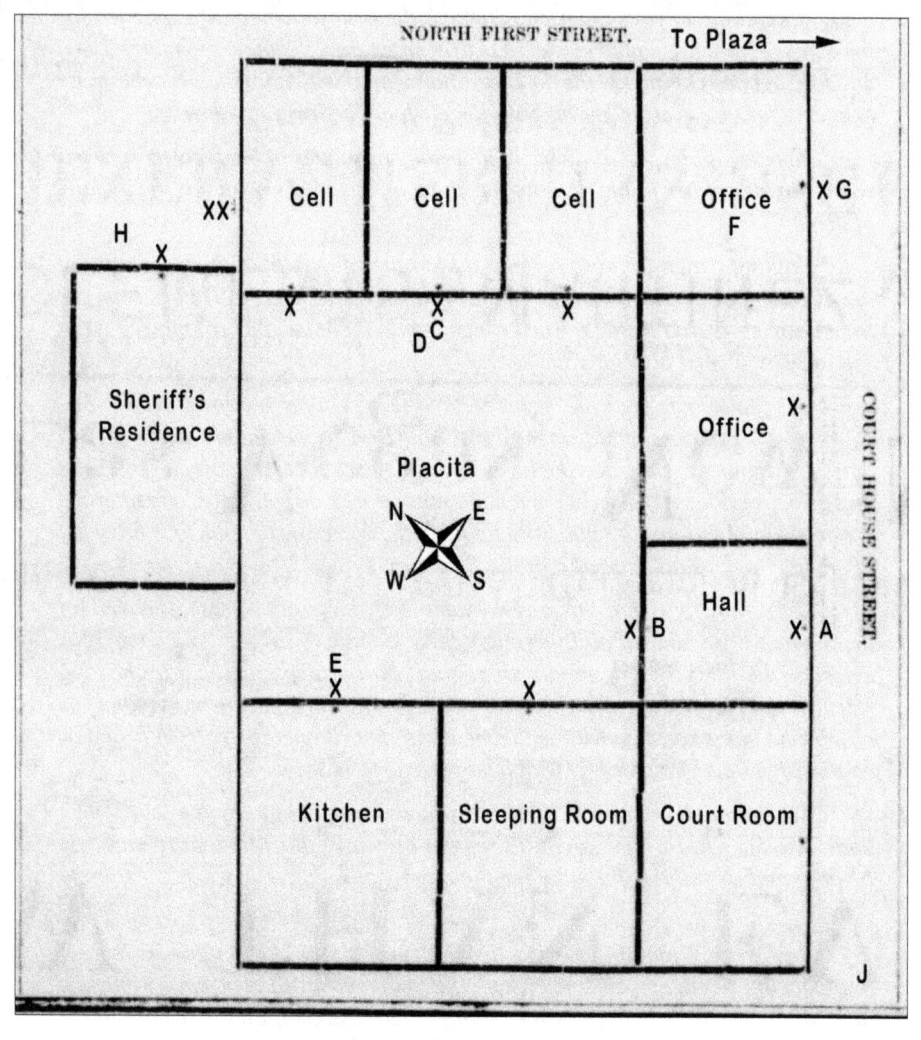

Drawing of Las Vegas courthouse complex in 1881. The complex was located in Old Town (West Las Vegas), one block northwest of the plaza.

"X" marks doors. "XX" marks the outside exit for the jail cells. (A) marks the Hall entrance into the complex. (B) marks the Hall entrance into the placita. (C) marks the spot (best guess) where Rudabaugh was standing when Allen shot jailer Valdez. (D) marks where Valdez fell after being shot. (E) marks where jailer Ramirez exited the kitchen. (F) marks the Probate Court office where Tafoya and Duran were when they heard the shot that mortally wounded Valdez. (G) marks where Tafoya and Duran exited the Probate Court office. (H) marks where Sheriff Romero was when he heard the shot. (J) marks where Rudabaugh and Allen were seen by Sheriff Romero running toward the plaza.

The only entrances into the windowless jail cells were from the placita. The cells had no windows. *Las Vegas Daily Gazette*, December 4, 1881.

- The court improperly commented upon the evidence in its instructions to the jury (instructing that there was no evidence of any degree of murder less than first)
- The verdict was against the evidence
- The verdict was against the law
- The was no evidence introduced *"whatever"* to sustain the verdict[274]

Most of these alleged errors appear to be routine complaints with little chance of success. But, surprisingly, Judge Prince approved the appeal.[275] Under New Mexico law, the trial judge, and only the trial judge, had the power to approve an appeal to the Supreme Court. If the judge said no, no appeal could be filed.

The Supreme Court scheduled a hearing for the case for the January, 1882, term of the Court. The case was never heard because of Rudabaugh's later "jail delivery." [276]

Rudabaugh's lawyers also filed a request with the court that Rudabaugh be allowed to remain in the Santa Fe jail until his appeal was heard, because of the high likelihood that he would be lynched if sent to Las Vegas. That request was denied. On April 22, he was was put on a train for transport to Las Vegas. To his and his escort's great surprise, also on the train:

"...was the officer that conducted the arrest at the time of the Kinsley train robbery in 1878.... The gentleman was the one who secured Dave's confession which led to the arrest and conviction of the gang." [277]

The "officer" is not named, but it is almost certainly Bat Masterson:

"The recognition this morning was almost electrical, and to his former custodian Rudabaugh talked freely, and while he acknowledged that he was deeply disappointed at the way the trial terminated, he was inclined to cherish fondly the possibility of the appeal being granted. His defeat, he thought, was all owing to a prejudiced jury, who had individually arrived at the conclusion that the verdict should read 'murder in the first degree.' He spoke about the unfortunate members of the train robbers and wondered how they were 'coming on,' as he put it." [278]

Reconstructing the Crime

The sequence of events leading to the fatal shooting of jailer Valdez begins with Rudabaugh and Allen going to Sumner House in New Town (East Las Vegas) to see Tom Pickett, who owed Rudabaugh money. Rudabaugh does not say so, but perhaps Pickett was working at Sumner House – a *"first class house in every respect."* Pickett had quit his job as a city constable the previous month, from reasons unknown.

At Sumner House, Rudabaugh learns that Pickett was at home, *"sick in bed."* Leaving the hotel, Rudabaugh and Allen hail hack driver J. C. Cauldwell, who had just dropped off several clients. Rudabaugh hires Cauldwell to drive him and Allen to Pickett's home. The time is about 2 pm.

Rudabaugh and Allen go in to see Pickett and spend, by Rudabaugh's account, fifteen minutes inside. Cauldwell says they spent about *"half an hour."* Rudabaugh, Allen, and Pickett leave the house. Cauldwell says there was a fourth, unidentified man with them, but that assertion is not supported by Rudabaugh's testimony.

82 ~ "Dirty Dave" Rudabaugh

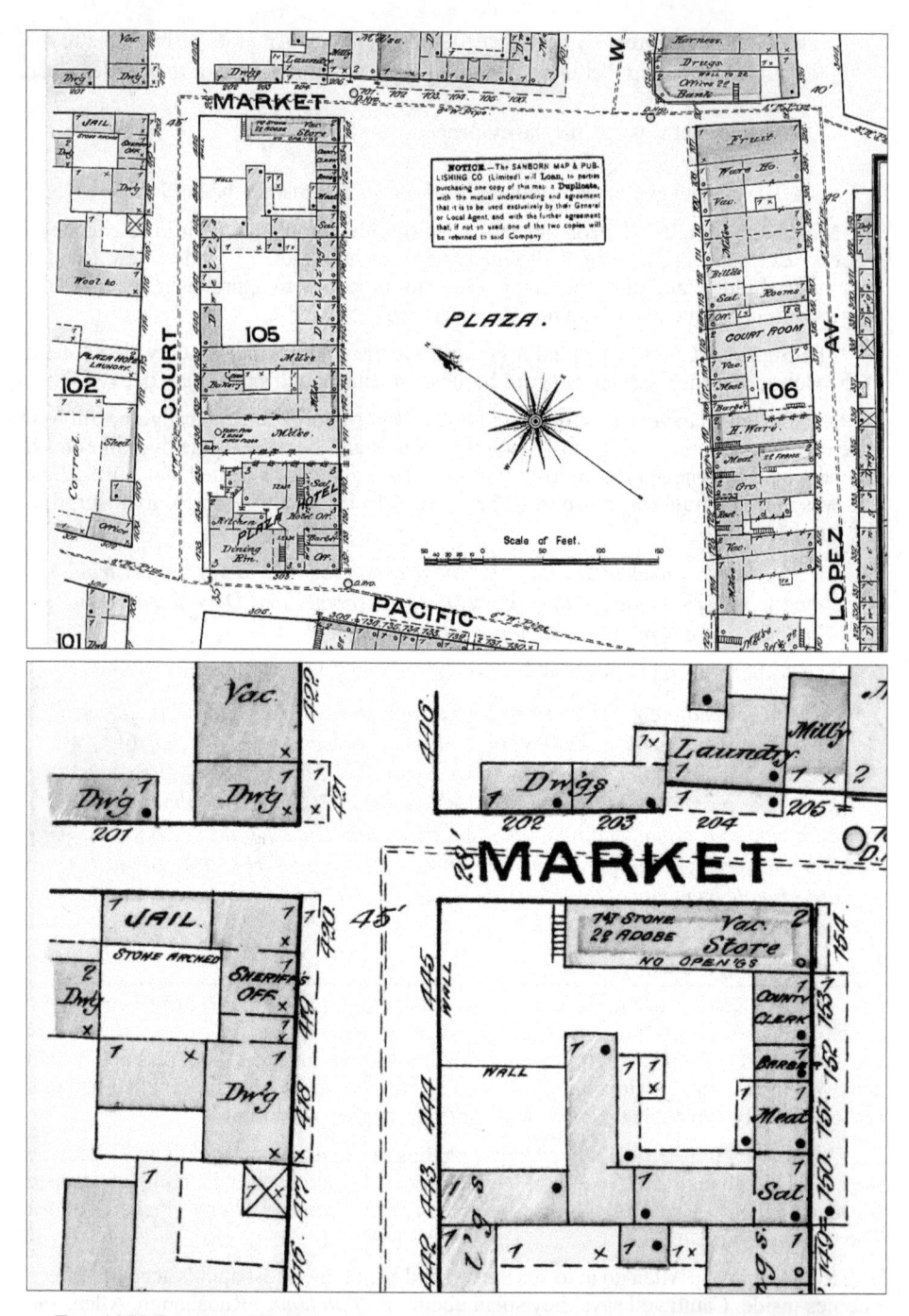

Top: 1883 Sanborn Fire Insurance map of Las Vegas, showing the area around the Old Town plaza. The jail complex is shown in the upper left corner. Bottom: Detail of Sanborn map showing jail complex. Market Street is identified as First Street in the drawing on page 80. Courtesy Library of Congress, Geography and Map Division.

San Miguel County jail, cell doors. Each jail cell had an outer door made of reinforced wood and an inner door made of crisscrossed iron bars. As described on page 30, the barred doors had two locks, which can be seen clearly on the right door. The doors opened into the jail placita. From Rudabaugh's trial testimony, Webb and Mullen were confined in the center cell and Rudabaugh was standing with his hands on the cell bars. Both Allen and Valdez were to Rudabaugh's left. When Allen shot Valdez, he fell to the placita ground just to the left of the center jail door. The persons are unidentified. Photo by Frank Evans, probably taken in 1881.
Courtesy Joseph Lordi.

Cauldwell drives the three men to Mendenhall's livery stable, in Old Town (West Las Vegas), where Pickett gets out. Rudabaugh tells Cauldwell to drive to the county jail. At the jail, Cauldwell is told to wait. Rudabaugh and Allen knock on the outside door of the jail, marked (A) on the drawing on page 80. The outside door is unlocked and opened by jailer Valdez, and they are let into the entry hall.

Valdez escorts the men through the hall into the placita. Rudabaugh approaches the cell where Webb and his cellmate Mullen are confined. The men's cell is never identified, but from Tafoya's map (page 65), it is the center cell, marked (C).

Rudabaugh passes some newspapers through the cell bars (the purpose of his visit). He is standing in front of the cell door, gripping the bars, speaking with Mullen, when Allen abruptly shoots Valdez. On hearing the shot, Rudabaugh berates Allen, *"What did you do that for."*

In Mullen's account, Allen first demanded of Valdez, *"Give me those keys you son of a bitch."* When Valdez replies in Spanish, Allen shoots him.

Whether witness Mullen actually saw Allen fire the shot is unsure from his testimony. He says explicitly, *"I saw Allen fire the shot."* But he may be inferring that action from the fact that he could see with certainty that Rudabaugh did not fire the shot.

Valdez falls to the ground, bleeding badly, at the spot marked (D). He would later be carried to the kitchen by two prisoners, where he would die about seven hours later. Allen grabs the keys from Valdez's pocket (or possibly his belt), returns to the cell, and attempts to unlock the cell door. Failing to open the door after trying for about two or three minutes, he tosses the keys at or through the bars toward Webb, saying, *"take these and unlock the door, I have to go."* Mullen did not actually see Allen take the keys from Valdez; but he did see him throw them at Webb.

Jailer José Ramirez is in the kitchen asleep when he hears the gunshot. He jumps up and runs into the placita through the door marked (E). According to his testimony, he had no gun. Rudabaugh, responding to Ramirez's appearance, *"jumped out of range,"* and pulled his gun.

Jesus Tafoya, the county clerk, is in the Probate Court office, marked (F), with jailer Benedito Duran when Allen's shot rings out, which *"thundered very much."* Duran runs out of the office at door marked (G), down Courthouse Street, and begins hammering on the locked hall entrance door (A). Tafoya, hearing Duran beating on the door, exits the office and goes toward the hall door. When there is no response from inside to Duran, Tafoya pounds on the door himself. He can hear the *"grunts or complaints of someone inside the jail."* After several minutes, Rudabaugh bursts out of the hall door. He is holding his pistol, which he points at Tafoya, telling him, *"Look out Jesus."* Rudabaugh and Allen then run toward Pacific Street, which leads to the Plaza.

Sheriff Romero is in front of his residence, marked (H), when he hears the shot. He runs around the outside of the jail to the hall entrance, a distance of *"about fifty yards."* When he turns onto Court Street, he sees Rudabaugh and Allen sprinting toward the plaza, in the direction marked (J).

At the plaza, Rudabaugh and Allen encounter Cauldwell *"just as [he] was in the act of getting out of [his] hack."* They force him to drive to New Town. During the drive, Allen tries to reload his pistol, but he is too drunk to do so. Rudabaugh replaces the spent cartridge for him.

In New Town, they make Cauldwell stop at Goodlett and Roberts' Saloon, where Rudabaugh retrieves a double-barreled shotgun belonging to Allen. Next, they go to Houghton's Hardware and buy more guns (and probably ammunition).

Cauldwell is forced out of the hack and Rudabaugh and Allen drive east for about ten miles, where they *"gave the hack to two Mexican herders."* Cauldwell, in his testimony, says he watched them go *"for about twelve or fourteen miles."*

Analyzing Rudabaugh's Trial

By today's standards, the lawyering in the trial was poor: the questioning of witnesses, shallow; the number of witnesses, tiny. Critical details were not explored in any depth and were not challenged in the rebuttals.

The trial transcript, which was located in the records of the Territorial Supreme Court, does not include the attorneys' closing arguments. Territorial Law required that a trial transcript be provided with the case records if a case was appealed.[279] Why are there no transcripts of the closing arguments in the trial record? Evidently, because closing arguments were not considered part of the trial evidence. The primary purpose of a closing argument was to remind the jury of the evidence supporting the speaker's case, to instruct the jury on how to interpret that evidence, and to show why the other side's evidence and interpretation were wrong. The Territorial Supreme Court apparently thought it only needed to consider witness testimony and judge's instructions to decide an appeal.

The prosecution, although not directly admitting it, was not claiming that Rudabaugh fired the fatal shot (or any shots). They were asserting that Rudabaugh was guilty of murder in the first degree because he was an accomplice to the killing (although the word accomplice was never used in the trial).

The defense was arguing that Rudabaugh did not know of the killing in advance and was innocently present when a drunken Allen shot Valdez. Why did the defense counsel not emphasize Allen's drunken state, which was evidence suggesting that Allen acted impulsively and without Rudabaugh's foreknowledge?

Judge Prince in his instructions told the jury that Rudabaugh was guilty if he was *"aiding or abetting"* the killing. There was no evidence introduced that Rudabaugh had physically or verbally aided or abetted the killing. The only evidence of "aiding" – and it is a stretch – was that Rudabaugh went to the jail armed, so perhaps a "reasonable person" might expect something like a killing to occur. And fleeing afterwards was indirect evidence of guilt.

To convict Rudabaugh of murder because he should have known that going to the jail armed might lead to a killing has no evidential weight. It was routine for Rudabaugh to visit the jail armed. And further, not even mentioned in the testimony, Rudabaugh was a city constable at the time, with legal permission (and a duty) to carry arms.

Do the events surrounding the killing, including fleeing, constitute enough evidence of *"aiding and abetting"* to convict Rudabaugh of first degree murder? Not if you believed Rudabaugh, according to Judge Prince's explicit instructions:

> *"If the jury believes that at the moment of the shooting the defendant was engaged in conversation with Mullen and Webb and was uninformed of any intent on the part of Allen to commit murder, then they must find for the defendant."* [280]

If any jury member believed Rudabaugh, that juror *"must find for the defendant"* and acquit. It matters not that Rudabaugh fled the crime scene.

If a jury member did not believe Rudabaugh, that person would have to convict based on implied – not direct – evidence of aiding and abetting. The prosecution failed to present any evidence of aiding and abetting that met the standard of *"certainty beyond a reasonable doubt."*

The other condition that Judge Prince included in his instructions, *"present,"* is not, in itself, evidence of guilt. Imagine if Prince had told the jury, *"if a felony is committed by one man and another is present, [the person who was present] is as guilty as the first."* Obviously, on its face, being *"present"* is not evidence in itself of guilt.

In the author's opinion, the prosecution did not present evidence of Rudabaugh's guilt that met the standard of proof beyond a reasonable doubt. Rudabaugh should have been acquitted!

Territorial law required that to convict a defendant of first degree murder, the jury must satisfy two requirements: they must be certain beyond a reasonable doubt that the defendant did it, and they must be equally certain that the act was premeditated.

The premeditated *"intention to kill"* must be present to convict a person of first degree murder. If there was no such premeditation, as in an unpredictable fatal accident, then murder in the second degree or less may be pursued by the government, but not first degree murder.

Judge Prince, in his instructions to the jury, failed to address the legal requirement of premeditation at all. Hence, it was not considered in the jury's deliberations. Under the Territorial Law, premeditation had a weight equal to that of being *"certain beyond a reasonable doubt."*

Here is how Judge Warren Henry Bristol addressed this requisite in his instructions to the jury in Billy the Kid's trial for killing Sheriff William Brady, held April 9, 1881, in Mesilla:

> *"As I have already instructed you to constitute murder in the 1st degree it is necessary that the killing should have been perpetrated from a premeditated design to effect the death of the person killed."*

> *"As to this premeditated design I charge you that to render a design to kill premeditated it is not necessary that such design to kill should exist in the mind for any considerable length of time before the killing."*

> *"If the design to kill is completely formed in the mind but for a moment before inflicting the fatal wounds it would be premeditated and in law the effect would be the same as though the design to kill had existed for a long time."* [For details on Billy's trial, see *"The Trial of Billy the Kid"* by the author.]

The omission of explaining this requirement to the jury would appear to be sufficient error on the part of the trial judge to render the verdict invalid on appeal. This was a surprising error on the part of the trial judge, Judge Prince, who was also the Chief Justice of the Territorial Supreme Court and widely recognized as a legal scholar. Nevertheless, this was not one of the grounds on which Rudabaugh's lawyers appealed.

Rudabaugh Nearly Escapes – September 19, 1881

On September 19, Rudabaugh, Thomas Duffy, H. S. Wilson, and Murphy (not otherwise identified) came within a hair's width of escaping the Las Vegas jail. About three o'clock that morning, Rudabaugh succeeded in picking the door lock of his cell with a bent wire.

> *"...it seemed that the much desired liberty had been gained, and but for the foolishness of Rudebaugh in approaching the sleeping guards and calling the chief of them by name, instead of attempting instant flight, the issue would probably have been different."*

> *"Florenzo Mares, the chief jailer..., was sleeping in the hallway leading to the jail placita; he was awakened by hearing a voice call 'Florenzo! Florenzo!' several times and upon opening his eyes, saw Rudabaugh standing over him with a revolver pointed in his face. Immediately realizing the situation and correctly divining that a break for liberty was being made, the guard sprang to his feet and grappled with the desperate prisoner."* [281]

Rudabaugh responded to Mares' seizing him by firing a shot, *"which glanced along the wash-board and entered the bed so recently vacated."*

"Rudebaugh, although a powerful man, was no match for the sinewy guard, and though he fired a second shot which glanced along the stone floor and entered a post in the placita, he was over-powered and disarmed." [282]

The noise of the shots alerted the two other guards in the jail. When they ran to Mares' aid, they were attacked by Duffy. In the desperate struggle that followed, Duffy was shot twice, once through the leg and once in the forehead *"about an inch and a half above the right eye."*

While Rudabaugh. Duffy and the guards were fighting, Wilson and Murphy were:

"...very sensibly [attempting] to scale the low walls, keeping as far from the hall as possible, and, while under ordinary circumstances the feat would not be difficult, their natural excitement and haste prevented its accomplishment." [283]

The would-be escapees were tightly bound and dragged back to their cell.

During the nearly-successful escape attempt, Webb, who was incarcerated in the same cell as the four aspiring escapees, refused to leave the cell. Asked about that by the *Las Vegas Gazette*, he said:

"...that he did not participate in the attempt to get away. That he had had many better opportunities to escape than last night. That his case was in the courts and he proposed whatever might be the issue to abide by it."

"He said he knew of the plans to escape and would have given it away but that he feared personal injury at the hands of the other prisoners.... He said that it seemed that when anything turned up he always got the worst of it." [284]

Rudabaugh was asked about the breakout attempt:

"[He] seemed willing to talk and very apprehensive of his personal safety. When we suggested that it would have been an easy matter for him to have made his escape after opening the door of his call without attacking the guards, he declared that he had no intention of harming them and that owing to his weakness from long confinement he was unable to climb the wall." [285]

"[Rudabaugh said he] assumed the entire responsibility [for the escape attempt]. That he was in a desperate hole and had to take desperate chance to get out of it. When asked how and where he got the pistol he replied that it was a leading question, that he would not give any one away, but that he had had it concealed in his cell for more than a month." [286]

The pistol was not the only thing Rudabaugh had stashed in his cell. When it was searched, a *"large quantity of bent wire, a brand new file and an old cold chisel"* were found. (Why was the cell not searched before – or regularly?)

When the deputy sheriff in charge of the jail was asked why the guards were so poorly prepared for a jailbreak, he replied:

"...that it is not usual to allow all of the guards to sleep at the same time, but that the usual number, five, had been reduced by sickness to three, and by an accident they all fell asleep [at once]." [287]

The next morning Duffy was still alive, but would he not live out the day. The *Gazette* reported of his wound:

> *"The ball entered a little to the left of the center of the forehead, the ball ranging downward and toward the right, and lodging in the fleshy part of the right neck. He has lost to-day through the wound and though the nasal passages about two ounces of brain."* [288]

Duffy was in jail waiting trial for the brutal killing of Tommy Bishop, an ex-Star line driver, in Liberty, New Mexico on August 27, 1881.[289] H. S. Wilson and Murphy were in jail charged with robbery.

Rudabaugh, Webb, and Five Others Escape – December 3, 1881

On Saturday, December 3, when the Las Vegas jailers *"made their first round at 7 o'clock"* in the morning, they discovered that seven of eleven prisoners in the jail had escaped during the night:

> *"[An] investigation led to the discovery that the prisoners had dug their way out through the walls. Six men were confined in the corner cell and five in the next cell to it, separated by a wall two feet thick – a hole was first dug through this wall and those who wanted to get out gathered in the corner cell, and commenced work on the outside wall, each taking his turn."*

> *"They commenced work about six o'clock, just as soon as the guards had locked up for the night, according to the testimony of four of the prisoners who remained, they worked steadily, dropping the stones and mortar on a mattress on the floor, until about one o'clock in the morning, when the hole, about seven by eighteen inches, was large enough for the smallest to go through."*

> *"During the work the four guards were quietly sleeping in the guard room across the placita, and the two dogs kept in the yard never uttered a bark."* [290]

The escaped prisoners were: Rudabaugh, Webb, Thomas Quillan, Frank Kearney, Edward M. "Choctaw" Kelly, William Goodman, and S. Schroeder.

> *"Goodman was the first fellow to make his exit. He was perhaps chosen because he is smaller, however, it was a tight squeeze for him and the other inmates of the cell, now growing uneasy for fear of being discovered, at once concluded to undress rather than to attempt to remove any more stones. This they all proceeded to do, with the exception of Webb, who left on his underclothes and went through the aperture in the following order: Kelly, second; Schroeder, third; Webb, fourth; Quillan, fifth; Kearney, sixth; and Rudabaugh, seventh and last...."*

> *"Rudabaugh, who had been kept heavily ironed, did not succeed in removing his wristlets and shackles, but cut the chains. He probably made a raid upon a blacksmith shop soon after getting out. None of the other prisoners were embarrassed with iron jewelry with perhaps the exception of Quillan, who may have had on a pair of bracelets with the chain broken when he left the jail."* [291]

Webb's escape shocked the people of Las Vegas. He had stoutly resisted gifted jailbreak offers twice before, the last time just 75 days earlier. As the *Daily Gazette* noted, out-going Governor Wallace had opined that he deserved pardon consideration, and it was generally expected that the new, incoming governor, Lionel A. Sheldon, would pardon him (from life in prison to something considerably less). [292]

Thomas Quillan had only been in the jail three days. He had been arrested by Sheriff Pat Garrett November 30 in Santa Fe on a warrant out of Clay County, Texas, where he had killed Deputy Sheriff James Bodenhemn. He had a $1000 reward on his head.[293]

"Tom Quilian [Quillan], immediately after getting out of jail, went to the St. Nicholas [hotel] and requested the night clerk to tell his wife that he wanted to see her. She hastily came down and they had a short interview. The two men, probably Rudabaugh and Webb, who accompanied him, were very nervous, and they hurried on." [294]

"Choctaw" Kelly was in jail for killing John Reardon in a drunken barroom fight at Carbonateville on October 17, 1880. He was recaptured a few days after his escape.[295]

The other escapees were in jail for minor offenses.

The tools used in the escape were:

"...an old pick, a case knife and an iron rod. The pick, rusty, dull and without a handle, was picked up by Goodman in the garden of the plaza, when he was out sweeping the streets, and brought in by him under his coat. The case knife was procured by Webb, who had been cook for some time, and had access to all the knives and kitchen utensils. The iron rod or poker was about two feet long and three-fourths of an inch thick, and was used in the cell as a poker. None of the articles used were furnished by outside parties." [296]

Could there have been a more ineptly managed jail in New Mexico? The *Mora County Pioneer* thought not and wrote:

"The arrest and conviction of these men has cost the Territory no small sum.... It is just such breaks as these that induce law-abiding citizens to take the law in their own hands.... the Territory must be rid of this class of lawless men and the quickest and cheapest is the one to enforce." [297]

The jail was built in 1872.[298] The *Gazette* at the time described it as *"the strongest and costliest edifice of its kind in the Territory,"* adding *"our jail is compact and strong enough for any one man to guard all and every outlaw confined therein."* [299] (The jail was replaced with a new jail December 28, 1885.[300])

Merchant Isidor Stern, capitalizing on the *"jail jugglery"* news, published the following advertisement for his store:

"The excitement over the escape of the prisoners does not interest the people of East and West Las Vegas as much as the astonishing low prices of the splendid stock of goods at Isidor Stern's, West Las Vegas." [301]

Governor Sheldon issued a $500 reward for the capture of Rudabaugh and the same for Webb.[302]

On December 8, 1881, Quillan was captured in Santa Fe. He was picked up and returned to Las Vegas by Sheriff Garrett. Several days later, Garrett escorted him to Clay County, Texas.[303]

Parral, Mexico. Undated photo. Courtesy Archives and Special Collections, NMSU.

Webb Dies of Smallpox – April 12, 1882

Both Rudabaugh and Webb got away clean. Webb, however, was only able to enjoy 130 days of freedom: On April 20, 1882, the *Dodge City Times* published the following letter:

> *"Dear Sir: John J. Webb is dead. He died on the 12th inst., of small pox, in Winslow, Arkansas. He was there working for J. D. Scott & Co., on the St. L. & S. F. R. R. He had the best of attention and care, but there came a very sudden change in the weather and I suppose he caught cold, and he died very suddenly. He was going under the name Sam King, after he came here. I suppose you would like to hear from him. You can tell the friends of his death." [signed] J. A. Scott"* [304]

The author of the letter, J. A. Scott, who expresses great sympathy for Webb, appears to be related to Webb's employer, J. D. Scott & Co., suggesting they knew Webb's real identify before his sudden death.

After this death report, the saga of Webb's life appeared to be over. Then, reports of Webb still being alive began to appear. The biggest shock happened March 25, 1884:

> *"When the train from the south pulled in yesterday afternoon, Deputy U.S. Marshal Toney [Tony] Neis stepped off, having in charge a prisoner manacled at the ankles, and who had the appearance of being a hardened criminal. Marshal Neis took a hack and started with his charge for the county jail, followed by a Gazette reporter...."* [305]

At the jail, Neis told the sheriff that he had John J. Webb who he had captured in El Paso. Asked his name, the prisoner replied, R. H. Clum.

The *Gazette* reporter decided to find someone who could definitively identify Webb. He located U.S. Marshal Arthur Jilson and took him to the jail:

"'That's not Webb,' said Marshal Jilson, 'but I believe I know you.'"

"'I expect so,' returned the prisoner. 'I know you, but I'm not Webb. My name is Clum. I was down on the Mexican Central railroad, and had just crossed the river at El Paso, when I was arrested by Toney (sic) and two other men, who shackled me, put me on the train and started for Las Vegas. I told Toney he was mistaken in his man, but he wouldn't listen....'" [306]

Clum later successfully proved his identity, and none of the reports of Webb still being alive proved to be true.

Rudabaugh's Life on the Run – 1881 to 1886

On May 23, 1882, the *Ford County Globe* published a letter from attorney Edward P. Colborn in which he claimed that Wyatt Earp of O.K. Corral fame had seen Rudabaugh among the men who had attempted to assassinate his brother, Virgil:

"Wyatt says after the first shock he could distinguish David Rudabaugh and Curly Bill [Brocius], the latter's body showing well among the bushes." [307]

This brief mention of a second-hand report caused many early researchers to assert that Rudabaugh went to Arizona after his Las Vegas escape. There is zero evidence of that and it is not believed by most Earp historians today. [308]

After his escape, Rudabaugh made straight for Mexico, by way of Rincon, New Mexico. The *Las Vegas Gazette* reported that when he was seen in Rincon, *"He looked well. The free air of the Jornada agrees with him much better than looking through bars into a slip noose."* [309]

In January, 1883, the *Santa Fe Daily New Mexican* reported that Rudabaugh talked to the editor of the *Chihuahua Mail*, in Chihuahua, Mexico. He suggested to the editor that he might come back to New Mexico. The *Daily New Mexican* responded:

"Better not, Dave. The climate of old Mexico is more healthy for you than ours would be." [310]

In April, 1884, the *Daily Commonwealth* reported that Rudabaugh *"was seen three weeks ago at Amoco, Mexico. He was following the butcher business and said he was going to Parral."* [311]

In May, 1884, an unnamed *Philadelphia Times* correspondent reported speaking with Rudabaugh in El Paso, Texas. He gave this description of Rudabaugh:

"Dave is still a young man and his handsome face and well-knit form would attract attention and excite comment anywhere. His hair was long, curly and black as a raven's wing. He sported a moustache, neatly trimmed and waxed, of the same color as his hair, and his semi-civilized dress was of the richest possible description." [312]

The final newspaper mention of Rudabaugh appears in November, 1884. Dick Carrolton, a range detective, who was in Mexico tracing some horses stolen from William "Buffalo Bill" Cody's ranch near North Platta, Nebraska, told the *Wichita Daily Eagle* that he saw Rudabaugh in Pardo, Mexico. He said Rudabaugh was *"keeping a saloon"* there.[313]

92 ~ "Dirty Dave" Rudabaugh

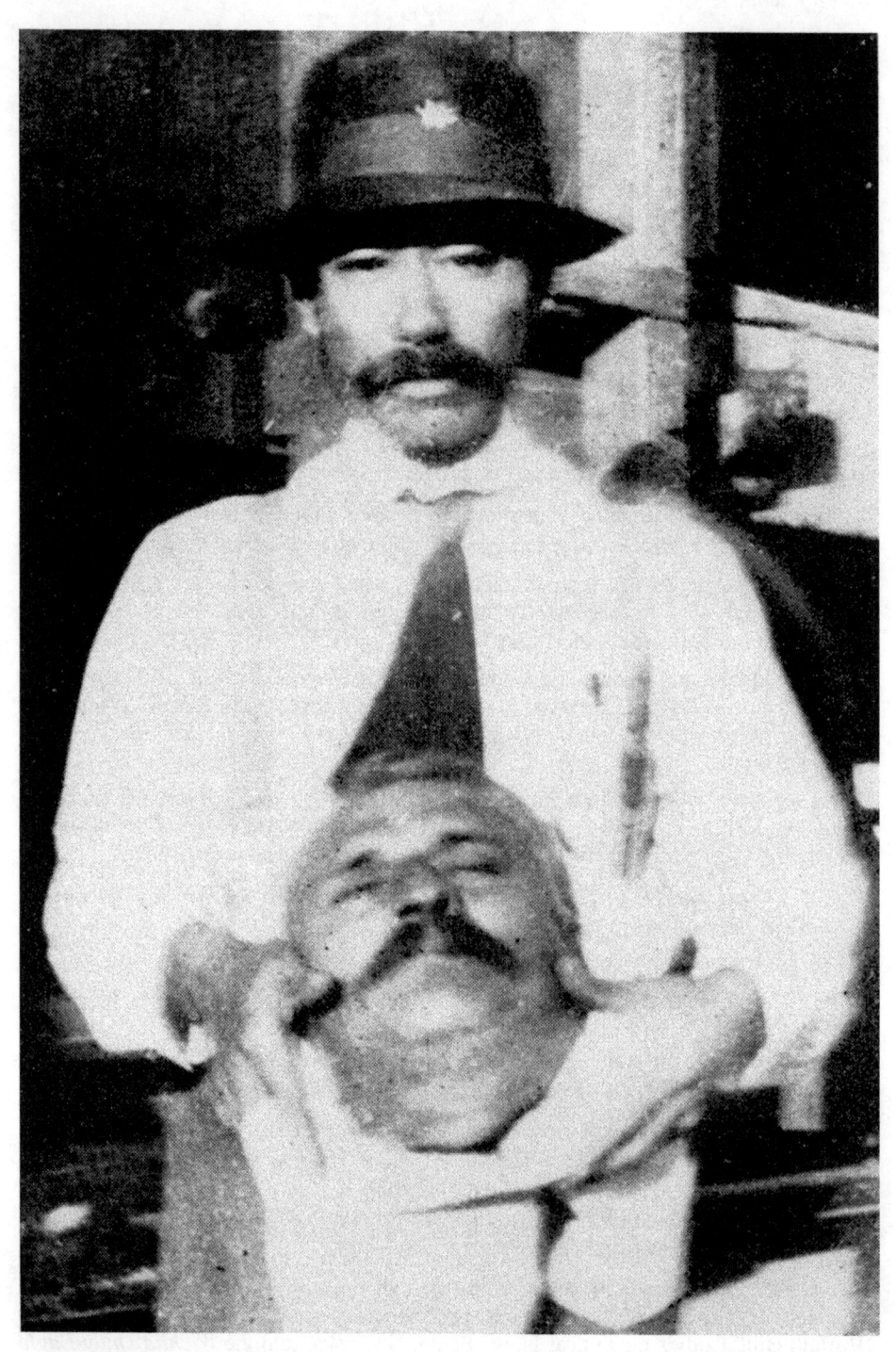

Head of David Rudabaugh, held by a Rurales. February 18, 1886, photo by Albert W. Lohn. Courtesy Fred M. Mazzulla Collection, History Colorado-Denver Colorado.

"Dirty Dave" Rudabaugh ~ 93

Rudabaugh's head on a pole. February 18, 1886, photo by Albert W. Lohn. Courtesy Fred M. Mazzulla Collection, History Colorado-Denver Colorado.

Rudabaugh Meets his Fate – February 18, 1886

On February 18, 1886, Rudabaugh was killed by a Winchester rifle shot to the chest in Parral, Mexico.

Parral, originally San José del Parral, later Hidalgo de Parral, was founded in 1631 when silver was discovered in the surrounding hills. It is 375 miles due south of El Paso, Texas. In 1886, silver mining was still the largest single source of area income, and the town had a rough, easy-money character.[314]

The only known existing eye-witness account of Rudabaugh's violent death is once-removed. This account, by William McGaw, is based on information supplied to McGaw by Fred M. Mazzulla, who got his depiction of the event from Albert W. Lohn, who was present at the killing.[315]

According to this account, Rudabaugh was working for Chihuahuan land baron Luis Terrazas as a ranch manager. Terrazas at the time owned millions of acres of ranch land in the Mexican State of Chihuahua and controlled millions more. He was an ex-governor of Chihuahua (1879–1884), and a retired Mexican general.[316]

Fred Milo Mazzulla, 1981 photo by Myron Woods. Courtesy Amon Carter Museum of American Art.

In McGaw's retelling, in the evening of February 18, Rudabaugh was in a Parral cantina behaving abominably:

> "[He] ordered a bottle of tequila. He elbowed a halfscore of customers from the bar, spat some on the floor, cussed out the bartender, shoved a couple of peons against the wall and then bellowed for a poker game."
>
> "He played poker four or five minutes, screamed that he had been cheated, stood up and shot two of the players dead...." [317]

That Rudabaugh *"fatally shot two persons"* just before his killing was confirmed in a brief *Las Vegas Optic* notice of his death, although the circumstances surrounding the event are unstated.[318]

After killing the two cantina patrons and wounding another, Rudabaugh left the bar for the town plaza and began drunkenly taunting the residents. Infuriated by the prior killings and Rudabaugh's grossly insulting behavior, *"a grocerman named José"* shot Rudabaugh through an open window of his grocery store, striking him in the chest:

> "The grocerman [grocery man] picked up a boning knife from a meat block and walked out into the plaza, picking up a broom stick as he left his shop."

"He walked to the prostrate form which had been Rudabaugh and coolly severed the head from its shoulders with his boning knife. He placed the head on [a] broomstick [a pole] and by this time all the lights in the town were on and the people were pouring out of their homes and shops into the middle of the plaza, many bearing torches...." [319]

"The natives of Parral got up a procession in honor of the event, and Dave's head, which had been severed from his body, was carried on a pole and exhibited about the streets." [320]

"[His] body was dumped in a hole at the edge of town." [321]

Rudabaugh's Obituary - March 23, 1886

On March 23, 1886, the *Tombstone Democrat*, of Tombstone, Arizona, published Rudabaugh's obituary.

"The Deeds of a Desperado"

"Dave Rudebaugh, who was reportedly killed at Parral, in the state of Chihuahua, Mexico, was what might be called an 'all around' desperado. He was equally proficient in holding up a railroad train or stage coach, or as occasion offered robbed [robbing] a bank, 'shooting up' a frontier settlement, or running off stock. He indulged in these little peculiarities for a year or two in Arizona, and inasmuch as many of our old-timers doubtless remember him, some of them to their cost, the following sketch of the antecedents of Rudebaugh, communicated to the Democrat by one who knows, will prove of interest:"

"Ten years ago just after the Santa Fe railroad had invaded western Kansas a train was 'held up' near Kinsley, and robbed of everything of value that it contained. Detective Hudgens got after the gang and soon had them all in the Leavenworth penitentiary, with the exception of Dave Rudebaugh, who turned state's evidence."

"After that Dave became a desperado, and finally outlawed at Las Vegas for numerous other crimes. In 1880 he became a member of the famous 'Billy, the Kid' gang, which eventually got him into jail. He escaped the jail at Las Vegas and fled to Arizona, where he 'rustled' with varying success for nearly two years, when he was driven out of the Apache country and struck for Old Mexico, where he became manager of the cattle interests in Chihuahua of the governor thereof. Dave continued to be a desperado, however, and became engaged in his final difficulty in the ancient town of Parral. He fatally shot two persons before the buzzing ball caught him in a fatal spot and ended his life. The natives of Parral got up a procession in honor of the event, and Dave's head, which had been severed from his body, was carried on a pole and exhibited about the streets." [322]

Almost all the "facts' in this obituary are wrong, and it initiates some of the myths that have defined Rudabaugh's life to writers, researchers, and the public ever since.

Rudabaugh robbed one train and two stage coaches during his life. Hardly an example of "proficiency." He never robbed a bank or shot up a *"frontier settlement."* Rudabaugh and his fellow train robbers got nothing from the Kinsley train robbery – it was a spectacular failure. It was Bat Masterson and not Hudgens who captured him afterwards. After being released from that charge due to turning state's witness, he spent only a few weeks in Dodge City, and then went to Las Vegas and became a city constable, not a *"all-around desperado."* Following his escape from the Las Vegas jail, he went directly to Mexico. He did not go to Arizona and spend *"nearly two years"* rustling cattle. The details of his decapitation and having his head paraded through the streets of Parral on a pole are true.

Rudabaugh's Death Photos

The pictures of Rudabaugh's decapitated head reproduced on pages 92-93 were taken by Albert W. Lohn, a nineteen-year-old, traveling, professional photographer who was in Parral the day Rudabaugh was killed.

"Shortly after the ferocious Dave quit breathing, Long [Lohn] got out his camera and took four pictures of the event. Two of the photographs were of better quality than the other two, so Long printed only the two best shots he obtained." [323]

Albert W. Lohn, 1919 photo. Courtesy Pimeria Alta Historical Society.

When the governor of the Mexican State of Durango (the state located south of Parral) learned that Lohn was selling post cards of Rudabaugh's severed head, he demanded that the photos and negatives be turned over to him. Lohn acceded to the governor's request (order) and gave him the two negatives he had printed. He retained the negatives of the two poorer photographs, which he had not printed.[324]

Lohn put the negatives away and totally forgot about them. In 1943, Fred W. Mazzulla, an avid collector of Western memorabilia, met Lohn in Nogales, Arizona, where Lohn was operating a photography studio.[325] The two became good friends. During one of their conversations, Lohn mentioned that he had been present in Parral when Rudabaugh was decapitated and he had taken photos of the event. Prompted by Mazzulla's collector's interest, Lohn located the two negatives he had put away 57 years earlier and gave them to Mazzulla.[326]

Of the two negatives, the one of the mob carrying Rudabaugh's head on a pole is dark (because it was taken at night) and poorly focused (but artfully composed). The one of a man, an unknown Mexican Rurales (Federal policeman), holding Rudabaugh's head is good. In this second photo, Rudabaugh has a black *"moustache, neatly trimmed and waxed,"* as described in the newspaper article about him two years earlier.[327]

In 1961, F. Stanley published the two photos in his *"David Rudabaugh, Border Ruffian"* book, which he had obtained from Mazzulla.

The beheading of Rudabaugh is known among Western History enthusiasts, but it is not the most famous beheading in Parral. On July 20, 1923, Mexican revolutionary Pancho Villa (birth name José Doroteo Arango Arámbula) was assassinated in Parral, where he had gone for a visit from his nearby ranchero. He was riding in a 1919 Dodge touring car. Near the city center, Villa and three of his entourage were ambushed by seven gunmen. Villa got one pistol shot off before dying of multiple wounds, killing one of his assassins.[328]

On February 6, 1926, the *Arizona Daily Star* reported:

"The body of Francisco Villa, the late bandit chief, was exhumed and decapitated last night by a band of five men, according to reports reaching here from Parral."

"The headless body was found near the grave this morning and nearby was a note saying the head would be sent to Columbus, N.M., which was raided by Villa's bandit band about ten years ago." [329]

Villa had been buried in the Parral city cemetery. After his body was dug up and beheaded, the recovered headless remains were reburied in a purposely-unmarked grave to prevent further desecration. In 1976, according to one account, they were dug up at the instigation of then Mexican President Luis Echeverría and moved to the Revolution Monument in Mexico City, Mexico.[330]

Where Rudabaugh's body and head were buried is unknown, and almost certainly will remain unknown forever.

Appendix A | Trial Testimony – Territory vs David Rudabaugh, Murder

Rudabaugh's trial for killing jailer Antonio Lino Valdez opened April 19, 1881, in the First District Court in Santa Fe, Judge L. Bradford Prince presiding. The charge was murder in the first degree, the penalty death by hanging.

Rudabaugh's defense attorneys were Marshal A. Breeden and George G. Posey (the lawyers that had handled his change of venue motion were sick). The attorney for the Territory (the prosecution) was William Breeden. Rather oddly, especially for a criminal trial, Prosecutor William Breeden was the older brother of Defense Attorney Marshal Breeden.

The jurors were: H. F. Swape, Walter N. Hoyh, Manuel Sandoval, A. M. Dettelbach, Benito Bacheco, R. M. Stephens, Jesus Torres, Bisente Garcia, G. Felgard, R. A. Biersuth, Juan Luis Gallegos, and Fasmundo Duran.

Testimony

Be it remembered that upon the trial of the above entitled cause at the April AD Term of the District Court for the County of Santa Fe, the following proceedings were had, to wit:

The following evidence which was all of the evidence given in the case was given upon the trial of the cause.

Prosecution Witness – San Miguel County Sheriff Hilario Romero

Hilario Romero Sworn:

Direct Examination by Col. Wm. Breeden

Wm. Breeden: Do you know the defendant?
Romero: Yes sir.

Wm. Breeden: Did you know Antonio Lino Valdez?
Romero: I did.

Wm. Breeden: Do you know where he is?
Romero: He is dead.

Wm. Breeden: Where did he die?
Romero: In Las Vegas.

Wm. Breeden: What time?
Romero: On the second day of April 1880.

Wm. Breeden: Do you know what occupation he pursued when he died?
Romero: He was a jailer.

Wm. Breeden: In the San Miguel County jail?
Romero: Yes sir.

Wm. Breeden: Where is the jail in San Miguel County?
Romero: In Las Vegas.

Wm. Breeden: Did he die at the jail?
Romero: I suppose so.

Wm. Breeden: Do you know how he came to his death?
Romero: I do.

Wm. Breeden: State how.
Romero: From a shot.

Wm. Breeden: In what part of the person?
Romero: I think it was either in the right or the left side.

Wm. Breeden: Do you know who fired the shot?
Romero: No sir.

Wm. Breeden: Where was it you saw the deceased after his death?
Romero: I saw him before his death.

Wm. Breeden: Where was it you saw him after he was shot?
Romero: I saw him in one of the guard rooms of the jail.

Wm. Breeden: Do you know how long after he received the shot that you saw him the first time?
Romero: From five to ten minutes.

Wm. Breeden: Had he been moved from the place where he received the shot?
Romero: Yes sir. They had either moved him or he had gone himself into a room.

Wm. Breeden: What time was it?
Romero: About one o'clock in the afternoon.

Wm. Breeden: Did you see the defendant that day?
Romero: I did.

Wm. Breeden: Where was it you saw him?
Romero: I saw him running from the hall of the Court House to the corner, as he turned around.

Wm. Breeden: Was he running.
Romero: Yes sir.

Wm. Breeden: Any one with him?
Romero: Yes sir.

Wm. Breeden: Who was with him?
Romero: Another man whose name I did not know at the time.

Wm. Breeden: Did he have anything with him?
Romero: They had pistols in their hands.

Wm. Breeden: Did the defendant have pistols?
Romero: Yes sir.

Wm. Breeden: You saw them running out of the hall of the Court House?
Romero: I saw them running until they turned the corner.

Wm. Breeden: How far was this hallway from the place where deceased was shot?

Romero: The hall was about six or eight yards inside the enclosure [placita].

Wm. Breeden: Did this hallway lead from the enclosure where the deceased was shot.

Romero: Yes sir.

Wm. Breeden: Had you at the time shortly before seeing the defendant, or had you seen or heard anything that attracted your attention?

Romero: Yes sir.

Wm. Breeden: What?

Romero: I heard a shot.

Wm. Breeden: Where did the sound of the shot come from?

Romero: From inside the enclosure.

Wm. Breeden: The enclosure where the man was shot?

Romero: Yes sir.

Wm. Breeden: How long after you heard the shot did the defendant run out?

Romero: About six or seven minutes.

Wm. Breeden: Do you know what defendant did then?

Romero: I know what I was told. I did not see.

Wm. Breeden: What County did this occur in?

Romero: San Miguel County, Territory of New Mexico.

Wm. Breeden: You say you saw Antonio Lino Valdez afterward?

Romero: I saw him wounded and saw him dead.

Wm. Breeden: How long after he was wounded did he die?

Romero: I was not there.

Wm. Breeden: How long after was it you saw him dead?

Romero: I saw him dead the next day. I was not in town that night [he was leading the posse that went after Rudabaugh and John J. Allen]. *When I returned he was dead.*

Wm. Breeden: Did you know him before?

Romero: Yes sir.

Wm. Breeden: When did you see him last?

Romero: We had been at our store about 12 minutes before.

Wm. Breeden: What was his condition as to health?

Romero: Good condition.

Wm. Breeden: Was he a jailer?

Romero: Yes sir.

Wm. Breeden: How long after you saw the defendant run out did you go into the jail?
Romero: As soon as he turned the corner.

Wm. Breeden: How far were you from it?
Romero: I was about eight yards.

Wm. Breeden: You immediately went in where the wounded man was?
Romero: Yes sir.

Wm. Breeden: In what condition was the wounded man?
Romero: He was lying down on a bed. He attempted to speak and shake hands with me but could not. It appears he wanted to talk to me but could not.

Cross examination by Mr. Posey

Posey: Where were you Mr. Romero when you heard the shot fired?
Romero: I was in front of my house.

Posey: How far is your house from the jail?
Romero: The south wall of my house is the north wall of the jail.

Posey: What portion of your house were you in?
Romero: I was in front in the street. [Marked H on the map on page 80.]

Posey: Is the jail in front or on the side of your house?
Romero: On one side of my house. On the South side.

Posey: How far was the place where you found the deceased from where you were standing?
Romero: About twenty yards, twenty yards in a direct line.

Posey: How many walls are between your house and the jail?
Romero: One.

Posey: I mean from the spot where you found the deceased?
Romero: If you go around, there are several walls. If you go straight through there is one.

Posey: How many shots did you hear?
Romero: One.

Posey: Do you know how long he had been shot where you found him?
Romero: I did not have a watch in my hand at the time but from six to seven minutes.

Posey: What door did the defendant come out of?
Romero: He came out of the door of the hall.

Posey: How is that door situated with reference to your house?
Romero: The door is on the south side and my house is on the north.

Posey: How far is the door from your house?
Romero: Going around it is about fifty yards.

Posey: The first place you saw the defendant he was coming out of the door?
Romero: When they came out of the hall I saw them for the first time.

Posey: Where did they go?
Romero: They went inside the Plaza.

Posey: How did they go?
Romero: They were running.

Posey: How long did you see them after they left the hall?
Romero: Just about the time it took them to run twenty four or thirty yards.

Posey: Is the Plaza in front of your house?
Romero: It is South.

Posey: Can you see the Plaza?
Romero: From in front I can.

Posey: That is the extent of the Plaza?
Romero: I don't know.

Posey: Is it as large as this Plaza [meaning Santa Fe]?
Romero: I think it is a little larger.

Posey: You can see all the way across that Plaza?
Romero: No you can't see the whole but a part from the alley which communicated with the street on the East side.

Posey: Did you make any effort to arrest these men at that time?
Romero: No sir.

Defense Witness – County Clerk Jesus Maria Tafoya

Jesus Maria Tafoya Sworn

Direct Examination by Col. Breeden

Wm. Breeden: Do you know this defendant?
Tafoya: I do.

Wm. Breeden: Did you know him last April?
Tafoya: I did.

Wm. Breeden: Did you know Antonio Lino Valdez?
Tafoya: Also.

Wm. Breeden: Do you know he is dead?
Tafoya: He is dead.

Wm. Breeden: Where did he die?
Tafoya: In the jail of San Miguel County.

Wm. Breeden: When?
Tafoya: On or about April 5 1880.

Wm. Breeden: *Do you know how he came to his death?*
Tafoya: *I don't know any more but what he told me before he died.*

Wm. Breeden: *Did he make a statement before he died?*
Tafoya: *Yes sir.*

Wm. Breeden: *What was his condition?*
Tafoya: *He could understand everything I asked him.*

Wm. Breeden: *What condition was he in regard to heath?*
Tafoya: *He was badly wounded.*

Wm. Breeden: *How was he wounded?*
Tafoya: *By means of a shot.*

Wm. Breeden: *Did he understand his condition?*
Tafoya: *Yes sir.*

Wm. Breeden: *You say he was badly wounded. In what part of the person?*
Tafoya: *On the breast. Somewhere on the breast.*

Wm. Breeden: *Did he say anything about his condition?*
Tafoya: *Yes sir.*

Wm. Breeden: *What did he say as to his condition?*
Tafoya: *He said he was very ill or sick.*

Wm. Breeden: *Did he say anything more?*
Tafoya: *He answered to the questions I asked him.*

Wm. Breeden: *Do you know how he felt or whether he knew he was very ill or not?*
Tafoya: *He told me he expected to die.*

Wm. Breeden: *How long after did he die?*
Tafoya: *He died about nine or ten o'clock at night of the same day.*

Wm. Breeden: *When did he make the statement as to how he received the wounds?*
Tafoya: *About two o'clock in the afternoon.*

Wm. Breeden: *What statement did he make?*
Tafoya: *I believe I am going to die. I am very sick.*

Answer and question objected to.

Wm. Breeden: *What did he say about it?*
Tafoya: *When I saw him he was wounded. I asked him who gave him that shot and the said that it was the smallest man of the two, who went inside the jail. He fired the shot at me, and the other man took the keys which I had tied at my belt and threw them into Webb's cell. That is all he told me.*

Wm. Breeden: *Did you see the defendant about there that day?*
Tafoya: *Yes sir.*

Wm. Breeden: *State where and under what circumstances you saw him.*

Tafoya: *I was at that time at the office of the Probate Court. One of the jailers, Benito Duran, was with me. A few moments after he had been there we heard a shot. I heard that the shot thundered very much. I told the jailer I thought that shot was inside the jail and he went out and I heard a noise at the door of the hallway to the jail. He rapped it for the second time. When I heard him rap the door the second time I came out and looked towards the door. Then I went towards the door myself. I stood there until he turned around. He told me the prisoners were going out on the other side. Few minutes after I rapped two times and no one responded. I heard the grunts or complaints of someone inside the jail, I did not know who. A few minutes afterwards Rudabaugh opened the door with his left hand. He opened the door and with his right he had a pistol which he pointed at me and said "Look out Jesus." Then I turned to one side of the door and he kept pointed the pistol at me and Allen came out of the hallway and went under his arm and then they went away together. After they went away, I went inside the jail. There I met Ramirez, one of the witnesses in this case, with a sharp shooter in his hand. I went on further in and saw the pool of blood where the deceased first fell. I tracked the blood or spots of blood to the kitchen where he was lying down. I found him lying down on a bed there.*

Wm. Breeden: *Can you make a map of the premises there?*

Witness draws a map of the premises which is attached to his testimony and marked Exhibit A [shown on page 106].

Wm. Breeden: *This main entrance is the south side?*
Tafoya: *Yes sir.*

Wm. Breeden: *What is the open space?*
Tafoya: *It is the placita.*

Wm. Breeden: *The cells of the jail open onto the placita?*
Tafoya: *Yes sir.*

Wm. Breeden: *What sized man was Allen?*
Tafoya: *He was smaller than Rudabaugh.*

Wm. Breeden: *Did you see the prisoner again after you went inside?*
Tafoya: *No sir.*

Wm. Breeden: *How long before you saw the deceased wounded had you seen him before?*
Tafoya: *I had seen him in the morning.*

Wm. Breeden: *What was his condition?*
Tafoya: *He was in good health.*

Wm. Breeden: *What kind of a pistol did the defendant have?*
Tafoya: *From what I could see they were new pistols, 44 Cal.*

Wm. Breeden: *He said when he pointed the pistol at you, he said, "Look out Jesus." Did he say anything more?*
Tafoya: *No sir.*

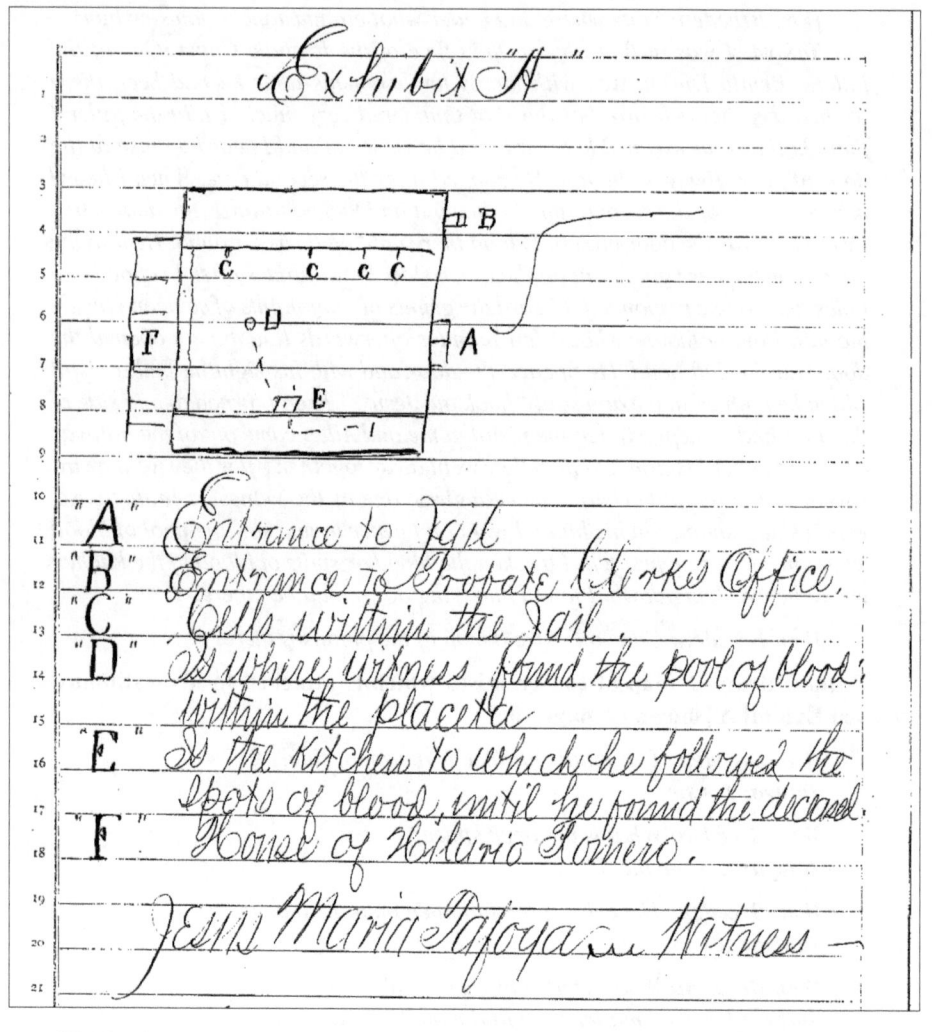

"Exhibit A" drawn by witness Jesus Maria Tafoya. Note that the map mistakenly shows four jail cells. Territory of New Mexico vs David Rudabaugh, Case No. 128.

Wm. Breeden: *This all occurred in Las Vegas, San Miguel County, New Mexico?*
Tafoya: *Yes sir.*

Cross Examination by Mr. Posey

Posey: *When you went into the jail who was there?*
Tafoya: *The first man I saw was Ramirez after they went out.*

Posey: *Where was Ramirez?*
Tafoya: *He was coming out of the kitchen to the hallway.*

Posey: *The kitchen is the place where you found the deceased?*
Tafoya: *Yes sir.*

Posey: Ramirez was there with him?
Tafoya: I suppose so.

Posey: Was there anybody else there?
Tafoya: Yes sir.

Posey: Who?
Tafoya: I saw Martin Kozlowski and somebody I did not know.

Posey: Where were they?
Tafoya: Kozlowski was standing at the kitchen door.

Posey: Anybody else there?
Tafoya: Yes sir.

Posey: Who else?
Tafoya: I don't know the names of the other persons.

Posey: How far was the pool of blood from the [jail cell] door?
Tafoya: Five or six feet at the most.

Posey: Were there any persons in the cells?
Tafoya: Yes sir.

Posey: Could a person standing at the door of the cells see the spot where you saw this pool of blood?
Tafoya: Yes sir.

Posey: Could he see all over the placita?
Tafoya: No sir.

Posey: What was the condition of the deceased when he spoke to you, was he weak?
Tafoya: He did not appear to be weak.

Posey: Could he breathe freely?
Tafoya: Yes sir.

Posey: No blood came out of his mouth?
Tafoya: No sir.

Posey: Have any trouble talking?
Tafoya: The pain only.

Posey: What effect did the pain have on his mind?
Tafoya: The blood spurted out of the wound when he spoke.

Posey: Did he seem much excited?
Tafoya: Yes sir.

Posey: He told you the man who shot him was the little fellow?
Tafoya: Yes sir.

Posey: Allen was much smaller than Rudabaugh?
Tafoya: Not much but some smaller.

Posey: Where is the house of Mr. Romero situated?
Tafoya: On the North side of the jail.

Witness located the house on the map

Posey: Tell me which way Romero's house fronts.
Tafoya: It fronts East.

Posey: Could a man stand at Romero's front door and see a man come out of the door?
Tafoya: No sir.

Posey: When these men came out of the jail where did they go?
Tafoya: They went down the street East to the street which is in front of the jail and then to the Plaza.

Posey: How long did you see them?
Tafoya: I saw them until they turned the corner.

Posey: How did they go there?
Tafoya: They were trotting.

Posey: You did not see any of the shooting yourself?
Tafoya: No sir.

Posey: How long was it after the shot was fired that you went into the jail?
Tafoya: About fifteen minutes.

Posey: Did you go into the jail immediately after these men came out?
Tafoya: I entered inside. I did not stay only long enough to ask Ramirez what was the matter.

Posey: This was bout fifteen minutes after the shot was fired?
Tafoya: Yes sir.

Prosecution Witness - Jailer José Ramirez

José Ramirez Sworn

Direct Examination by William Breeden

Wm. Breeden: Do you know the defendant?
Ramirez: Yes.

Wm. Breeden: Do you know Antonio Lino Valdez?
Ramirez: I did.

Wm. Breeden: Do you remember the day Antonio Lino Valdez was shot?
Ramirez: Yes.

Wm. Breeden: Where were you at that time?
Ramirez: I was a jailer in Las Vegas.

Wm. Breeden: Were abouts in Las Vegas were you at the time of that occurrence?
Ramirez: I was in a room inside the jail.

Wm. Breeden: *State what you heard and saw then?*
Ramirez: *I heard a shot and then I saw the defendant and another one running out of the jail.*

Wm. Breeden: *Immediately after hearing the shot?*
Ramirez: *Yes.*

Wm. Breeden: *What were they doing?*
Ramirez: *When I heard the shot, I stepped out of the door of the kitchen and went out. I saw two men, they had pistols.*

Wm. Breeden: *Did this man have a pistol? (indicating defendant)*
Ramirez: *Yes sir.*

Wm. Breeden: *How did he have it?*
Ramirez: *In his hand.*

Wm. Breeden: *Do you know where Antonio Lino Valdez was?*
Ramirez: *He was at the door of a cell.*

Wm. Breeden: *Well what did you do then?*
Ramirez: *I followed them to see where they were going.*

Wm. Breeden: *Where did they go?*
Ramirez: *They went out and went to the new town [East Las Vegas].*

Wm. Breeden: *What did you do then?*
Ramirez: *I followed them.*

Wm. Breeden: *Where did you again see Antonio Lino Valdez?*
Ramirez: *In the night.*

Wm. Breeden: *Is that all you know about it?*
Ramirez: *Yes sir.*

Wm. Breeden: *What jail did you say this was?*
Ramirez: *The Las Vegas jail.*

Wm. Breeden: *About what time did this occur?*
Ramirez: *In April.*

Wm. Breeden: *What year?*
Ramirez: *1880.*

Wm. Breeden: *Last year?*
Ramirez: *Yes sir.*

Cross Examination by Mr. Posey

Posey: *When you came out of the room after you heard the shot, what did you do?*
Ramirez: *I stood at the door.*

Posey: *Did you pull your pistol?*
Ramirez: *No.*

Posey: *Didn't you have a pistol?*
Ramirez: *I did not.*

Posey: *Was you a jailer there?*
Ramirez: *I was.*

Posey: *You say the deceased was standing in front of a cell when you came out?*
Ramirez: *He had fallen down in front of a cell.*

Posey: *Who was in the cell?*
Ramirez: *There were several persons there. I don't remember their names.*

Posey: *Was Mullen there?*
Ramirez: *Yes sir.*

Posey: *Could he see the man that was shot?*
Ramirez: *Yes sir.*

Posey: *Did these men say anything to you?*
Ramirez: *No sir.*

Posey: *I mean the men who went out?*
Ramirez: *No sir.*

Posey: *Did they offer to do anything to you?'*
Ramirez: *No sir, they just passed out of the door.*

Posey: *Was this man who was shot able to talk?*
Ramirez: *Yes sir.*

Posey: *Did he say anything to you?*
Ramirez: *No sir.*

Posey: *What was his appearance. Did he look as if he was frightened and excited?*
Ramirez: *When I saw him the first time he said nothing to me.*

Posey: *You saw him fall?*
Ramirez: *I saw him falling.*

Posey: *How long after the shot was fired did you see him falling?*
Ramirez: *Just as I stepped to the door, I saw him falling?*

Posey: *How long was that after the shot was fired?*
Ramirez: *About a minute.*

Posey: *Just about the time it took you to step out of the door?*
Ramirez: *Yes sir.*

Posey: *Were you standing near the door?*
Ramirez: *I was laying down asleep.*

Posey: *Which was the larger of these two men?*
Ramirez: *This man. (indicating defendant)*

Posey: Allen was smaller?
Ramirez: Yes sir.

Prosecution Witness - Hack Driver J. C. Cauldwell

J. C. Cauldwell Sworn

Direct Examination by William Breeden

Wm. Breeden: Where do you live?
Cauldwell: In Las Vegas

Wm. Breeden: Do you know this defendant?
Cauldwell: Yes sir.

Wm. Breeden: Where were you in the early part of April 1880?
Cauldwell: In Vegas.

Wm. Breeden: Do you know this man here? (indicating defendant)
Cauldwell: Yes sir.

Wm. Breeden: Do you remember the time a jailer was killed Las Vegas?
Cauldwell: Yes sir.

Wm. Breeden: Were you in Las Vegas at the time?
Cauldwell: Yes sir.

Wm. Breeden: What was your occupation?
Cauldwell: I was a hack driver.

Wm. Breeden: Did you see the defendant that day?
Cauldwell: Yes sir.

Wm. Breeden: Now state all you know about the circumstances connected with this case that you know of.

Cauldwell: I don't know as I can call the day of the month. Somewhere between the third and the fifth. I have been driving a hack ever since Las Vegas had a new town. I was driving a hack at that time. It was between one and two o'clock. It was might have been after two in the afternoon that I saw this man Rudabaugh and John Allen. I came from the new town with a load of passengers and drove them to the Sumner House. Rudabaugh and Allen told me to wait. And they would go to the new town. And I waited and they told me to drive around by the jail, as they wanted to see Webb. After they got in, I drove around to the jail and stopped and Allen spoke to Rudabaugh and said something to Rudabaugh about he is not here and told me to drive up on the hill to the house of Tom Pickett. And I drove up there and they got down out of the hack and went in and had a conversation for half an hour. And then Rudabaugh and Allen and Pickett and another man, I never learned his name, came out of Pickett's house and got into the hack. They then told me to go on and I came down the back street to Mendenhall's and from there I intended to drive into the stable but they said "hold on we want to see Webb."

Then Pickett and the other man got out of the hack and went out into the Plaza and I went down to the jail with Rudabaugh and Allen. Then they got out of the hack and told me to wait. They went and rapped on the jail door and the man who was killed let them in. In a few minutes I heard a pistol shot and got a little frightened, and as I had an idea that something was the matter, I drove my team around to the Plaza. I did not know whether they had done anything, and I was kind of anxious to find out, so I stopped my team as soon as I got in the plaza. I thought I would tie my team and go back on foot and see what they had done. Just as I was in the act of getting out of the hack they came running around the corner and jumped into my hack and Allen said "drive to the new town." And I drove them over to the new town.

Wm. Breeden: *What kind of pistol were they?*
Cauldwell: *Large pistols.*

Wm. Breeden: *Six shooters?*
Cauldwell: *Yes.*

Wm. Breeden: *Did they have arms when they went through the jail?*
Cauldwell: *They had revolvers in their belts and before we got to the jail, I saw Allen's revolver.*

Wm. Breeden: *You drove them to the new town?*
Cauldwell: *Yes sir.*

Wm. Breeden: *Any thing occur on the road?*
Cauldwell: *They each held their pistol in their hands from the old to the new town. Where we crossed the creek, Allen was pointing his revolver at me and I turned around to push it away. As I turned around Rudabaugh is the man who loaded his revolver at that time.*

Wm. Breeden: *Was it a cartridge pistol or what?*
Cauldwell: *Yes sir.*

Wm. Breeden: *How many loads did he put in?*
Cauldwell: *One load.*

Wm. Breeden: *Did he remove anything?*
Cauldwell: *He took out a shell.*

Wm. Breeden: *You saw him remove a shell from the pistol and afterwards put in a new cartridge?*
Cauldwell: *Yes sir.*

Wm. Breeden: *You afterwards found an empty shell in the carriage?*
Cauldwell: *Yes sir.*

Wm. Breeden: *What was done with the cartridge?*
Cauldwell: *He put into the pistol.*

Wm. Breeden: *Well?*

Cauldwell: *When we got to the new town Rudabaugh jumped out and went into Goodlett's and I wanted Allen to get out and let me go. He wouldn't do that and then I wanted him to take the hack and let me go. Then Rudabaugh came out with a double barrel shot gun and laid it in the back and I started to get out. Allen said, "you son of a bitch, if you make a move I will blow your brains out." Then I said to Rudabaugh, you can take the team and go as far as you please, and he did not make any reply. So I jumped out of the hack and Allen was going to shoot and Rudabaugh said, "don't make a fool of yourself, I will drive." Then Rudabaugh took the lines and drove across to Houghton's Hardware store. They went in and Rudabaugh got some guns, I don't know how many, and put them in the hack and drove off.*

Wm. Breeden: *Who was Webb?*
Cauldwell: *Webb was a prisoner then and is now.*

Wm. Breeden: *In the Las Vegas jail?*
Cauldwell: *Yes sir.*

Wm. Breeden: *When they rode in the hack after leaving the jail and between there and the new town, did they say what they had done?*
Cauldwell: *I asked Allen what he had done and he said, "that Greaser wouldn't give us the keys and we killed the son of a bitch."*

Cross Examination by Mr. Posey

Posey: *Allen said that?*
Cauldwell: *Yes sir.*

Posey: *Where did Rudabaugh sit?*
Cauldwell: *He sat in the back seat.*

Posey: *Did he hear what Allen said?*
Cauldwell: *He could have heard it. Allen was in the middle seat and Rudabaugh in the back seat and I in front.*

Posey: *Did Rudabaugh say anything?*
Cauldwell: *Not that I heard.*

Posey: *Did he say anything about what had happened during the ride?*
Cauldwell: *No sir.*

Posey: *Is that all that was said at that time?*
Cauldwell: *Yes sir.*

Posey: *How did you go back from the old town to the new town?*
Cauldwell: *We went about as fast as the horses would take us.*

Posey: *What kind of a road is it?*
Cauldwell: *Very good road, except rocky at the creek.*

Posey: *What is the character of the road generally between the towns?*
Cauldwell: *Good.*

Posey: Where did this conversation between you and Allen about killing the son of a bitch occur?
Cauldwell: While crossing the creek.

Posey: That was in the rocky part of the road?
Cauldwell: I had just crossed the rocky part.

Posey: You were going pretty fast?
Cauldwell: Yes sir.

Posey: How did you happen to see Rudabaugh loading the pistol?
Cauldwell: He might have put all of the loads in at that time.

Posey: He might have had his pistol empty for all you know?
Cauldwell: Yes sir.

Posey: Allen was the man who made all these hostile moves?
Cauldwell: Yes sir.

Posey: Rudabaugh made no threats to you?
Cauldwell: He made no threats but only spoke to me about driving faster.

Posey: How long was it after you heard that shot until these men came up and wanted you to take them to the new town?
Cauldwell: I should judge about three or four minutes.

Posey: You say Rudabaugh made no reply when Allen said, we have killed this man?
Cauldwell: I did not hear him.

Posey: What became of these other men you spoke of?
Cauldwell: They went out in the Plaza. I saw Pickett the same evening and talked to him.

Posey: Are you well acquainted with the town over there?
Cauldwell: Yes sir.

Posey: Do you know the location of the different houses?
Cauldwell: I know the situation of a great many of them.

Posey: Is there any porch in front of the jail?
Cauldwell: Yes sir.

Posey: Where is it located?
Cauldwell: The porch runs along the front of the jail all the way along.

Posey: How long is the front of that building?
Cauldwell: I should judge some fifty feet.

Posey: How far is it from the front of the Court House or jail to the Plaza?
Cauldwell: It is not over a hundred yards, probably seventy-five yards.

Posey: Is the square in sight of the porch?
Cauldwell: You can go down on the lower side of the porch and see the Plaza.

Posey: You did not notice whether all the chambers of Allen's pistol was full or not?
Cauldwell: No, he had them in his hand.

Posey: He might have had some empty?
Cauldwell: Yes sir.

Posey: Might not that have been Allen's pistol that Rudabaugh loaded?
Cauldwell: They must have changed.

Posey: Might not Allen have passed his pistol back to Rudabaugh while you were driving?
Cauldwell: It might have been done.

Redirect by William Breeden

Wm. Breeden: You say Rudabaugh and Allen went off with your hack after coming out of Houghton's Hardware store?
Cauldwell: Yes sir.

Wm. Breeden: Did you see where they went?
Cauldwell: I was in sight of them for about twelve or fourteen miles.

Wm. Breeden: You kept in sight for about fourteen miles?
Cauldwell: From twelve to fourteen.

Wm. Breeden: Which way did they go?
Cauldwell: They went East.

Wm. Breeden: At what rate did they go?
Cauldwell: I don't know. They went pretty fast.

Wm. Breeden: When did you again see your hack?
Cauldwell: After I lost sight of it I did not see it again until after sundown.

Wm. Breeden: Where did you see it then?
Cauldwell: It was then about twenty four miles East of Vegas.

Wm. Breeden: Where did you again see Rudabaugh?
Cauldwell: I never saw him again until they brought him back to Vegas.

Wm. Breeden: Recently?
Cauldwell: Yes, within the last week.

Defense Witness - Prisoner William Mullen

William Mullen Sworn

Direct Examination by Mr. Posey

Posey: What is your name?
Mullen: William Mullen

Posey: Where do you live?
Mullen: I live in Santa Fe now.

Posey: Where were you on the second day of April 1880?
Mullen: In Las Vegas.

Posey: Where in Las Vegas?
Mullen: In jail.

Posey: You say you were in jail?
Mullen: Yes sir.

Posey: Will you state to the jury whether you saw Rudabaugh that day?
Mullen: Yes sir.

Posey: Were you there when the jailer was killed?
Mullen: Yes sir.

Posey: Was Rudabaugh there?
Mullen: Yes sir.

Posey: State all you know about the circumstances connected with the killing.
Mullen: Rudabaugh and Allen came in there one afternoon abut two o'clock and had some tobacco and newspapers. They came in and Rudabaugh had his hand on the door of the cell. The first thing I heard was Allen saying "Give me those keys you son of a bitch." I don't know what the jailer said in Mexican. Then Allen shot him and ran behind and took the keys. And Rudabaugh ran out of the door.

Posey: Did Allen give the jailer any time to give up the keys?
Mullen: No sir. The pistol went off immediately.

Posey: What was Rudabaugh doing at that time?
Mullen: He had his hands up on the door talking to me and Webb.

Posey: Do you know what Rudabaugh came there for?
Mullen: No sir.

Posey: It was his habit to come there with papers?
Mullen: Yes sir. He came there two or three times a week.

Posey: What happened after the shot was fired and Rudabaugh ran out?
Mullen: Allen threw the keys down to Webb, and said "take these and unlock the door, I have to go."

Posey: Were there any of the jailers in sight?
Mullen: No sir. I believe there was one in the kitchen.

Posey: Did any of them come on the firing of the shot?
Mullen: Yes in two or three minutes.

Posey: Was Rudabaugh there when they came out?
Mullen: Yes sir.

Posey: How far were these men from you when the shooting took place?
Mullen: Not over two feet. Allen might have been four feet.

Posey: Where was the man who was shot?
Mullen: He was standing on the left side of Rudabaugh.

Posey: *On which side of Rudabaugh was Allen standing?*
Mullen: *On the left.*

Posey: *What did the jailer do when he came out?*
Mullen: *I seen him run out of the kitchen with a pistol in his hand.*

Posey: *Did you see him point it at anybody?*
Mullen: *Yes sir.*

Posey: *How did this man get from the place where he was shot to the kitchen?*
Mullen: *Two prisoners carried him in.*

Posey: *Could you see this man where he fell from where you were in the cell?*
Mullen: *No sir. He fell backwards. I could see him after they picked him up and carried him to the kitchen.*

Posey: *Did Rudabaugh say anything when the shot was fired?*
Mullen: *I didn't hear him.*

Posey: *He ran out immediately?*
Mullen: *Yes sir.*

Posey: *Did Rudabaugh have a pistol in his hand.*
Mullen: *I didn't see any.*

Posey: *Could you have seen one?*
Mullen: *Yes sir.*

Posey: *When that shot was fired what was the position of his hands when the shot was fired?*
Mullen: *He had them on the cell door.*

Posey: *He was talking to you and Webb through the grating?*
Mullen: *He was asking us how we got along.*

Posey: *Did you hear any information from either Allen or Rudabaugh that they were coming that day?*
Mullen: *No sir.*

Posey: *As far as you know their coming there was not by appointment?*
Mullen: *No.*

Posey: *Did you hear any conversation between Rudabaugh and Webb at that time?*
Mullen: *No.*

Posey: *Did they have any private talk there?*
Mullen: *No.*

Posey: *You heard everything then said?*
Mullen: *Yes sir.*

Posey: *What was the substance of their conversation?*
Mullen: They didn't stand there but a minute or two and shook hands with me and Webb and the next thing I heard was a shot.

Posey: *The conversation was how you felt and if you wanted anything?*
Mullen: Yes sir.

Posey: *You could not see the man after he was shot and fell?*
Mullen: I seen him about the time Allen pointed the pistol and he fell back.

Cross Examination by William Breeden

Wm. Breeden: *What were you in jail for?*
Mullen: Train robbery.

Wm. Breeden: *What was Webb in for?*
Mullen: Murder.

Wm. Breeden: *You say Rudabaugh was in the habit of visiting you frequently?*
Mullen: Yes sir, nearly every day.

Wm. Breeden: *How long have you known Rudabaugh?*
Mullen: I had known Rudabaugh four months.

Wm. Breeden: *How long had you been in there?*
Mullen: Somewhere between eight and ten months.

Wm. Breeden: *He visited you all that time?*
Mullen: Not every day.

Wm. Breeden: *He is a friend of yours?*
Mullen: Yes sir.

Wm. Breeden: *As soon as the shot was fired Rudabaugh ran off?*
Mullen: Yes sir.

Wm. Breeden: *Turned and ran did he?*
Mullen: Yes sir.

Wm. Breeden: *How long did Allen remain there after Rudabaugh left?*
Mullen: Two or three minutes, just long enough to –

Wm. Breeden: *Never mind what he did, you answer my questions.*

Wm. Breeden: *Where did you say he got the keys?*
Mullen: Out of the jailer's pocket.

Wm. Breeden: *After he fell?*
Mullen: Yes sir.

Wm. Breeden: *How do you know he got them out of the jailer's pocket?*
Mullen: I saw him come back with them.

Wm. Breeden: *You did not see him take them out of the pocket?*
Mullen: No sir.

Wm. Breeden: *Can you swear positively that Rudabaugh did not take them?*
Mullen: *Yes sir.*

Wm. Breeden: *How can you swear?*
Mullen: *Because Rudabaugh was standing at the door when the shot was fired and turned and ran out.*

Wm. Breeden: *Rudabaugh was not at the door where the keys were taken out of the dead man's pocket?*
Mullen: *No sir.*

Wm. Breeden: *You could not see the dead man?*
Mullen: *No sir.*

Wm. Breeden: *Then you did not see who did take them out. How are you able to swear Rudabaugh did not?*
Mullen: *Because he was in that part of the jail. (gesture)*

Wm. Breeden: *How can you swear to that when you could not see the man when he fell?*
Mullen: *The jailer fell on that side and Rudabaugh was this way. (gesturing)*

Wm. Breeden: *How do you know Rudabaugh did not go back there where the dead man was?*
Mullen: *He did not came back there.*

Wm. Breeden: *How can you swear when you could not see that far?*
Mullen: *Simply because the jailer fell on this side and Rudabaugh ran out that way.*

Wm. Breeden: *You just swore that Rudabaugh did not do it and now you undertake to swear he did not do it when you did not see him.*
Mullen: *I saw Allen fire the shot.*

Wm. Breeden: *You said you could not see the dead man. Now how can you swear positively that Allen was the man who took the keys and not Rudabaugh?*
Mullen: *Allen jumped on top of he jailer and took the keys.*

Wm. Breeden: *How do you know he jumped on top of him when you couldn't see? You can swear positively to what you did not see? How do you manage to do that?*
Mullen: *The jailer fell on that side and Rudabaugh ran out on that side.*

Wm. Breeden: *Have you talked about his case before today?*
Mullen: *No sir.*

Wm. Breeden: *Tell anybody what you could testify?*
Mullen: *Yes sir.*

Wm. Breeden: *Tell Rudabaugh?*
Mullen: *No.*

Wm. Breeden: *When were you subpoenaed?*
Mullen: *This morning.*

Wm. Breeden: *You talked to these lawyers about it?*
Mullen: *I believe this gentleman called me outside and talked to me about it.*

Wm. Breeden: *Didn't you talk to Rudabaugh?*
Mullen: *No. I spoke to Mr. [Marshal] Breeden. The first time I spoke of it, I told them what I said here.*

Wm. Breeden: *How far around the placita was it?*
Mullen: *I should think about ten steps across it.*

Wm. Breeden: *You say Rudabaugh ran when he went?*
Mullen: *He ran right out of that room.*

Wm. Breeden: *He ran at the firing of the shot?*
Mullen: *Yes sir. Allen remained there until he had taken the keys from the dead man and attempted to unlock the door. He dropped the keys in front of the door and said, "take these and unlock the door. I have to go."*

Wm. Breeden: *Who was in the there beside you and Webb?*
Mullen: *The Stokes brothers [Joseph and William].*

Wm. Breeden: *And then Allen left?*
Mullen: *Yes. About two minutes behind Rudabaugh.*

Wm. Breeden: *All Rudabaugh said was, "how are you and do you want anything?"*
Mullen: *Yes sir.*

Wm. Breeden: *A minute?*
Mullen: *A minute or a minute and a half.*

Wm. Breeden: *What did Allen say?*
Mullen: *He did not speak at all.*

Wm. Breeden: *They came in together?*
Mullen: *Yes sir.*

Wm. Breeden: *Did Rudabaugh draw a pistol when he ran?*
Mullen: *No sir.*

Wm. Breeden: *Did you see that he had a pistol?*
Mullen: *I did not see any pistol about him.*

Redirect Examination by Posey

Posey: *Were these last charges against you dismissed at the last term of court?*
Mullen: *Yes sir.*

Posey: *You are not under indictment now?*
Mullen: *No sir.*

Posey: Explain to me if you can the position of the door through which Rudabaugh went out of that placita or courtyard.
Mullen: There is a kind of a middle door and an outside door.

Posey: Did you see him come back?
Mullen: No sir.

Posey: If he had come back could you have seen him?
Mullen: Yes sir.

Posey: Did Rudabaugh go out of that courtyard or placita in the same direction that the jailer fell?
Mullen: Yes sir.

Posey: Which way did he go?
Mullen: The jailer fell off that way and Rudabaugh went this way.

Posey: What did Allen do after he had fired the shot?
Mullen: He went toward this man after the keys.

Posey: Did he have the keys when he came back?
Mullen: Yes sir.

Defense Witness - Defendant David Rudabaugh

David Rudabaugh sworn

Direct Examination by Mr. Posey

Posey: What is your name?
Rudabaugh: David Rudabaugh.

Posey: You are the defendant in this cause?
Rudabaugh: Yes sir.

Posey: You were in Las Vegas in April 1880?
Rudabaugh: Yes sir.

Posey: You were present in the killing referred to?
Rudabaugh: Yes sir.

Posey: State to the jury how you came to be there?
Rudabaugh: I had been a police officer in Las Vegas prior to the killing of the jailer and was a personal friend of Webb who had got into a difficulty there and I used to go and see him and take him tobacco and newspapers and see how he was getting along. I was well acquainted with this jailer as well as the rest and was never refused admittance. I went over this day to the Sumner House in East Las Vegas. Allen went with me. We went to see a man who owed me some money. Mr. Allen wanted to go to the jail to see Webb, and I said I was going too.

The man I wanted to see was not at the Sumner House. This man was Tom Pickett. I went up where he lived. He was sick in bed and I went up to see him. I was there fifteen or twenty minutes and he said he was going down town and got into the hack and went with us to Menden Hall's stable. There he got out. I told the hack driver to drive us to the jail. I wanted to see Webb. When we got there I got out and knocked at the door. The jailer admitted us. He asked me if I wanted to see Webb. I said I did. He showed us the cell he was in. I had some newspapers which I gave them and asked them how they were getting along, and stood there talking to them. I was standing there with my hands crossed on the door and Allen shot the jailer. I turned around and said, "what did you do that for?" I looked round and saw the jailer fall. I started to go out when a jailer drew a pistol on me. I jumped out of range and pulled my pistol. By that time men were knocking at the front door. I opened the door and ran out. The hack I left at the door was gone. I ran down and overtook it in the Plaza, and asked him why he didn't wait. I never looked back.

By the time I got into the hack Allen was there. He got in the hack and told the driver to drive as fast as he could drive. On the way to the new town he tried to load his pistol but could not as he was under the influence of liquor. He gave me the pistol and asked me to load it and I loaded it. We drove over to the new town and I went into Goodlett's Saloon, where he told me there was a double-barrel shot gun belonging to him. Then we drove to Houghton's Hardware store and got these other guns. He brought them out, got into the hack and we left the town going in an Easterly direction. We drove about ten miles and gave the hack to two Mexican herders.

Posey: What did Allen do after the firing of the shot?
Rudabaugh: I don't know.

Posey: Why don't you know?
Rudabaugh: Because I left the jail.

Posey: How did you go?
Rudabaugh: I went pretty fast.

Posey: How came Allen to be with you going to the jail?
Rudabaugh: He said he would like to go in and see Webb and the Stokes. He said that he couldn't get in and knowing that I had admittance when I wanted to, asked me to take him in.

Posey: It is testified that on your way to the new town, Allen said to the driver of the hack, "I killed the son of a bitch" or words to that effect. Did you hear such a remark?
Rudabaugh: No sir.

Posey: How do you account for such a remark?
Rudabaugh: I think if he had said it, I should have heard it.

Posey: Did you [know] anything about it?
Rudabaugh: No sir.

Posey: Did you make any threats to any body?
Rudabaugh: None whatever.

Posey: And you only pulled your pistol when you were threatened by another jailer?
Rudabaugh: Yes sir.

Posey: Were you in the habit of carrying pistols?
Rudabaugh: Yes sir.

Cross Examination by Wm. Breeden

Wm. Breeden: Do you know Jesus Maria Tafoya?
Rudabaugh: I know him when I see him.

Wm. Breeden: Did you meet him at the doorway that day?
Rudabaugh: Not that I know of.

Wm. Breeden: Did you threatened him with a pistol?
Rudabaugh: No sir.

Wm. Breeden: Did you not point a pistol at him?
Rudabaugh: No sir.

Wm. Breeden: When did you see Allen again?
Rudabaugh: When he got into the hack.

Wm. Breeden: Was that the first time you saw him after the shot was fired?
Rudabaugh: Yes sir.

Wm. Breeden: What did you go the jail for?
Rudabaugh: I went there to see Webb.

Wm. Breeden: Didn't you go there to help Webb escape?
Rudabaugh: No sir, I did not.

Wm. Breeden: You say Allen went into Houghton's Hardware store after guns?
Rudabaugh: Yes sir.

Wm. Breeden: Are you not the man who went after the guns?
Rudabaugh: No sir.

Wm. Breeden: You did not go in?
Rudabaugh: No sir.

Instructions to the Jury:

The defendant by his attorneys asked that the following instructions be given to the jury:

> *"That if the jury believe from the evidence that the deceased just prior to his death from such shooting recognized that one Allen fired the shot that caused his death, and then and there, knowing his death to be close at hand, as stated, then they must find for the defendant."*

Which request for said instructions was denied by the Court, to which ruling of the Court the defendant by his Counsel excepts. The Court gave the following instructions to the jury:

Gentlemen of the Jury:

The defendant David Rudabaugh was indicted by the Grand Jury of San Miguel Co. together with John Allen for the murder of Antonio Lino Valdez at Las Vegas on April

5th, 1880. The defendant took a change of venue to this Court in order to obtain a jury entirely unprejudiced.

The evidence has been brief and the whole case has been brought before you within a shorter time than is usual in cases of such gravity so that the facts as testified to are all fresh in your memory.

Certain facts are undisputed and this simplifies your labors. It is undisputed that the deceased Valdez died from a wound received in the placita of the Las Vegas jail, on the day alleged in the indictment and that at the time of the firing of the pistol shot, the defendant and Allen were in such placita and soon after went out rapidly from the gateway thereof.

Here the indisputable evidence may be said to cease and you are to judge from all the evidence before you as to the other facts connected with the killing. You are first to decide whether the deceased was killed, and if you agree as to that, then as to who it was who killed him.

There is no evidence at all tending to show that the killing in any case was justifiable or excusable or that the circumstances existed to make such killing any degree of murder less than first.

The statuary definition of Murder in the First Degree is the unlawful killing of a human being perpetrated from a premeditated design to effect the death of the person killed and the penalty death.

It is a principle of law founded on reason, that if a felony is committed by one man and another is present, aiding and abetting such person in the commission thereof, the abettor is as guilty as the first. The act in such case is the act of both, and both are equally guilty.

If then, from all the evidence you are satisfied beyond a reasonable doubt that the defendant killed the deceased in such a manner as to constitute murder in the first degree, or that that crime was committed by Allen, the defendant now on trial, being present, aiding and abetting in the commission of such murder, it is your duty to find a verdict of Guilty of Murder in the First Degree.

If you do not so believe beyond a reasonable doubt, then it is your duty to acquit.

In this as in all criminal cases you are to remember that the law presumes every man to be innocent until he is found to be guilty. That the defendant is entitled to the benefit of every reasonable doubt and that unless you are satisfied of the guilt of the accused beyond such reasonable doubt, he is entitled to an acquittal.

A reasonable doubt, however, in the view of the law is a substantial doubt founded on the evidence, and not a mere fancy or the possibility of a doubt.

From various requests to charge, I give you the following, asked by the defendant's counsel:

If the jury believes that at the moment of the shooting the defendant was engaged in conversation with Mullen and Webb and was uninformed of any intent on the part of Allen to commit murder, then they must find for the defendant.

To all of which the defendant by his Counsel excepted. After the verdict had been rendered in the cause, the defendant by his Counsel moved the Court to set aside the verdict and grant him a new trial for the reasons set forth in said motion [see pages 79-80]. Which motion was overruled by the Court, to which ruling the defendant by his Counsel excepted.

The defendant now prays that his bill of acceptance may be signed and sealed by your honor and made a part of the record herein which is accordingly done.

L. Bradford Prince
Chief Justice of N. M.

Certification of Trial Record

Territory of New Mexico
County of Santa Fe

I, Clerk of the First Judicial District Court of said Territory in and for said County certify that the foregoing seventy three pages and nine lines contain a true copy of the record and of all the proceedings in the cause of Territory of New Mexico versus David Rudabaugh, as the same are of record in the my office.

Witness my hand and seal of said Court this 21th day of December, 1881.

R. W. Clancy, Clerk

Office a bill of exceptious, which said bill of exceptious is in the words and figures following, to wit:

Territory of New Mexico
County of Santa Fe
The Territory vs David Rudabaugh, Murder

Be it remembered that upon the trial of the above entitled cause at the April A.D. Term of the District Court for the County of Santa Fe, the following proceeding here had to wit:

The [preceding] evidence which was all of the evidence given in case was given upon the trial of the cause.

Appendix B | Billy Wilson's Counterfeiting Case

On August 3, 1880, Billy Wilson sold his livery stable in White Oaks for $400 to William H. West. West paid Wilson with four $100 counterfeit bills. Wilson did not recognize the bills as fake. William West was one of several people who were distributing phony bills created by a New York counterfeiter named William E. Brockway.[1] The bills were being passed in a number of Western states. Responding to the appearance of the fake bills, the U.S. Treasury Department sent Special Operative Azariah F. Wild to New Mexico to investigate and, if possible, arrest the bill passers. Wild arrived in New Mexico September 19 or 20, 1880, and left December 23, 1880.[2]

On August 5, 1880, Wilson changed one of the fake bills in James J. Dolan's store in Lincoln. He asked Dolan to put the other bills he had received from West in his safe (see Dolan's letter following).

Ten days later, August 15, Wilson, retrieved the locked-up bills from Dolan's safe. He spent one of them in José Montaño's store in Lincoln. On September 1, Wilson changed one of the bills with merchant William Robert in Anton Chico. By that time, Wilson suspected the bills were fake, according to sworn testimony given by Robert in Wilson's later trial.[3]

From Anton Chico, Wilson went to Fort Sumner.

On October 3, Operative Wild met with Dolan and positively identified the note Wilson changed with Dolan as counterfeit.[4] It quickly became known that Wilson had or was passing counterfeit notes, giving Wilson ample reason to remain in Fort Sumner and to link his fate with Billy the Kid.

On December 23, 1880, Wilson, Billy, Rudabaugh, and Pickett were captured at Stinking Springs by Sheriff Pat Garrett.

Wilson's Federal trial for passing counterfeit bills was held February 28, 1882, in Santa Fe. In defending himself, Wilson said that he had been given the bills by West in exchange for his livery stable and he did not know that they were fake. The witnesses against him were James J. Dolan, José Montaño, David Easton, Pat Garrett, Ira Leonard, and William Robert.

The bill that Wilson gave Robert was introduced as evidence. About the bill, the *Santa Fe New Mexican* wrote:

> *"The hundred dollar bill which he is alleged to have given Mr. Robert is from the only counterfeit plate of that denomination ever made, and it is so perfect as to deceive the most expert bank officers. It was compared yesterday with various other notes of the same amount, and not one person in ten could tell it from the others."* [5]

Wilson was convicted and sentenced to 7 years in the penitentiary, half the maximum penalty of 15 years. Wilson appealed his case.

Grave of David L. Anderson (Billy Wilson), Saint Mary Magdalene Cemetery, Brackettville, Texas. 2008 photo by author.

On September 9, 1882, Wilson escaped jail in Santa Fe, where he was being held while he waited for his appeal to be heard. The *Santa Fe New Mexican*, in reporting his escape, wrote:

> "Billy Wilson always protested that he was innocent of crime.... He says he passed the counterfeit notes, but swears he did not know that they were not good money. A short time before he escaped, Wilson reiterated this, saying that never in his life had he knowingly violated the law. He had been induced to join the Kid through fear, there being indictments against him which his friends told him would result in his being sent to the penitentiary. He tried to avoid this by joining the outlaws. Of course, Billy's statements are of no consequence, but his pertinacity in clinging to them through thick and thin is to be remarked." [6]

After escaping, Wilson did not immediately leave New Mexico. In January, 1884, he, Tom Pickett, and two others killed four unarmed Hispanic men in cold blood at Seven Rivers. One newspaper described it as *"one of the most blood curdling crimes ever executed in frontier history."* The dead men were buried in a common grave.[7]

Wilson went to Texas and assumed the name of David L. Anderson.

In 1896, Wilson contacted his defense lawyer from the counterfeiting trial, William T. Thornton, who in the meantime had been elected Governor of New Mexico, and asked for help in obtaining a pardon for his conviction. Governor Thornton agreed, and put together a campaign that involved soliciting 25 letters from his Texas acquaintances as to his good character. Thornton also got Garrett and Dolan to write letters supporting Wilson's pardon request. He submitted those letters plus his own personal plea to U.S. Attorney General Judson Harmon on July 7, 1896. On August 25, 1896, President Grover Cleveland granted Wilson a pardon.[8]

In 1915, Wilson became sheriff of Terrell County, Texas. On June 14, 1918, Wilson was killed by Ed "Red" Valentine in a saloon in Sanderson, Texas. Wilson entered the saloon to arrest Valentine, who was dunk and shooting up the place. Valentine, who had been telling patrons he would kill Wilson if Wilson attempted to arrest him, beat Wilson to the draw and shot Wilson's gun out of his hand. Wilson *"ducked behind the bar and Red ran to the end of the bar and shot again,"* killing Wilson. In retaliation for Wilson's wanton killing, a man named Bob Gatlin shot and killed Valentine.[9] Wilson was buried in the Saint Mary Magdalene Cemetery in Brackettville, Texas.

Here is the letter that Pat Garrett wrote supporting Wilson's request for a pardon (Garrett was not yet sheriff of Dona Ana County):

Office of Numa Reymond,
Sheriff, Dona Ana County,
Las Cruces, New Mexico

Las Cruces, N.M.
May 24, 1896

Hon. W. T. Thornton

Dear Sir

I write you for the purpose of stating the facts with reference to Billy Wilson who was convicted in 1881 for passing Counterfeit Money & afterward escaped from the Jail at Santa Fe. I was the principal witness in the case & Jimmy Dolan was the other important witness against him. I worked hard for his conviction, from the fact that I believed him guilty, but from positive evidence since that time, I am now fully convinced that he was innocent. I have made it an object to fully investigate every thing pertaining to Wilson & while I must admit that I was somewhat prejudiced against him from the fact that he was arrested with "Billy the Kid" – He was at that time quite young & engaged in the Livery Stable business at White Oaks, when a man by the name of [William H.] West undoubtedly brought the Counterfeit money into the Country & bought Wilsons (sic) stable, paying him therefore with this money – I have since 1891 known Billy Wilson in Texas as D. L. Anderson, where he has enjoyed the reputation of being a good, honest, & straight forward citizen, has occupied many positions of trust & for a long time employed as Manager of the Dolores Cattle Co. in Kinney Co Texas. I know of nothing he had done which would be discreditable to him since his escape. He is a man of family, all of whom command the respect of all the people with whom they come in contact.

Yours Very Truly
P. F. Garrett [10]

Here is the letter that James J. Dolan wrote supporting Wilson's request for a pardon (punctuation uncorrected):

FELIZ CATTLE CO.
Feliz Ranch, N.M.
June 30, 1896

Hon W. T. Thornton
Governor of New Mexico
Santa Fe, N.M.

Dear Governor:

I write you in behalf of Billy Wilson, who was Convicted some years ago at Santa Fe of the crime of passing Counterfeit Money. And who, from information which has come to me Since his Conviction, I believe has been wrongfully Convicted. You were his Attorney at the time. And Pat Garrett, who at that time was the Sheriff of Lincoln County and myself were the principal Witnesses Against Wilson.

The Circumstances Connected with his trial and Conviction are about as follows: He had Sold just prior to that time a Livery Stable at White Oaks to a man by the Name of [William H.] West. A few days afterwards he came to Lincoln And Came into my Store With Several One hundred dollar bills; he asked me to change one of them, which I did; the other bills he put in my safe, and left them there for some time; when he took them out he wanted me to change another one of them, but I could not make the Change, and he took it to José Montaño, bought a few articles there, and received the balance of the change for the bill; he then staid around Lincoln for some time after which he went up to [Fort] Sumner, where I understand one of the other bills were passed [it was Anton Chico]. He remained in Sumner until Pat Garrett went to arrest "Billy the Kid", a noted outlaw and desperado, who had killed Several men. And whom Garret Killed in arresting him. And Wilson was arrested at the same time in Company with the Kid. [Strangely, Dolan has conflated Billy and Wilson's arrest at Stinking Springs with Billy's killing at Fort Sumner.]

I am ready to admit that the fact that Wilson was in Company with this Outlaw prejudiced me against him and did much to induce me at the time to believe he knew the character of the Money he passed. I fell certain that it was this prejudice existing in the Minds of the Jurors and the Excitement in the County, owing to his Association with this Outlaw, for several Weeks prior to his arrest that tended to his conviction. I now have grave doubts as to Wilson's knowledge of the character of the Money passed. And I have information which I consider very reliable that he has lived the life of an honorable and upright Citizen Ever Since his Escape from Jail, a few days after his Conviction. And I write You this letter to ask you to aid me in securing his pardon. And Also to forward this letter, or statement of the Case to the Attorney General for his information.

Wilson at the time was but a boy. I think perhaps abut eighteen years of age. Certainly not over twenty. I have Never heard of his Committing any other Crime Either before or Since this, and had many friends in this County up to the time that he was accused of this Crime and found in Company with the "Kid."

Hoping that you may be able to Secure this pardon, I remain

Yours Very Respectfully
Jas. J. Dolan
Ex Member of Territorial Council [11]

Here is the letter Governor Thornton wrote supporting Wilson's request for a pardon:

TERRITORY OF NEW MEXICO
Office of the Executive
July 7th, 1896
Santa Fe, N. Mex.

Hon. Judson Harmon
Attorney General
Washington, D.C.

Sir:

I have the honor to call your attention to the case of "Billy Wilson", who was convicted in the District Court in the Territory of New Mexico sitting at Santa Fe, N.M. in the year 1881, of the crime of passing counterfeit money, and beg leave to make application for pardon; I was his attorney and desire to state to you the following facts: Mr. Wilson at that time was young, and a cowboy about 18 years of age, who had but newly come to the territory, and had had very little experience except upon the range. He was the owner of a livery stable in the then new town of White Oaks; he sold this stable to a man by the name of West, and received in payment therefore four $100.00 new greenback bills.

Shortly after this, he went to the county seat, and passed one of these bills upon a merchant by the name of James J. Dolan, placing the other three bills in an envelop and putting it in the safe of this merchant, Mr. Dolan, where he left them for some weeks. He afterwards drew out one of the bills and passed it upon a man named Montoya [Montaño], and a few days after went to Ft. Sumner, in an adjoining county where he remained four or five months, when he was arrested in company with a notorious outlaw known as "Billy the Kid", whose real name, I cannot at this time give you [!!]. This outlaw had just prior to this time killed a deputy marshall (sic) and sheriff of Lincoln County, and there was great indignation felt towards him by the people of the territory. This prejudice extended to all parties in his company and naturally reached Billy Wilson.

I believe at that time and I still believe that this boy was absolutely innocent that the money he received from the sale of his livery stable, and passed upon Mess. Dolan and Montoya, was counterfeit. I could not conceive how it was possible for a man of ordinary sense to pass a counterfeit $100 bill, and place the remaining counterfeit bills in the safe of the man upon whom he had passed the money. The prejudice against him arising from his association with this outlaw was so great that the conviction was obtained upon evidence showing the above state of facts. An appeal was taken to the Supreme Court, but a few weeks after the conviction there was a jail delivery at Santa Fe when Wilson made his escape and has ever since remained at large.

I have followed his course for a number of years, and am able to state upon information and belief, that he had during the past 15 years, since his conviction lived an honest and honorable life; he is married, and has a wife and two children, and enjoys the respect and esteem of the community in which he lives. He has held several positions of trust under the government, and also in the control of private property, and has in every instance acted honorably and given perfect satisfaction.

He now lives in Texas under the name of D. L. Anderson, and I herewith submit to you for your consideration the letters of about twenty-five of the most responsible citizens who have known him during the many years he has lived amongst them, and showing the character which he has borne. I also enclose you letters from the two principal witnesses against him, Sheriff Pat F. Garrett and Hon. J. J. Dolan, the last named being the person upon whom he passed the money; each of these witnesses upon investigation, have concluded that he was wrongly convicted. I also submit a letter from Chief Justice Prince, late Governor of this Territory, before whom Wilson was tried and convicted, recommending his pardon. Mr. Wilson at my suggestion has agreed to surrender himself to the authorities, and submit his case upon its merits, and either receive executive clemency or submit to the punishment which has been adjudged against him.

This is one of the few cases where I have been interested in which I would feel perfectly justified in saying that from the beginning to the end, I have always felt and still feel and believe implicitly in the innocence of Billy Wilson, and that his punishment would be an outrage. His whole life since his conviction has proven to me the justice of my feelings in the matter.

I therefore submit these papers with the request that you give them your careful attention, and if you desire any further papers setting forth the circumstances, I shall be glad to place them before you so that you may become thoroughly familiar with his case, which I feel upon a thorough investigation, you will look at it as I do. I realize the unfortunate condition which surround it from the fact that he is an escaped prisoner, but I cannot blame a boy of 18 yrs of age, who felt that he was wrongfully convicted in undertaking to escape an unjust punishment.

The information that he is under this cloud, has only been known to his wife for a short time, and the knowledge of it has so affected her as to almost drive her to distraction.

I desire further to say that the parties who have written these letters with reference to the character of Wilson, are in utter ignorance of his former name, or that he is an escaped convict. The letters were obtained upon the idea that he desired to receive an appointment, or to go to another country, and simply desired to take letters with him showing his character and standing in that community. Mr. Garrett, Mr. Dolan and Judge Prince alone are aware of the true purpose for which the letters were obtained.

Hoping you will give this matter your prompt attention, and thanking you in advance, I remain,

Respectfully,
W. T. Thornton
Governor [12]

Several researchers have argued that David Anderson was not really Billy Wilson. Rather, Wilson took the name Robert Levi Martin and died September 30, 1935, in New Madrid, Missouri. If Anderson was not Wilson, why would he have solicited a pardon for something he did not do, and even more unanswerable, why would he have offered to serve out the remainder of Wilson's seven year Federal sentence if he was not granted the requested pardon, as he told Governor Thornton he would (see Thornton's letter)?

Appendix C | Timeline

Here are the dates of the most important events related to *"Dirty Dave" Rudabaugh, Billy the Kid's Most Feared Companion*.

- 1829 – Anna Radenbaugh (census spelling), David Rudabaugh's mother, born in Ohio
- April 5, 1835 – Señora de Los Dolores de Las Vegas founded by thirty-seven brave pioneers from San Miguel del Vado, Mexico
- February 13, 1847 – John Joshua Webb born in Keokuk County, Iowa
- July 14, 1854 – David Rudabaugh born in Fulton County, Illinois
- 1856 – "Z" (Zeth or maybe Zadek) Radenbaugh, David's brother, born in Iowa.
- 1860 – "I" (Ida) Radenbaugh, David's sister, born in Iowa
- 1861 – "J" (John) Radenbaugh, David's brother, born in Iowa
- October 2, 1862 – James W. Rodenbaugh, Rudabaugh's father, inducted into Company G, 103rd Illinois Infantry, as a musician
- January 15, 1863 – James W. Rodenbaugh leaves military service
- 1872 – San Miguel County jail built in (Old) Las Vegas
- June or July, 1872 – Dodge City, Kansas, founded
- March 1, 1875 – Census: Rudabaugh, mother Anna, and three siblings living in Spring Creek Township, Kansas
- 1877 – Rudabaugh living in Dodge City, Kansas
- January 27, 1878 – Rudabaugh, Michael Roarke, Dan Dement, Edgar J. West, Thomas Gott, and J. D. Green attempt to rob a train at Kinsley, Kansas, a few minutes before four pm
- January 27, 1878 – Posse led by ex-sheriff Robert McCause fails to find Kinsley robbers
- January 29, 1878 – Sheriff Bat Masterson and posse leave Dodge City after robbers
- January 30, 1878 – Masterson and posse arrive at Lovell's cattle camp
- January 31, 1878 – Rudabaugh, West, and William Tilghman captured by Sheriff Masterson – Tilghman released because he was not one of the robbers
- February 1, 1878 – Masterson, posse, Rudabaugh, West, and Tilghman arrive in Dodge City at 6 pm
- February 2, 1878 – Rudabaugh and West taken to Kinsley, Kansas, by train
- February 18, 1878 – John Henry Tunstall murdered by Tom Hill and William "Buck" Morton
- February 26, 1878 – Rudabaugh signs a confession admitting to the Kinsley train robbery and turns state's witness
- March 15, 1878 – Kinsley train robbers Gott and Green arrested at Dodge City

- June 12, 1878 – Rudabaugh, Gott, West, and Green attempt to break out of Emporia jail
- June 19, 1878 – Trial begins for Rudabaugh, Gott, West, and Green
- June 20, 1878 – Gott, West, and Green plead guilty to second degree robbery. Each gets five years at hard labor
- June 21, 1878 – Gott, West, and Green transported to penitentiary. Rudabaugh let go
- July 15, 1878 – First day of 5-day shootout in Lincoln
- July 19, 1878 – Last day of 5-day shootout in Lincoln. Alexander A. McSween house burned and McSween and four others killed.
- August 13, 1878 – Roarke, Dement, William Tillman, and William Kersey rob the Winthrop Junction Train
- October 20, 1878 – Roarke arrested and Dement killed by Secret Agent Evander Light
- February 04, 1879 – Masterson files pardon request for Thomas Gott
- March 2, 1879 – West writes letter to *Valley Republican* newspaper
- March 13, 1879 – Roarke found guilty of Kinsley train robbery and sent to pen for 10 years
- March 18, 1879 – Rudabaugh in Dodge City looking for a honest job
- April, 1879 – Rudabaugh hired as an East Las Vegas city constable
- July 4, 1879 – First train arrives at East Las Vegas.
- August 14, 1879 – Rudabaugh, Joe Martin, and Joe Carson rob the Tecolote stage four miles south of Las Vegas. They get $90. Sixteen months later, Rudabaugh confesses to this crime.
- November 3, 1879 – Rudabaugh and Joseph Martin brought before judge to answer charge of robbing the Tecolote stage. The prosecution fails to show, so they are released.
- January 1, 1880 – Hilario Romero begins term as San Miguel County Sheriff
- January 9, 1880 – Michael Kelliher and William Brickley leave Deadwood, SD.
- January 14, 1880 – Pat Garrett marries Apolinaria Gutierrez at Anton Chico
- January 14, 1880 – Barney Mason marries Juana María Madrid at Anton Chico
- January 15, 1880 – Roarke granted a new trial
- January 22, 1880 – Joe Carson killed in Close & Patterson's dance hall at 11 pm. Eight bullets in body.
- February 6, 1880 – James West, Henry, and Dorsey captured at Buena Vista
- February 8, 1880 – James West, Henry, and Dorsey lynched on Las Vegas plaza
- February 16, 1880 – First train arrives in Santa Fe. Governor Wallace drives last spike.
- February 29, 1880 – Michael Kelliher and William Brickley arrive at Las Vegas
- March 2, 1880 – Kelliher killed in Goodlett and Robert's Saloon
- March 2, 1880 – James Morehead killed by James Allen in St. Nicholas Hotel
- March 3, 1880 – Coroner's jury led by Hoodoo Brown rules Kelliher killing justified

- March 3, 1880 – James Allen jailed after preliminary examination
- March 3, 1880 – Hoodoo Brown and "Dutchy" Schunderberger skip town
- March 4, 1880 – John J. Webb indicted by grand jury for killing Kelliher
- March 4, 1880 – $300 reward offered for capture of Hoodoo Brown
- March 8, 1880 – Hoodoo Brown captured at Parsons, Kansas
- March 9, 1880 – Hoodoo Brown released at Parsons on writ of Habeas Corpus
- March 10, 1880 – Webb tried and convicted of murdering Kelliher
- March 10, 1880 – Webb appeals his murder conviction
- March 11, 1880 – Mrs. Carson arrives in Houston with husband's body

- April 2, 1880 – Rudabaugh and John J. Allen visit the Las Vegas jail. Allen decides to break Webb from jail. Webb refuses to leave jail cell. Jailer Antonio Lino Valdez killed by Allen.
- April 2, 1880 – Rudabaugh and John J. Allen steal Cauldwell's hack and flee town
- April 3, 1880 – Posse led by Sheriff Hilario Romero chases after Rudabaugh and John J. Allen. They return that evening without having found them.
- April 8, 1880 – George Davidson kills hack driver Charles Nelson Starbird
- April 9, 1880 – Date set for Webb's hanging for killing Kelliher

- May, 1880 – Thomas Pickett resigns job as East Las Vegas constable, makes his way to Fort Sumner

- August 3, 1880 – Billy Wilson sells his livery stable in White Oaks to William H. West. West pays him with four $100 counterfeit bills
- August 3, 1880 – James Allen convicted in Santa Fe court of killing James Morehead
- August 4, 1880 – William Mullen and brothers Joseph and William Stokes falsely convicted of Tecolote stage robbery, each sentenced to 1-½ years – this is the robbery Rudabaugh later admits that he, Joe Martin, and Joe Carson committed
- August 5, 1880 – Billy Wilson "breaks" a counterfeit $100 bill in James J. Dolan's store for smaller bills. He also asks Dolan to put three other (counterfeit) bills in his safe.
- August 10, 1880 – James Allen transferred to Las Vegas jail
- August 15, 1880 – Billy Wilson spends counterfeit note in José Montaño's store

- September 1, 1880 – Billy Wilson changes counterfeit note with William Robert in Anton Chico
- September 19 or 20, 1880 – Special Operative Azariah F. Wild arrives in Santa Fe to investigate the passing of counterfeit notes

- October 16, 1880 – Rudabaugh, Wilson, and Pickett rob stage four miles north of Fort Sumner. Weston and Mrs. Deolatere arrested for the robbery
- October 17, 1880 – James Allen writes letter begging for warm clothes
- October 17, 1880 – "Choctaw" Kelly kills John Reardon at Carbonateville, New Mexico
- October 30, 1880 – Robbery case against Weston and Mrs. Deolatere dismissed

- November 2, 1880 – Garrett elected sheriff of Lincoln County. His term begins January 1, 1881. He appointed deputy sheriff by Sheriff George Kimbrell so that he could begin hunting Billy the Kid (William Henry McCarty).

- November 11, 1880 – Webb, James Allen, George Davidson, John Murray, William Mullen, and George Davis escape from Las Vegas jail
- November 13, 1880 – James Allen and Davidson killed by possemen
- November 15, 1880 – Rudabaugh, Billy Wilson, Edwards, and Cook steal eight horses from Grzelachowski at Puerto de Luna. Seven of the horses are eventually recovered and the eighth is killed at Coyote Springs.
- November 19, 1880 – Las Vegas records record temperature of 12 degrees below zero
- November 20, 1880 – Garrett and Mason meet with Secret Service Agent Azariah F. Wild to discuss capturing Billy the Kid and his companions
- November 21, 1880 – Wild hires Mason as an "informer" at $2 a day plus expenses
- November 22, 1880 – Rudabaugh, Billy the Kid, and Wilson attempt to steal horses at Jason B. Bell's place at White Oaks
- November 22, 1880 – Record low temperature reported in Santa Fe
- November 22, 1880 – Agent Wild writes about his visit to Greathouse's roadhouse
- November 22, 1880 – Rudabaugh, Billy the Kid, Wilson, Edwards, and Cook reported at Blake's Saw Mill
- November 22, 1880 – Rudabaugh, Billy the Kid, Wilson, Edwards, and Cook camp at Coyote Springs
- November 23, 1880 – Posse led by Deputy Sheriff William Hudgens finds Rudabaugh, Billy the Kid, Wilson, Edwards, and Cook at Coyote Springs. In the resulting shootout, Billy the Kid's and Wilson's horses are killed. Rudabaugh's horse is captured. The three are left horseless. Edwards and Cook escape separately on their horses.
- November 24, 1880 – Rudabaugh, Billy the Kid, and Wilson sneak into White Oaks, having walked from Coyote Springs, a distance of six miles. They obtain new horses from Dedrick and West's livery stable.
- November 24, 1880 – Billy the Kid (or someone) fires at Jim Redmond loitering in front of Hudgen's saloon in White Oaks
- November 24, 1880 – Garrett, leading a posse of twelve men, sets out from Roswell "after dark" to search for Billy the Kid and his "gang"
- November 25, 1880 – Joseph Cook captured by Garrett near John Chisum's ranch
- November 25, 1880 – Webb and Davis captured by Garrett at Dan Dedrick's house at Bosque Grande
- November 26, 1880 – Longworth and Carlyle lead a posse after Rudabaugh, Billy the Kid, and companions
- November 27, 1880 – James Carlyle killed at James Greathouse's roadhouse
- November 28, 1880 – Carlyle buried in a blanket by Steck and Kuch
- November 28, 1880 – Greathouse's roadhouse burned by posse led John Hurley
- November 29, 1880 – Spencer's roadhouse burned down by same posse
- November 29, 1880 – Hurley's posse rebury Carlyle in a coffin in another location

- December 12, 1880 – Billy the Kid writes Governor Wallace about Carlyle killing
- December 12, 1880 – Garrett brings Webb and Davis to Las Vegas
- December 12, 1880 – Garrett gives interview to *Las Vegas Gazette* about Greathouse
- December 13, 1880 – Governor Wallace issues a $500 reward for Billy the Kid's capture

- December 14, 1880 – Garrett leaves Las Vegas with Stewart and Mason to look for Billy the Kid
- December 15, 1180 – Garrett joins up with Texas posse at Anton Chico
- December 16, 1880 – Garrett and posse arrive at Puerto de Luna at 9 am
- December 17, 1880 – Garrett and posse arrive at Gerhardt's ranch at 9 pm in a severe snow storm
- December 18, 1880 – Garrett and posse arrive at Fort Sumner just before dawn
- December 19, 1880 – Tom O'Folliard killed at Fort Sumner, Rudabaugh's horse shot.
- December 23, 1880 – Charlie Bowdre killed at Stinking Springs
- December 23, 1880 – Rudabaugh, Billy the Kid, Wilson, and Pickett captured at Stinking Springs
- December 23, 1880 – Special Operative Wild leaves New Mexico
- December 25, 1880 – Christmas dinner at Grzelachowski's in Puerto de Luna
- December 26, 1880 – Garrett delivers prisoners to Las Vegas jail
- December 26, 1880 – Rudabaugh and Billy the Kid interviewed by *Las Vegas Daily Optic*
- December 27, 1880 – Rudabaugh, Billy the Kid, and Wilson taken by train to Santa Fe, locked in jail there by 7:30 pm
- December 28, 1880 – Rudabaugh pleads guilty to robbing stage coaches and U.S. Mail

- January 1, 1881 – Garrett's first day as Lincoln County Sheriff
- January 6, 1881 – Webb's murder conviction upheld by Territorial Supreme Court
- January 15, 1881 – J. F. Morley was sworn in as a Las Vegas city constable
- January 18, 1881 – Rudabaugh and Billy the Kid interviewed by *Las Vegas Gazette*
- January 29, 1881 – Acting Governor Ritch signs Webb's death warrant

- February 11, 1881 – Webb tried for robbing stage at Tecolote
- February 12, 1881 – Rudabaugh testifies for Webb – says he was not at the Tecolote stage robbery
- February 13, 1881 – Webb acquitted of Tecolote stage robbery charge
- February 14, 1881 – William Mullen and Joseph and William Stokes, the three men falsely convicted of robbing the Tecolote stage, are released from jail
- February 18, 1881 – Petition presented to Acting Governor Ritch asking that Webb's death sentence be commuted to life in prison
- February 22, 1881 – Governor Wallace grants Webb a 20-day stay of execution
- February 22, 1881 – Billy Wilson indicted for passing counterfeit bills
- February 25, 1881 – Date set for Webb's hanging by Acting Governor Ritch
- February 25, 1881 – *Las Vegas Optic* publishes Webb's life story
- February 26, 1881 – *Las Vegas Daily Gazette* reports that John J. Allen was killed by Rudabaugh at Martin's Well. Years later Rudabaugh is quoted as saying he killed Allen at Alkali Wells
- February 26, 1881 – Rudabaugh convicted of robbing U.S. Mail during Tecolote and Fort Sumner stage robberies and sentenced to life in prison. His sentence is suspended so he can be tried for killing Valdez
- February 27, 1881 – Rudabaugh names who robbed the Tecolote stage: himself, Joe Martin, and Joe Carson

- February 28, 1881 – Rudabaugh, Billy the Kid, and Wilson nearly escape from the Santa Fe jail
- March 4, 1881 – Deputy U.S. Marshal Tony Neis interviewed about Rudabaugh
- March 4, 1881 – Webb's death sentence commuted to life in prison
- March 5, 1881—San Miguel County Sheriff Hilario Romero takes train to Santa Fe to get Rudabaugh
- March 7, 1881 – Rudabaugh and "Choctaw" Kelly brought to Las Vegas to be tried
- March 12, 1881 –Hanging date for Webb after 20-day extension (moot after Webb's commutation to life)
- March 18, 1881 – Rudabaugh's trial for killing Valdez opens in Las Vegas
- March 18, 1881 – Rudabaugh's lawyers ask for a change of venue to Santa Fe
- March 18, 1881 – J. F. Morley files affidavit supporting Rudabaugh's change of venue
- March 19, 1881 – Rudabaugh granted a change of venue to Santa Fe
- March 21, 1881 – Rudabaugh taken to Santa Fe for Valdez murder trial
- March 28, 1881 – "Choctaw" Kelly found guilty of killing John Reardon
- March 29, 1881 – Billy the Kid transported to Mesilla to be tried for killing Andrew "Buckshot" Roberts and Sheriff William Brady

- April 6, 1881 – Charges against Billy the Kid for killing Roberts are dropped
- April 9, 1881 – Billy the Kid convicted of killing Sheriff Brady
- April 13, 1881 – Billy the Kid sentenced to hang on May 13, 1881
- April 16, 1881 – A posse led by Robert Olinger leaves Mesilla with Billy the Kid for Lincoln, where Billy is to be hanged
- April 18, 1881 – Charges dropped against John J. Allen as he is declared dead
- April 18, 1881 – Stewart travels to Santa Fe to observe Rudabaugh's trial
- April 19, 1881 – Rudabaugh tried and convicted of killing Antonio Lino Valdez
- April 20, 1881 – Rudabaugh sentenced to death by hanging on May 20, 1881
- April 20, 1881 – Rudabaugh files for new trial
- April 20, 1881 – Rudabaugh appeals case – gives 7 reasons – appeal granted
- April 20, 1881 – Roarke pleads guilty to Winthrop train robbery and sentenced to jail
- April 21, 1881 – Billy the Kid delivered to Sheriff Garrett at Fort Stanton
- April 22, 1881 – Rudabaugh files request with court that he not be sent to Las Vegas
- April 22, 1881 – Rudabaugh sent to Las Vegas
- April 28, 1881 – Billy the Kid escapes from Lincoln jail, killing guards James W. Bell and Robert Olinger

- May 8, 1881 – Lincoln County Deputy Thomas "Kip" McKinney kills Bob Edwards
- May 13, 1881 – Date set for Billy the Kid hanging for killing Sheriff Brady
- May 30, 1881 – Date set for Rudabaugh's hanging for killing Valdez. Automatically stayed by Rudabaugh's appeal to Territorial Supreme Court.

- July 14, 1881 – Billy the Kid killed in Pete Maxwell's bedroom at Fort Sumner by Deputy Sheriff Pat Garrett

- August 8, 1881 – Rudabaugh and Wilson indicted for killing Carlyle
- August 27, 1881 – Thomas Duffy kills Tommy Bishop in Liberty, New Mexico

- September 19, 1881 – Rudabaugh attempts to escape jail – Duffy mortally wounded

- December 3, 1881 – Rudabaugh. Webb, Thomas Quillan, Frank Kearney, Fred "Choctaw" Kelly, William Goodman and S. Schroeder escape from Las Vegas jail
- December 5, 1881 – $500 Reward offered for Rudabaugh's capture
- December 5, 1881 – $500 Reward offered for Webb's capture
- December 8, 1881 – Thomas Quillan recaptured by Garrett
- December 15, 1881 – Greathouse killed by Harry A. "Joe" Fowler
- February 28, 1882 – Billy Wilson convicted of passing counterfeit bills and sentenced to seven years
- March 1, 1882 – Billy Wilson appeals his counterfeit conviction to the Territorial Supreme Court. The appeal was pending when Wilson escaped jail.
- April 12, 1882 – Webb dies in Winslow, Arkansas, of small pox
- May 23, 1882 – Colborn publishes letter claiming Rudabaugh was seen in Arizona riding with the men who attempted to assassinate Wyatt Earp (a false claim)
- June 16, 1882 – Rudabaugh seen in Rincon, New Mexico
- September 9, 1882 – Billy Wilson escapes from the Santa Fe jail
- January 14, 1883 – Rudabaugh speaks to the *Chihuahua Mail*
- January 19, 1883 – Rudabaugh seen in El Paso, Texas
- November 7, 1883 – Joe Fowler kills James E. Cale in Grand Central Hotel in Socorro
- January 22, 1884 – Fowler taken from jail and lynched at Socorro
- March 25, 1884 – Deputy U.S. Marshal Neis brings false Webb to Las Vegas
- April 1, 1884 – Rudabaugh reported in Amoco, Mexico, working as a butcher. He says he intends to go to Parral, Mexico.
- May 20, 1884 – Rudabaugh seen in El Paso
- December 28, 1885 – New Las Vegas jail opens
- February 18, 1886 – Rudabaugh killed by a Winchester rifle shot to the chest in Parral, Mexico, by a grocery man named José
- February 18, 1886 – Albert W. Lohn takes four pictures of Rudabaugh's decapitated head
- August 25, 1896 – Billy Wilson pardoned by Governor Thornton
- November 13, 1910 – Hoodoo Brown dies in Torreón, Mexico
- 1918 – Albert W. Lohn buys photography studio in Nogales, Arizona
- July 20, 1923 – Pancho Villa assassinated in Parral by seven gunmen
- February 5, 1926 – Villa's body dug up in Parral cemetery and decapitated. Head stolen.
- 1943 – Fred M. Mazzulla meets Lohn in Nogales, Arizona, and obtains death photos of Rudabaugh
- November 16, 1956 – Lohn dies in Nogales, Arizona

- 1961 – F. Stanley publishes *"David Rudabaugh, Border Ruffian"*

Appendix D | Cast of Characters

Here are brief biographies of the most important persons appearing in this book..

Allen, James. Born in 1857 in Pennsylvania. The *Las Vegas Daily Gazette* described him as *"slender built, 5 feet 11 inches high, dark complexion, dark hair and blue eyes."* He arrived in Las Vegas from Leadville, Colorado, in August, 1879. On March 2, 1880, he killed James Morehead at the St. Nicholas Hotel following a physical fight that started because of an insult given the day before, when Allen, who was working as a waiter, refused to serve Morehead any eggs for breakfast. He was convicted of killing Morehead August 3, 1880, and sentenced to death. He escaped jail November 11, 1880, along with Webb and four others. He was killed November 13, 1880, by a sheriff's posse sent to capture the escaped prisoners.[1]

Allen, John J. "Jack." Real name may have been John Lewelling. Also known as "Little Allen." Born in Atlanta, Georgia. Allen's early life is unknown. On November 10, 1871, in Topeka, Kansas, he was convicted along with Jessie Evans of passing counterfeit 50-cent notes. He was sentenced to one year in the state penitentiary.

Allen shows up next in Las Vegas in 1879 working as a mechanic. He and Rudabaugh became good friends. On April 2, 1880, the two men go to the Las Vegas jail to visit their mutual friend John J. Webb, convicted of murdering Michael Kelliher. When they arrived at Webb's jail cell, Allen abruptly pulled his pistol and mortally wounded jailer Antonio Lino Valdez. Rudabaugh, in his trial testimony, said he had no advance knowledge of Allen's murderous intention. Allen then tried to get Webb to escape, but Webb refused to be sprung, because he expected to have his conviction reversed on appeal. There are two accounts of Allen's death, both of which allege that he was killed by Rudabaugh. One report says he was killed at Martin's Well in the Jornada del Muerto (Journey of Death) north of Las Cruces. The other, that he was killed at Alkali Wells. He was declared dead April 18, 1881, by the Santa Fe Court.[2]

Bell, James W. "Long Bell." Born in 1853 in Maryland. Bell was a Texas Ranger before moving to New Mexico. He was one of the two deputies that Garrett left guarding Billy in the Lincoln County Courthouse when he went to White Oaks. Bell was shot with his own pistol (probably) by Billy on April 28, 1881, during Billy's escape. He has a memorial marker in the Cedarvale Cemetery in White Oaks.[3]

Billy the Kid. See William Henry McCarty.

Bowdre, Charles. Born about 1848 in Mississippi. Bowdre married Manuela Herrera, the younger sister of "Doc" Scurlock's wife, in 1879. At the fight at Blazer's Mill, Bowdre fired the shot that fatally wounded William "Buckshot" Roberts. He was killed December 23, 1880, at Stinking Springs by Pat Garrett's posse. Bowdre was buried the next day in the Fort Sumner Cemetery, in a new suit paid for by Garrett.[4]

Bowdre, Manuela Herrera. Her parents were José Fernando Herrera and María Juliana Martin. Manuela was the wife of Charles Bowdre. She was 14 when Bowdre was killed at Stinking Springs. Manuela married three times after Charles' death: to José Portillo, Maximiano Corona, and James Salsberry. She died February 13, 1939.[5]

144 ~ Appendix D

Manuela Herrera Bowdre. Undated photo. Courtesy Donald Cline Collection, image 74326, box 10422, f. 157, New Mexico State Records Center and Archives.

Brazil, Manuel Silvestre. Born June 12, 1850, in Rosais, Sao Jorge Island, Azores Archipelago. Brazil came to the U.S. about 1865 and to the Fort Sumner area about 1871. He began ranching at a spring that became known subsequently as Brazil Springs, and he soon formed a ranching partnership with Thomas Wilcox. Brazil sold his ranch and moved to Las Vegas about 1893, then to Texas, and then to Hot Springs, Arkansas, where he died June 17, 1928.[6]

Brown, Hoodoo, real name Hyman Graham Neill. Born May 20, 1856, in Lexington, Missouri, the oldest son of Henry and Sarah Neill. His sobriquet "Hoodoo" is a corruption of "voodoo," an appellation first applied to "charmed" gamblers in New Orleans who seemed to possess more than normal "good luck." Although Hoodoo's early life is obscure, he is known to have "worked" as a gambler in Denver, Colorado, prior to his arrival in Las Vegas. By 1878, he was the East Las Vegas Chief of Police, Coroner, and Justice of the Peace. After Kelliher was killed by Webb on March 2, 1880, Hoodoo skipped town with $860 of Kelliher's money. (Some sources say it was Webb who stole Kelliher's money – not true.) Hoodoo was arrested in Parsons, Kansas, but released due to lack of sufficient evidence to hold him. From Kansas, Hoodoo relocated to Mexico. There he lived as Henry Graham, and later, "Santiago" Graham. He died November 13, 1910, in Torreón, Mexico. His body was returned to and buried in Machpelah Cemetery in Lexington beside his brother.[7]

Carlyle, James. Born in 1854 in Ohio, possibly in Trumbull County. His parents were born in Scotland. Some sources say Carlyle participated in the fight at Adobe Walls in Texas as "Bermuda Carlisle," and later spent many years as a buffalo hunter and hide trader. By 1880, he was working as a blacksmith in White Oaks. In the early morning of November 27, 1880, a posse of White Oaks' men led by Thomas Longworth and Carlyle crept up on Jim Greathouse's roadhouse, located on the road from Las Vegas to Anton Chico. Their intention was to arrest Billy, Rudabaugh, and Wilson, known to be sheltering there. By sunup they had the roadhouse surrounded. In the standoff that followed, to show each side's good faith, the two sides agreed to exchange hostages. Carlyle entered Greathouse's roadhouse and Greathouse surrendered to the posse outside. Both men left their arms behind. After a number of hours, it was still a standoff. A sudden, accidental pistol firing by one of the possemen spooked Carlyle, who had been drinking heavily, causing him to leap through the top sash of a window. His crashing exit caused the posse to open up, and in the wild firing of the two sides that followed, Carlyle was killed. The indictment issued for his killing stated that Carlyle was shot three times, once each in the *"head, breast and body,"* which would confirm that he was shot by posse members and not by someone in the roadhouse. Garrett described Carlyle as "honest, generous, merry-hearted, quick-witted and intelligent." For details on the recent marking his grave, see page 42.[8]

Carson, Joe W. Born in 1840 in Knoxville, Tennessee. He came to Las Vegas from Sherman, Texas. In Las Vegas, he was a city constable by under Chief Constable Hoodoo Brown. On August 14, 1879, he, Rudabaugh, and Joe Martin robbed the Tecolote stage four miles south of Las Vegas. They got $90. Three innocent men were convicted of the robbery and served six months and ten days before being freed by Rudabaugh's confession to the crime.

Carson was killed January 22, 1880. Earlier that day, four Texas Panhandle cowboys, Tom "Dutch" Henry, James West, William Randall, and Jim "Loco" Dorsey, rode into Las Vegas with the intention of settling a score with Carson. Belligerently drunk and heavily armed, they entered Close and Patterson's dance hall, where they found City Constables Carson and Dave Mather. Constable Mather ordered them to disarm. In response, Henry drew his gun and shot Carson in the left arm. In the furious firing that followed, Carson was killed and Randall was mortally wounded. Carson's widow loaded her husband's body on the train and left for Houston, Texas, where he had relatives. Whether it was a coincidence or a planned event is unknown, but Mrs. Carson met up with Hoodoo Brown in Parsons, Kansas, where she was *"rather more affectionate than would be expected under the circumstances"* with Hoodoo. On March 11, 1880, Mrs. Carson arrived in Houston by train with her husband's body. He was buried a few days later in Houston's Glenwood cemetery in an unmarked grave.[9]

Cook, Joseph "Joe." Cook was with Billy the Kid, Rudabaugh, Billy Wilson, and Bob Edwards when they got into the shoot-out with Deputy Sheriff William H. Hudgens and his posse at Coyote Springs. Edwards and Cook escaped on horseback, Cook with a second horse. Billy, Rudabaugh, and Wilson had their horses killed and had to escape on foot. On November 24, 1880, *"after dark,"* Garrett and his posse left Roswell to begin their hunt for Billy and his "gang" Just outside of Roswell, they encountered:

"...a man riding one horse and leading another. He was heading south, in the direction of [John Simpson] Chisum's ranch. We went to Roswell, and found that this way farer had avoided that place, and concluded he was dodging. Knowing that the Kid's party had become separated we thought he might be a straggler from that band, trying to get out of the county."

"... we pursued and caught up with the fugitive near Chisum's ranch [the next morning]. [Possemember] Mason at once recognized him as Cook, who had fled from the fight at Coyote Springs. We disarmed him, took him back to Roswell and put him in irons. Capt. J. C. Lea had Cook in charge for some three or four weeks then sent him to the jail it Lincoln, from whence he made his escape." [10]

What happened to Cook after his jail escape is unknown.

Cosgrove, Michael. Born in 1831 in Ireland. Michael was the brother of Con Cosgrove. He supervised the U.S. Mail delivery for the Cosgrove "Star" Line. Michael was staying in Fort Sumner when Thomas O'Folliard was killed and undoubtedly saw him buried. He donated new clothes to Billy, Rudabaugh, Pickett, and Wilson when they were jailed in Las Vegas following their capture at Stinking Springs. He helped Garrett transport Billy, Rudabaugh, and Billy Wilson to jail in Santa Fe. Michael was also in Fort Sumner when Billy was killed and saw him buried. He was interviewed about Billy's death in the *Las Vegas Daily Gazette* and confirmed that it was, without any doubt, Billy who was killed. In 1886, he moved to Kingston and opened a store. He died there in February, 1887.[11]

Crocchiola, Louis. Pen name "F. Stanley." "F" for Francis, not "Father." Born October 31, 1908, in Greenwich Village, New York. Stanley graduated from high school in 1927. He wanted to pursue a teaching career, but, because there was a surplus of teachers at the time, he was persuaded by his pastor to enter the priesthood. He enrolled in Catholic University in Washington, D.C. On February 10, 1938, he was ordained in the Order of the Atonement, a branch of the Third Order of St. Francis. As was traditional on ordination, Stanley had the option of taking another name or adding additional names to his birth name. He chose to add "Stanley" and "Francis," becoming Stanley Francis Louis Crocchiola. Three days after his ordination, *"doctors found two spots on my right lung. They gave me five years if I didn't go to a drier climate."* [12]

After two years struggling to get assigned to a diocese in the Southwest, Stanley was appointed assistant pastor of Our Lady of Guadalupe Church in Taos, New Mexico, in 1940. Over the next 12 years, he served in various parishes in New Mexico. In 1952, he was transferred to Texas. He served in sundry Texas parishes until his retirement, January 20, 1984. Stanley died February 5, 1996, in Amarillo, Texas.

During his life, Stanley published at least 190 books. In an interview in 1969, he said he *"hoped to do five hundred [books] before I die."* [13] Stanley financed his books himself, often going into debt to pay the printing costs. Concerning his Rudabaugh book, Stanley said he twice lost the completed manuscript: *"I started over and wrote [it] again, because I always felt – don't quit, don't quit."* [14]

Davidson, George. Born in 1855 in Missouri. In the early morning of April 8, 1880, Davidson killed Las Vegas hack driver Charles Nelson W. Starbird. Davidson *"was rather full, but not drunk."* Starbird picked up Davidson at an East Las Vegas dance hall and delivered him to Mackley's Stable. Along the way, Davidson threatened to kill a woman passing in another hack. When Davidson arrived at Mackley's Stable and found it closed, he became infuriated and began firing blindly, killing Starbird. On November 11, 1880, Davidson and five other men escaped the Las Vegas jail. Late that evening, a posse led by Desidero Apodaca came upon Davidson and three of his fellow escapees camped around a fire. Apodaca opened fire after shouting a brief warning in Spanish, which none of the escapees understood. In the firing that followed, Davidson and fellow escapee James Allen were killed.[15]

Davis, George. Born in 1849 in Illinois. Davis was one of the six men who escaped from the Las Vegas jail on November 11, 1880. He was employed as a teamster when he was arrested and jailed, after being accused of stealing a mule team. Following his escape, Davis made it to Fort Sumner. When Michael Cosgrove saw him there, he, surprisingly, readily identified himself. He was captured on November 25, 1880, by Garrett at Dan Dedrick's house at Bosque Grande. His actions after being returned to jail are unknown.[16]

Dement, Daniel W. "Dan." Born in 1848 in Dixon, Illinois. In early life, Dement was a buffalo hunter. On January 27, 1878, Dement, Rudabaugh, Roarke, West, Gott, and Green attempted to rob the westbound train at Kinsley, Kansas. The robbery was botched due to terrible planning and cold weather. Rudabaugh in his confession described Dement as:

> *"...about five feet eight inches high, thirty years of age, weight abut 150 pounds, black hair and eyes; wears a black mustache, very heavy; thin face."* [17]

On August 13, 1878, Dement, Roarke, William Tillman, and William Kersey robbed the train at Winthrop, Missouri, getting $5,100. While the four men were on the run,

Gravestone of Joseph Samuel Marion Edwards, buried on private land, Eddy County, New Mexico. Undated photo. Courtesy findagrave.com.

Kersey discovered that Dement was sleeping with his wife. In an act of revenge, he identified Dement and Roarke to the authorities. On October 20, 1878, Evander Light, working secretly as an agent for the Atchison, Topeka & Santa Fe Railroad, tracked Dement and Roarke to Brookville, Kansas. Roarke surrendered, but Dement fled and was shot and killed by Light.[18]

Dorsey, Jim "Loco," real name Jim Dawson. One of the four Panhandle Texas cowboys who entered Close and Patterson's dance hall January 22, 1880, looking for Constable Joe Carson. They were upset at being questioned the previous day about a stolen top buggy. They were asked to disarm by Constable Mather. Without warning, one of their number, Tom Henry, shot Carson. In the firing that followed, Carson was killed. Dorsey and Henry escaped, but were caught by a posse led by Hoodoo Brown February 6, 1880. On February 8, 1880, Dorsey was taken from his jail cell by a party of vigilantes and placed on the platform of the windmill in the Las Vegas plaza and *"perforated with bullets."* [19]

East, James Henry. Born August 30, 1843, in Kaskaskia, Illinois. East left home for Texas at the age of 16 for cowboying. He was working for the LX ranch when he joined the posse that captured Billy at Stinking Springs. He helped Garrett transport Billy, Rudabaugh, and Wilson to jail in Santa Fe. In 1882, he was elected sheriff of Oldham County, Texas. He served two terms. In 1903, he moved to Douglas, Arizona. There, he served as town marshal and later as municipal judge. East died May 14, 1930.[20]

Edwards, Joseph Samuel Marion "Bob." Born August 3, 1848, in Arkansas. Some time prior to 1860, Edwards moved with his parents to Hamilton, Texas. On November 23, 1870, he married Susan C. Fulkeson. Their first child was born in 1872. By 1880, Edwards, his wife, and their four children are living on a ranch near Seven Rivers.[21] About his background, the *Las Vegas Gazette* wrote:

> *"Bob Edwards, a notorious horse thief, [has] for the past two years been slyly depredating in this country.... after committing many crimes in southwestern Texas, [he] was finally lodged in the town of Uvalde. By the assistance of his wife, who by her devotion to him in all his troubles has proven herself worthy of a better husband, he effected his escape and came to this Territory. Since coming here, when not stealing himself, he was at his ranch on the Peñasco harboring thieves and taking care of their stolen property."* [22]

In mid-April, 1881, Edwards and several others stole 21 head of horses from John Slaughter's Ranch near Tombstone, Arizona. Learning that Edwards was driving the horses toward Seven Rivers, Garrett's deputy Thomas "Kip" McKinney went after him with a posse. On May 8, 1881, they encountered Edwards at Rattlesnake Springs on the Black River. Edwards sighted McKinney first and opened up with his Winchester. McKinney returned the fire. His second *"shot broke one of Edward's legs. Edwards dropped to the ground but continued firing. McKinney then sent a bullet through his brain...."* Ten of the stolen horses were recovered.[23]

Fowler, Harry A. "Joe or Joel." Born in 1849 in Indiana. He grew up in Azle, Texas. In 1877, he killed a man he discovered in bed with his wife. Before that, according to one account, he killed a man for sport and 25 cents. Fleeing the consequences of killing his wife's lover, he moved to Las Vegas, where he staged well-liked variety shows. He married one of his performers, Josie, there. In early 1880, he moved to Santa Fe and opened the Texas Saloon, and later, the Theatre Comique. At the time, the Comique was the only theatre in the city. Fowler and Josie both performed in the Comique. In June, 1880, Fowler moved to White Oaks, where he operated a saloon. He left White Oaks after killing a drifter named Virgil Collum. Although some in White Oaks claimed the killing was murder, it was accepted by city authorities as justified, because Fowler had been asked by the city constable to arrest Collum.[24]

Now a wealthy man, Fowler bought a large cattle ranch in the Gallinas Mountains, about 50 miles west of Socorro. On December 15, 1881, Fowler and his foreman Jim Ike encountered James Greathouse, Jim Finley and Jim Kay, who Fowler suspected of having stolen 40 head of his cattle. Greathouse, Finley, and Key agreed to accompany Fowler to his ranch, not knowing that Fowler owned the cattle the men had stolen. They stopped for lunch at the Point of the Rocks. At some point during that stop, *"Finley became suspicious that all was not right and opened fire."* Fowler replied with his shotgun, killing Greathouse and Finley. Ike killed Kay.[25]

On November 7, 1883, Fowler killed James E. Cale with a *"Spanish dirk"* in the Grand Central Hotel in Socorro (some accounts say it happened in the street). On January 22, 1884, while awaiting trial for Cale's killing, Fowler was taken from jail by a mob of 200 men and hanged from a nearby tree:

> *"The murderer was hanged with the chain which had held him to the log in the jail still dangling from his leg and the heavy shackle to which the chain was fastened had to be cut from his leg with a cold chisel. The disarrangement of his clothes was evidence that Fowler had struggled desperately for his life...."* [26]

Fowler's body was placed in a $250 casket and shipped to Ft. Worth, where Fowler had family.[27]

Garrett, Patrick Floyd Jarvis. Born June 5, 1850, in Chambers County, Alabama. Garrett was a Lincoln County Deputy Sheriff when he captured Billy at Stinking Springs. After leaving Lincoln, he lived in Roswell and then Uvalde, Texas. He returned to Las Cruces, New Mexico, February 23, 1896, after being hired to investigate the abduction and apparent murder of Colonel Fountain and his son. He served two terms as Dona Ana County sheriff and one term as El Paso Customs Collector. Garrett was killed by Jesse Wayne Brazel on Leap Day, February 29, 1908. For details on Garrett's killing and Brazel's trial, *"Killing Pat Garrett, The Wild West's Most Famous Lawman – Murder or Self-Defense?"* [28]

Gott, Thomas, alias "Dugan or Dagan." Born in 1856 in Pennsylvania. On January 27, 1878, Gott, Dement, Rudabaugh, Roarke, West, and Green attempted to rob the westbound train at Kinsley, Kansas. The robbery was botched due to terrible planning and cold weather. Gott and Green were captured March 16, 1878, by Sheriff Bat Masterson, after being sighted in a Dodge City dance hall. Gott was charged with first degree robbery, which carried a sentence of 10 years at hard labor. His trial opened June 18, 1878. After Rudabaugh had his case dismissed for turning state's evidence, Gott made a deal with the prosecution. He pleaded guilty and received 5 years at hard labor, to be served in Leavenworth. On February 4, 1879, Masterson applied to the Kansas governor for a pardon for Gott, which was denied. Gott's later life is unknown.[29]

Greathouse, James "Whiskey Jim." Birth date unknown. Greathouse earned the sobriquet "Whiskey Jim" in 1874 at Fort Griffin, bootlegging huge amounts of drinking alcohol to Native Americans. According to one account, he generally took buffalo robes in payment. His illicit liquor peddling was so aggravating that the commander of the fort, Colonel Ranald S. Mackenzie, ordered his arrest – dead or alive. Greathouse quickly moved on to stealing horses and cattle in West Texas, basing himself at Rath and Reynolds' trading post on the Double Mountain Fork of the Brazos River. When that became too hot after several rustlers were lynched, he moved north to the Texas Panhandle. There he hunted buffalo and dealt in stolen livestock. He moved to New Mexico shortly before building his roadhouse. The roadhouse was burned to the ground November 28, 1880, by a posse seeking revenge for the killing of James Carlyle.[30]

Greathouse was killed December 15, 1881, by a double-barreled shotgun blast at the Point of the Rocks in the foothills of the San Mateo Mountains by "Joe" Fowler.[31]

Green, J. D. Born in 1855 in Missouri. On January 27, 1878, Green, Gott, Dement, Rudabaugh, Roarke, and West attempted to rob the westbound train at Kinsley, Kansas. The robbery was botched. Green and Gott were captured March 16, 1878, by Sheriff Bat Masterson, after being sighted in a Dodge City dance hall. The *Dodge City Times* wrote about the two men:

"The two prisoners, Greene [sic] and Gott, are men of more than ordinary natural intelligence – especially Greene. It is said that he ranks next to Mike Roarke as a leader of the organized gang. He has an intellectual countenance, eyes rather sunken, protruding forehead and rather a stupid disposition." [32]

Green was charged with first degree robbery, which carried a sentence of 10 years at hard labor. His trial opened June 18, 1878. After Rudabaugh had his case dismissed for turning state's evidence, Green made a deal with the prosecution. In exchange for pleading guilty, he received 5 years at hard labor, to be served in Leavenworth. Green's later life is unknown.[33]

Henry, Tom "Dutch." Real name Thomas Jefferson House. One of the four Panhandle Texas cowboys who entered Close and Patterson's dance hall January 22, 1880, looking for Constable Joe Carson. They were asked to disarm by Constable Mather. Without warning, Henry shot Carson. In the firing that followed, Carson was killed. Henry was shot in the leg. Henry escaped, but was caught February 6, 1880, at Buena Vista twenty-seven miles north of Las Vegas by a posse led by Hoodoo Brown. On February 8, 1880, Henry was taken from his jail cell by a party of vigilantes and placed on the platform of the windmill in the Las Vegas plaza and *"perforated with bullets."* [34]

Hudgens, John Newton. John and his older brother William Harrison were born in Claiborne Parish, Louisiana, on a plantation a few miles distant from the plantation where Pat Garrett's family lived, so they likely knew each other as children. The two brothers came to New Mexico in 1878 with their wives and took over the operation of the Old Brewery at Fort Stanton. In the spring of 1879, they moved to White Oaks. The local newspaper credits John with building the first house in White Oaks, and John's wife with having the first child born in the town. In 1880, John and William opened the Pioneer Saloon in White Oaks.

Gravestone of William Harrison Hudgens, Hillsboro Cemetery, Hillsboro, New Mexico. 2013 photo by author.

On January 5, 1885, John killed Louis N. Monjeau, the mayor of a tiny, nearby settlement, outside the "Billiard Hall" Saloon in White Oaks. About 2 in the morning, Monjeau entered the saloon and challenged John to come outside. For reasons never explained, in the street outside, Monjeau suddenly drew his pistol on John. John got a bullet off first, *"the ball crashing through [Monjeau's] mouth, breaking his spine, causing instant death."* John was indicted for the killing but never prosecuted.[35]

In 1892, William Hudgens moved to Hillsboro, New Mexico. He died there October 11, 1894, and was buried in the city cemetery. In 1887, John moved to Nevada. He died December 16, 1923, in Searchlight, Nevada, and was buried there in the city cemetery.[36]

Kelliher, Michael. Born in 1851 in Colorado. On January 9, 1880, Kelliher and his hired man William Brickley left Deadwood, South Dakota, for Las Vegas, New Mexico. They were driving three freighting teams. Kelliher was carrying $2,115 that he intended to use to buy cattle in Las Vegas. The men arrived at Las Vegas on February 29, 1880, and camped on the *"west edge of town."* They went into Las Vegas at sundown. After partying in various drinking places, they went to Goodlett and Roberts' Saloon. What followed differs depending upon which side related the events. Brinkly said that City Constable John. J. Webb killed Kelliher without provocation. Webb and his supporters said that after Kelliher was politely asked to disarm, he refused and drew his pistol. Webb drew faster and killed Kelliher.

In the events that followed, Hoodoo Brown took Kelliher's unspent money, $1,950. He claimed in court that Kelliher only had $1090 on him. Webb was cleared of killing Kelliher by a coroner's jury led by Hoodoo Brown, but was later charged and convicted of murdering Kelliher.[37]

Lohn, Albert William. Born June 9, 1867, in Chicago, Illinois. Lohn learned photography at an early age and by 1886 was traveling the border towns of Mexico and the United States earning a living as an itinerant photographer selling family portraits. On February 18, 1886, Lohn witnessed the triumphal aftermath of the beheading of Dave Rudabaugh in Parral, Mexico. Earlier that evening, a drunken, belligerent Rudabaugh killed two men and wounded another in a Parral cantina. Rudabaugh carried his drunken rampage into the streets. Infuriated by Rudagaugh's deeds, *"a grocerman named José"* shot Rudabaugh through an open window of his grocery store, striking him in the chest. José then decapitated Rudabaugh, stuck his head on a long pole, and paraded it around the plaza.[38]

Lohn took four photographs of the gruesome event. He developed the best two. When the governor of the Mexican State of Durango learned that Lohn was selling post cards showing Rudabaugh's severed head, he demanded that the photos and negatives be given to him – Lohn felt he had no choice but to comply. He retained the negatives of the two poorer photographs. In 1943, Fred W. Mazzulla was given the two unprinted negatives by Lohn. The photos on pages 92 and 93 are prints of those negatives.[39]

In 1918, Lohn opened a photography studio in Nogales, Arizona, which he ran until his death November 16, 1956. Lohn is buried in the Nogales City Cemetery.[40]

Martin, Joseph. Martin was named by Rudabaugh in his confession as one of his confederates in the Tecolote train robbery (the other was Joe Carson). Martin and Rudabaugh were arrested and accused of the robbery. At their preliminary examination, the prosecuting attorney inexplicably failed to appear, leading to their charges being dropped. The author has found no other information on Martin.[41]

Mason, Barney. Born October 29, 1848, in Richmond, Virginia. Mason arrived in New Mexico about 1876. He began hanging out with Billy, who considered him a trusted friend. On November 29, 1879, Mason killed John Farris who fired three shots at him first. About the same time he became friends with Garrett. On January 14, 1880, in Anton

Chico, he married Juana María Madrid in a joint wedding with Pat Garrett, who married Apolinaria Gutierrez (Garrett's second wife). The 1880 census shows Mason living at Fort Sumner with Juana, aged 17.

When Garrett put together his posse to capture Billy, he included Mason, whom he deputized for the purpose. As Mason and Billy had been close friends, Garrett knew that Mason's intelligence on Billy would be invaluable. Secret Service Agent Azariah Wild hired Mason as a spy to help Garrett capture Billy. Mason helped Garrett transport Billy, Rudabaugh, and Billy Wilson to jail in Santa Fe. In 1886, Mason was hired by the residents of Fort Sumner to go to Las Vegas and buy Christmas supplies. He was given a large sum of money. When he returned months later, he had no supplies. He claimed that after buying the supplies he stopped in Anton Chico and eventually lost everything gambling.

On May 18, 1887, Mason was convicted of stealing cattle and sentenced to one year in the state penitentiary. It was a short year. On November 16, 1887, he was pardoned by Territorial Governor Edmund G. Ross. In 1903, he was charged and convicted of assault. In 1905, Mason was charged with bribing a guard in Albuquerque to help a prisoner escape. About 1910, he moved to California. Mason died April 11, 1916.[42]

Mazzulla, Fred Milo. Born December 14, 1903, in Trinidad, Colorado. Mazzulla, a practicing attorney, spent much of his adult life collecting historic photographs and memorabilia. In 1943, Mazzula was given two negatives taken by Albert W. Lohn of Rudabaugh's decapitated head. Mazzulla died January 28, 1981, in Reno, Nevada.[43]

McCarty, William Henry "Billy the Kid. Most historians believe Billy was born in New York City in 1859. Some authors have suggested he was born December 20, 1859. Billy's mother may not have been married. Billy, his younger brother Joseph, and his mother Catherine McCarty left New York in 1872 for Wichita, Kansas. There they lived with William H. Antrim, a farmer, who later would become Billy's stepfather. Catherine and her sons were probably taken on by Antrim as a charity case, and as free labor. Within a few months, Antrim and his three wards left Kansas for New Mexico, where Antrim married Catherine in Santa Fe on March 1, 1873.[44]

Shortly after the marriage, the family moved to Silver City, New Mexico.[45] There, on September 16, 1874, Catherine died of tuberculosis. One year after his mother's death, Billy was arrested and jailed for concealing stolen property. Billy was manipulated into hiding the purloined items by George Schafer, a much older tough known around Silver City as "Sombrero Jack." [46] Billy escaped from the jail by shinnying up a fireplace chimney in the corner of his cell. Following his escape, Billy fled Silver City, beginning his now famous life as an adult.

During his life, in court records, Billy was referred to as William Bonney, alias "Kid,' alias William Antrim. It is unknown why Billy began calling himself Bonney. It is possible that his birth father's surname was Bonney. Billy went by Henry Antrim while growing up in Silver City. In letters, Billy signed his name as W. H. Bonney, or occasionally, W. Bonney.[47]

Billy was killed about midnight, July 14, 1881, by Sheriff Pat Garrett in Pete Maxwell's bedroom at Fort Sumner.[48]

Morehead, James Aull "Jimmy." Born October 10, 1840, in Lafayette, Missouri. Morehead was a traveling salesman for Derby & Day, a liquor wholesaler, based in St. Louis, Missouri, when he was shot and mortally wounded by James Allen on March 2, 1880. The previous day, Allen, who was a waiter at the St. Nicolas Hotel, refused to serve Morehead any fried eggs for breakfast (something Morehead reportedly ate every morning). On the day of the killing, the two men got into a fight over the fried-egg insult. After being thrown to the floor, Allen jumped up and ran into an adjacent room. He returned with a "cocked" pistol and shot and mortally wounded Morehead. The *Las Vegas Daily Gazette* described Morehead as:

> "...a large, robust man between 35 and 40 years of age, but who looks considerably older from the fact that his hair and mustaches are quite gray. He is a gentleman of the most excellent family and comes from St. Louis, where his aged parents now live." [49]

Morehead died March 3, 1880. His body was shipped by train to Leavenworth, Kansas, where he had a brother living. He was buried in the Mount Muncie Cemetery in Leavenworth. Allen was convicted of killing Morehead August 3, 1880, and sentenced to death.[50]

Morley, J. F. Known as "Jumbo" from his "size and shape." Morley first appeared in New Mexico in 1880 as a postal inspector. In January of that year he was nearly killed in a fight at Close's Dance Hall in Las Vegas with "Texas Bill" Truelove and his girlfriend Mollie Deering. In October, 1880, he arrested and preferred charges against Fred Weston and Mrs. Deolatere for the October 16 mail robbery that Rudabaugh later confessed to. On December 27, 1880, when the train containing Garrett and his prisoners was surrounded by a mob, Morley rushed to Las Vegas at Garrett's request and piloted the train to Santa Fe. On January 15, 1881, Morley was sworn in as a Las Vegas constable. The remainder of his life was spent in law enforcement in various places. He died some time after 1922.[51]

Mullen, William. On August 4, 1880, Mullen and brothers Joseph and William Stokes were convicted of the Tecolote stage robbery and sentenced to two and a half years in prison. The men were innocent of the crime. They were released February 14, 1881, after Rudabaugh confessed that he, Joseph Martin, and Joe Carson committed the robbery.[52]

On November 11, 1880, Mullen, Webb, James Allen, Davidson, Murray, and Davis broke out of the Las Vegas jail. The men escaped by picking their cell lock with a telegraph wire. Two days later, a posse led by Desidero Apodaca came upon Mullen, Allen, Davidson, and Murray lying around a campfire seven miles east of Chaperito. After yelling a warning in Spanish, Apodaca opened up on the four men. Allen and Davidson were killed. Mullen and Murry escaped. Mullen walked back to Las Vegas and turned himself in.[53]

On April 19, 1881, Mullen testified as a defense witness in Rudabaugh's trial for killing Valdez. Mullen's testimony fully supported Rudabaugh's claim that he did not shoot Valdez. Mullen's willingness to testify for Rudabaugh is surprising, because the crime for which Mullen was convicted, robbing the Tecolote stage, was committed by Rudabaugh. Mullen served six months and 10 days on that false conviction.[54]

Murray, John. On November 11, 1880, Murray, Mullen, Webb, James Allen, Davis, and Davidson broke out of the Las Vegas jail. Murray was in jail awaiting trial for the murder of a railroad grader near Tecolote. Murray was never caught as far as the author can determine.[55]

O'Folliard, Thomas "Tom." Born in 1858 (or maybe 1854) in Uvalde, Texas. It has been suggested that his real name was "Folliard," but the evidence put forward to support that theory is not credible. Little is known about his life prior to his appearance in New Mexico in 1873. O'Folliard was killed December 19, 1880, when O'Folliard, Billy, Rudabaugh, Bowdre, Pickett, and Wilson rode into Fort Sumner, thinking that Garrett was in Roswell. That false information had been conveyed to Billy by Garrett in a note that Garrett had forced Billy's friend José Valdez to write. It was an ambush. O'Folliard, riding the lead horse, was shot in the chest, probably by Garrett. It took O'Folliard an agonizing 45 minutes to die. He was buried in the snow-covered Fort Sumner cemetery the next morning.[56]

Pickett, Thomas "Tom." Born May 27, 1856, in Wise County, Texas. Pickett was raised in a strong religious family (his father's middle name was Bible). On April 1, 1876, Pickett became a Texas Ranger. He was discharged August 31, 1877. In August, 1876, while still a Ranger, he was charged with stealing cattle. The case was dismissed. By the fall of 1879, he was working as a Las Vegas city constable. In May, 1880, he quit and left Las Vegas.

When he was captured with Billy at Stinking Springs he had only been riding with Billy for a short time. After being jailed overnight with Billy in Las Vegas, Pickett was released on bond with no charges related to being captured with Billy. In January, 1884, he and Billy Wilson and two others killed four unarmed Hispanic men in cold-blood at Seven Rivers. One of the men fired at, but not hurt, was José Roibal, who Garrett had hired to spy on Billy at Fort Sumner. (Roibal's brother Juan was with Garrett at Stinking Springs when Billy was captured.) One newspaper report said Pickett recognized José Roibal and fired upon him *"in retaliation for the aid he gave Garrett in capturing [him at Stinking Springs]."* No charges were ever filed. Pickett died May 14, 1935, at Pine Top, Arizona, of inflammation of the kidneys. His obituary said his only surviving relative was a brother living in Texas.[57]

Posey, George Gordon. Born February 5, 1850, in Wilkinson County, Mississippi. He was admitted to the Missouri bar in 1871. He moved to Santa Fe in early 1880, just a few months before he was appointed by the First District Court to serve as Rudabaugh's lead attorney for his trial for killing Valdez. After practicing two years in Santa Fe, he relocated to Silver City, where he continued to practice law until his death April 29, 1891, of paresis.[58]

Randall, William "Tom." Born in 1847. One of the four Panhandle Texas cowboys who entered Close and Patterson's dance hall January 22, 1880, looking for Constable Joe Carson. They were upset at being questioned the previous day about a stolen top buggy. They were asked to disarm by Constable Mather. Without warning, one of their number, Tom Henry, shot Carson. In the firing that followed, Carson was killed and Randall was mortally wounded, with shots in his "hip, arm, stomach, and bowels." Randall may have been born in New York, where he had a sister living at the time of his death.[59]

Roarke, Michael "Big Mike." Born in Tennessee in 1848. Roarke was a professional civil engineer. In 1873, he surveyed the Lawrence & Southwestern railroad line. He also surveyed and led the men that built the railroad line from Ellsworth, Kansas, to Newton, Kansas. On January 27, 1878, Roarke, Dement, Rudabaugh, West, Gott, and Green attempted to rob the westbound train at Kinsley, Kansas. The robbery was botched due to terrible planning and cold weather.[60]

On August 13, 1878, Roarke, Dement, William Tillman, and William Kersey robbed the train at Winthrop, Missouri, getting $5,100. The *Atchison Daily Champion* described Roarke as:

"...a large man, well built, good natured, and seemingly good hearted.... He is a Tennessean, a tip top marksman, and considerably inclined to sport, having a special liking for billiards, pool, and poker.... He dresses well and has much of the look of a man bred in the city, rather than one accustomed to pass a life of wild adventures on the border, such as are credited to him." [61]

While the four men were on the run, Kersey discovered that Dement was sleeping with his wife. In an act of revenge, he identified Dement and Roarke to the authorities. On October 20, 1878, Evander Light, working secretly as an agent for the Atchison, Topeka & Santa Fe Railroad, tracked Dement and Roarke to Brookville, Kansas. Roarke surrendered, but Dement tried to flee and was shot and killed by Light.

Roarke, after a change of venue from Kinsley, was convicted of robbery in the first degree and sentenced to ten years in the state penitentiary. He was given an equal sentence for the Winthrop robbery. His life after being released from the penitentiary is unknown.[62]

Romero, Hilario. Born January 13, 1844, in Real de Dolores, Santa Fe County, New Mexico (then part of Mexico). His father moved his family from Real de Dolores to Las Vegas in 1851. In 1865, Romero graduated from El Colegio de San Miguel in Santa Fe. The next year, Hilario started a freighting business, shipping goods between New Mexico and Westport, Missouri. Two years later he opened a mercantile business, which evolved into H. Romero & Brother. His partner was Benigno Romero. In 1878, he erected the Romero Building on the west side of the Las Vegas plaza. He was elected San Miguel County Sheriff twice, 1880-81 and 1894-1897. Hilario died July 20, 1903, in Las Vegas, after suffering for many months from incurable illness.[63]

Schunderberger, John "Dutchy." Nothing is known of Schunderberger's life prior to his appearance in Las Vegas in 1879. On February 8, 1880, Schunderberger was a member of the posse that went after Dorsey and Henry, two of the four Texas cowboys involved in the killing of Joe Carson. At the time, Schunderberger was Justice of the Peace Hoodoo Brown's clerk. He may have been a town constable also, although there is no confirmation of that. When Hoodoo skipped town March 3, 1880, with $860 of Kelliher's money, Schunderberger skipped with him. He fled because he was in on the plot to steal the money. Schunderberger's later life is unknown.[64]

Stanley, F. See Crocchiola, Francis Louis Stanley.

Starbird, Charles Nelson W. Born in 1857 in Pennsylvania. He was killed April 8, 1880, by George Davidson. At about 2 o'clock the morning of the killing, Davidson exited an East Las Vegas dance hall and hailed a hack. He asked to be taken to Mackley's Stable. When the hack passed another hack containing a pretty woman, Davidson drew his pistol yelling he *"wanted to hunt a woman."* He was blocked from firing by his driver. At Mackley's Stable, Davidson climbed out. To his raving frustration, the stable was closed for the night. When Starbird's hack passed by, Davidson opened up on it and killed Starbird. Starbird left a widow, Josie Nellie (Heard), who he had married in June, 1878, in Hutchinson, Kansas.[65]

Stewart, Frank. Real name John W. Green. Born October 23, 1852, in New York, New York. The original family name was Gruene. He moved to Kansas at a young age, probably about 1867. In July, 1880, Stewart was hired as a range detective by the Panhandle Cattleman's Association. In November of that year, Stewart led a group of men into New Mexico to recover stolen cattle. The foray was a failure. When Garrett was putting together his posse to capture Billy, Stewart joined him as one of the Texas contingent. He helped Garrett transport Billy, Rudabaugh, and Wilson to jail in Santa Fe. Newspaper reports show that in 1884 he was a Bernalillo County deputy sheriff. A couple of years later he was working as a ranch manager in the Las Vegas area. Some time after 1903 he seems to have gone back to using John Green. Around 1916, he settled in Raton, where he worked in the A.T. & S.F. round house and engine shop until he retired. Stewart died May 11, 1935.[66]

Stokes, William "Bill." Born in 1846 in Kentucky. On August 4, 1880, William, his brother Joe, and William Mullen were convicted of the Tecolote stage robbery and sentenced to two and a half years in prison. The men were innocent of the crime. They were released February 14, 1881, after Rudabaugh confessed that he, Joseph Martin, and Joe Carson committed the robbery.[67]

Stokes, Joseph T. "Joe." Born in 1854 in Kentucky. On August 4, 1880, Joe, his brother William, and William Mullen were convicted of the Tecolote stage robbery and sentenced to two and a half years in prison. The men were innocent of the crime. They were released February 14, 1881, after Rudabaugh confessed that he, Joseph Martin, and Joe Carson committed the robbery. Joe was lynched in April, 1881, in El Paso, Texas, for stealing horses.[68]

Tafoya, Jesus Maria. Born in 1837. During the Civil War, Tafoya fought for the Union, serving in the New Mexico Infantry, Company C, and the New Mexico Cavalry, Company E. On April 2, 1880, he was in the probate court office (he was the county clerk) when John J. Allen killed jailer Valdez. He testified for the prosecution at Rudabaugh's trial for killing Valdez. Tafoya died in 1904.[69]

Valdez, Antonio Lino. Born in 1836 in New Mexico. Valdez was killed by John J. Allen on April 2, 1880. He was shot once in the chest without warning by Allen shortly after 2 pm. He died seven hours later in the jail kitchen.

Webb, John Joshua. Born February 13, 1847, in Keokuk County, Iowa. His schooling in Iowa must have been almost non-existent, as he never learned to read or write. In 1862, Webb's family moved to Nebraska. Although only 15, Webb left home for Denver, Colorado. In 1875, he was in Ford County, Kansas, working as a teamster. In January,

1878, Webb was hired by Dodge City Sheriff Bat Masterson as a deputy. On the 27th of that month, Rudabaugh and five other men attempted to rob a train at Kinsley, Kansas. They were caught and jailed by a posse led by Masterson that included Webb. The next year Webb participated in the Royal Gorge War on the side of the Denver & Rio Grande railroad. The D. & R.G. and the A.T. & S.F. railroads were racing to be the first to build track through the Coloradoan Royal Gorge. The competition became violent and both sides hired armed "guards," who were little more than gunmen and saboteurs. Webb was the D. & R.G.'s Chief of Guards. When that ended, Webb moved to Las Vegas, New Mexico. He joined Rudabaugh as a city constable. On March 2, Michael Kelliher and two other men were in a Las Vegas saloon, acting wildly. Kelliher was armed in violation of city ordinance. Constables Webb, Rudabaugh, and Dutchy Schunderberger entered the saloon and asked Kelliher to surrender his weapon. He refused and drew on Webb. According to newspaper accounts, Webb then shot Kelliher in the breast and several more times as he fell to the floor. Webb was arrested, tried, and sentenced to hang on April 9, 1880. He appealed his case, delaying his execution.[70]

On November 10, 1880, he escaped from the Las Vegas jail using telegraph wire to pick the cell door lock. He was captured by Sheriff Garrett on December 8 at Dan Dedrick's house at Bosque Grande. Webb's appeal of his murder conviction for killing Kelliher was upheld by Territorial Supreme Court on January 6, 1881. On March 5, 1881, Governor Wallace commuted his death sentence to life in prison. On December 3, 1881, Webb, Rudabaugh and five others escaped from jail. Webb fled to Arizona, then Arkansas, where he died of smallpox on April 12, 1882, under the alias of Sam King.[71]

West, Edgar J. Born in 1856 in Aurora, Illinois. On January 27, 1878, West, Dement, Rudabaugh, Roarke, Gott, and Green attempted to rob the westbound train at Kinsley, Kansas. The robbery was botched. West and Rudabaugh were captured by Ford County Sheriff Bat Masterson January 31, 1878. After initially pleading "not guilty," West changed his plea to "guilty" in exchange for a reduced sentence of five years in the penitentiary at hard labor. The *Dodge City Globe* described him as *"tall, low browed, with black mustache and hair."* West's later life is unknown.[72]

West, James. Real name Anthony W. Lowe. One of the four Panhandle Texas cowboys who entered Close and Patterson's dance hall January 22, 1880, looking for Constable Joe Carson. They were upset at being questioned the previous day about a stolen top buggy. They were asked to disarm by Constable Mather. Without warning, one of their number, Tom Henry, shot Carson. In the firing that followed, West, was *"shot through the lower bowels and breast."* Too wounded to walk, West was carried to the Las Vegas jail. On February 8, 1880, a party of vigilantes forced their way into the jail intent on lynching West:

> *"Two men then opened the cell where West was. They put the rope around his neck and he exclaimed, "My God! I am suffering enough now, can't you let me alone." Two more men came in and carried him out. He groaned loudly with pain from his wound."* [73]

West was carried to the windmill in the Las Vegas plaza and hanged.[74]

Wild, Azariah Faxon. Born in 1835, in West Fairlee, Vermont. He served as a Union soldier during the Civil War. On June 15, 1877, he was hired as a Special Operative by the U.S. Secret Service. In late September, 1880, the Treasury Department dispatched Wild to Lincoln County to investigate counterfeit bills being circulated in the area. Convinced that Billy's the Kid's "gang" were ringleaders in the distribution of the bills, Wild tried to get Marshal John Sherman to hunt and arrest the men. Although Sherman declined, he convinced Garrett to take up the job. Garrett agreed to do it for no extra pay. During the hunt for Billy, Wild hired Barney Mason as a spy to provide Garrett with intelligence on Billy. Wild died June 10, 1920, in New Orleans.[75]

Wilson, William H. "Billy." Wilson was born November 23, 1860. He was killed June 14, 1918, by Ed "Red" Valentine in a saloon in Sanderson, Texas.[76] See Appendix B for details.

Notes

1 - Preface

1. 1875 Census, Spring Creek Township, Greenwood County, Kansas, ancestry.com, accessed Aug. 5, 2022.

2. https://www.nps.gov/civilwar/search-soldiers-detail.htm?soldierId=DFAE5BCA-DC7A-DF11-BF36-B8AC6F5D926A; https://www.fold3.com/image/293442249; accessed Aug. 5, 2022.

3. *Dodge City Times* (KS), June 29, 1878; *Weekly Commonwealth* (Topeka KS), June 27, 1878.

4. *LV Daily Optic*, Dec. 27, 1880.

5. Mary Jo Walker, *The F. Stanley Story* (The Lightning Tree, 1985), pp 21-23.

6. Chapter 3 of Stanley's book is about the Royal Gorge War. He asserts in this chapter that Rudabaugh was a participant in that war. He he was not!

7. 1875 Census, Spring Creek Township, Greenwood County, Kansas, ancestry.com, accessed Aug. 5, 2022.

8. Robert Barr Smith "The Short, Nasty Life of Dave Rudabaugh," Wild West, June, 1996, pp 40-44, 81.

9. *Ford County Globe* (Dodge City, KS), May 23, 1882.

10. *LV Daily Optic*, Feb. 23, 1886.

11. Southwesterner (Columbus NM), Aug. 1, 1962; Fred M. Mazzulla, "Don't Lose Your Head," 1964 Denver Westerners Brand Book (Johnson Publishing 1965), p 263.

12. Billy was convicted of killing Sheriff Brady on April 9, 1881. The date set for his hanging was May 13, 1881. He escaped from the Lincoln courthouse jail on April 28, 1881. He was killed at about midnight July 14, 1881, by Deputy Sheriff Pat Garrett. His jail escape permitted him to live 63 days past the May 13 date set for his execution.

2 - "Dirty Dave" Rudabaugh

1. 1875 Census, Spring Creek Township, Greenwood County, Kansas, ancestry.com, accessed Aug. 5, 2022.

2. F. Stanley, *David Rudabaugh, Border Ruffian* (World Press, Inc, 1961); *Daily Commonwealth* (Topeka KS), June 22, 1878.

3. https://www.nps.gov/civilwar/search-soldiers-detail.htm?soldierId=DFAE5BCA-DC7A-DF11-BF36-B8AC6F5D926A; https://www.fold3.com/image/293442249; accessed Aug. 5, 2022.

4. The 1850 census lists a James W. Radabaugh born 1843 living in Sycamore, Hamilton, Ohio. That same person appears in the 1860 census. This can not be the James W. that is David Rudabaugh's father, however, because he appears in the 1900 census living in the same city, but married to a Jeannette, who he married in 1876.

5. *Dodge City Times* (KS), June 29, 1878.

6. *Dodge City Times* (KS), June 29, 1878.

7. Rudabaugh's confession has the quality of a literary work. *Dodge City Times* (KS), June 29, 1878; *Weekly Commonwealth* (Topeka KS), June 27, 1878.

8. McCause's possemen were G. L. Hubbs, E. A. Noble, and N. Billings. *Wichita Weekly Beacon* (Wichita KS), Feb. 6, 1878.

9. Fuller's possemen included Clute, Wells, and "Calamity Bill." *Valley Republican* (Kinsley KS), Feb. 2, 1878.

10. *Valley Republican* (Kinsley KS), Feb. 2, 1878.

11. Bat's possemen were John J. Webb, David "Prairie Dog" Morrow, and Kinch Riley. *Hays City Sentinel* (Hays City, KS), Feb. 8, 1878.

12. For a full-length biography of William Tilghman, see *Outlaw Days, A True History of Early-Day Oklahoma Characters* by Zoe A. Tilghman (Harlow Publishing Company, 1926).

13. *Pawnee County Herald* (Larned KS), Feb. 7, 1878.

14. *Dodge City Times*, March 16, 1878.

15. *Weekly-News Democrat* (Emporia KS), June 21, 1878.

16. The correspondent is identified only as "Vilas." *Daily Commonwealth* (Topeka KS), June 22, 1878.

17. *Kinsley Graphic*, June 22, 1878, quoted in Kansas Historical Quarterly (Kansas Historical Society, Autumn, 1961).

18. *Kinsley Graphic*, June 22, 1878, quoted in Kansas Historical Quarterly (Kansas Historical Society, Autumn, 1961).

19. *Kinsley Graphic*, June 22, 1878, quoted in Kansas Historical Quarterly (Kansas Historical Society, Autumn, 1961).

20. *Daily Commonwealth* (Topeka KS), June 23, 1878.

21. *Kinsley Graphic*, June 22, 1878, quoted in Kansas Historical Quarterly (Kansas Historical Society, Autumn, 1961).

22. *Daily Commonwealth* (Topeka KS), Dec. 29, 1878.

23. The author was unable to further identify West's father.

24. *Kinsley Graphic*, June 22, 1878, quoted in Kansas Historical Quarterly (Kansas Historical Society, Autumn, 1961).

25. Kansas Historical Quarterly, (Kansas Historical Society, Autumn, 1961), p 257.

26. *Edwards County Leader* (Kinsley KS), Feb. 3, 1879.

27. *Valley Republican* (Kinsley KS), March 15, 1879.

28. *Rolla Herald* (Rolla MS), Oct. 31, 1878; *Saline County Journal* (Salina KS), Oct. 31, 1878.

29. *Daily Commonwealth* (Topeka KS), April 22, 1881.

30. *Weekly Kansas State Journal* (Topeka KS), April 28, 1881.

31. *Dodge City Globe*, March 18, 1879.

32. Las Vegas was officially founded April 5, 1835, by thirty-seven settlers from San Miguel del Vado. They were granted colonization permission by Mexico, which mandated that the settlement set aside land for a plaza (a well in the plaza was the first source of non-river drinking water – this well, expanded in 1874 by prisoners, was the well served by the windmill shown in the plaza picture on page 19). The structures lining the plaza were built in such a way that they made the plaza a defendable stockade. Each building had gun portholes in the outer-facing walls.

The new community was named Señora de Los Dolores de Las Vegas (Our Lady of the Sorrows of the Meadows). The location was chosen because the Gallinas River was fordable there.

The initial settlement was on the West side of the river. When Anglos began to arrive after the Mexican-American War ended in 1848, they chose to settle mostly on the East side of the river. This led to the two communities being considered different towns, West Las Vegas (Old Town) and East Las Vegas (New Town). The two sections officially consolidated in 1969. Milton W. Callon, *Las Vegas New Mexico… The Town That Wouldn't Gamble*, pp 7-8, 18-22; Joseph A. Lordi, *Las Vegas New Mexico* (Cartolina Press, 2010), pp 7-8.

33. *SF Weekly New Mexican*, Sept. 6, 1879.

34. *SF Weekly New Mexican*, Sept. 6, 1879.

35. *LV Daily Gazette*, Nov. 4, 1879.

36. *LV Daily Gazette*, Aug. 6, 1880; *LV Daily Gazette*, Aug. 11, 1880.

37. *Dallas Daily Herald*, May 11, 1881; *LV Gazette*, April 20, 1881.

38. *Chicago Tribune*, Jan. 24, 1880; *LV Daily Gazette*, Feb. 14, 1880.

39. *LV Daily Gazette*, Jan. 21, 1880; *Chicago Tribune*, Jan. 24, 1880; *The National Police Gazette*, Feb. 7, 1880, p 3.

40. *Chicago Tribune*, Jan. 24, 1880.

41. *Chicago Tribune*, Jan. 24, 1880.

42. *SF Weekly New Mexican*, Jan. 31, 1880.

43. *Chicago Tribune*, Jan. 24, 1880; *SF Weekly New Mexican*, Jan. 31, 1880; *The National Police Gazette*, Feb. 7, 1880, p 3.

44. *SF Weekly New Mexican*, Feb. 14, 1880.

45. *LV Daily Gazette*, Feb. 10, 1880.

46. *LV Daily Gazette*, Feb. 10, 1880.

47. *LV Daily Gazette*, Feb. 10, 1880.

48. *SF Weekly New Mexican*, Feb. 14, 1880.

49. *LV Daily Gazette*, Feb. 10, 1880.

50. Callon, *Las Vegas New Mexico… The Town That Wouldn't Gamble* (Las Vegas Daily Optic, 1962), pp 94-95.

51. *SF Weekly New Mexican*, Feb. 14, 1880.

52. *LV Daily Gazette*, Feb. 10, 1880.

53. *LV Daily Gazette*, Feb. 10, 1880.

54. *LV Daily Gazette*, March 5, 1880.

55. *LV Daily Gazette*, March 5, 1880.

56. *Dodge City Globe*, March 9, 1880.

57. *Dodge City Globe*, March 9, 1880.

58. *LV Daily Gazette*, March 5, 1880.

59. *LV Daily Gazette*, March 5, 1880.

60. *LV Daily Gazette*, March 5, 1880.

61. *LV Daily Gazette*, March 5, 1880.

62. Grand Jury True Bill, Territory of New Mexico vs John J. Webb, County of San Miguel, March 4, 1880, Case 1024, New Mexico State Records Center and Archives.

63. *LV Daily Gazette*, March 10, 1880.

64. *LV Daily Gazette*, March 10, 1880.

65. *LV Daily Gazette*, March 10, 1880.

66. *LV Daily Gazette*, March 10, 1880.

67. *LV Daily Gazette*, March 10, 1880.

68. *LV Daily Gazette*, March 10, 1880.

69. *LV Daily Gazette*, March 10, 1880.

70. *LV Daily Gazette*, March 10, 1880.

71. *LV Daily Gazette*, March 10, 1880.

72. L. Bradford Prince, ed., *The General Laws of New Mexico* (W. C. Little & Co., 1880), Chapter LI, Section 1, p 257.

73. *SF Weekly New Mexican*, March 15, 1880.

74. *Dodge City Times*, March 13, 1880.

75. *Parsons Daily Eclipse* (Parsons KS), March 9, 1880.

76. *Parsons Weekly Sun* (Parsons KS), March 11, 1880.

77. *Lexington Intelligencer* (Lexington Missouri, Nov. 27, 1910.

78. Charles H. Gildersleeve, *Reports of Cases Argued and Determined in the Supreme Court of the Territory of New Mexico From January Term, 1880, to January Term 1883, Inclusive*, Vol. II, (Callaghan & Co, 1911), pp 147-161.

79. *LV Daily Gazette*, March 10, 1880; Gildersleeve, *Reports of Cases Argued and Determined in the Supreme Court of the Territory of New Mexico From January Term, 1880, to January Term 1883, Inclusive*, Vol. II, (Callaghan & Co, 1911), pp 147-161; Territory of New Mexico vs David Rudabaugh, Case No. 128, January, 1882, NM Territory Supreme Court Collection 1982-135, Box 12, F 128, Serial 3360, New Mexico State Records Center and Archives.

80. Allen's real name was John Llewellyn. *LV Daily Gazette*, Feb. 26, 1881.

81. *LV Daily Gazette*, Nov. 11, 1880; Note: The mask head of this issue gives the date as November 10, but the typesetter had failed to update the issue's date. The newspaper is actually the November 11 edition.

82. *LV Daily Gazette*, April 4, 1880.

83. *LV Daily Optic*, Dec. 4, 1896.

84. Territory of New Mexico vs David Rudabaugh, Case No. 128, January, 1882, New Mexico Territorial Supreme Court Collection, Box 12, F 128, No. 3369, New Mexico State Records Center and Archives.

85. *SF New Mexican*, Oct. 31, 1880.

86. Azariah F. Wild Report, Oct. 2, 1880, Leon C. Metz Papers, UTEP. Wild in his October 20, 1880, report wrote: "The parties Kid, Wilson, O'Folliard, and Pickett who are undoubtedly the ones who robbed the mail on the 17th are out at a ranch twelve miles from Fort Sumner." In his October 28, 1880, report, Wild wrote: "I am informed this day by Judge Leonard that a lady passenger [Mrs. Deolatere] who was along at the time the stage was robbed near Fort Sumner that she recognized No. '80' [Wilson] and William Antrom [sic] alias 'Billy Boney' [sic] as two of the robbers who robbed her and the mails." Wild's reports are full of unsubstantiated, ridiculous assertions. For example, in his October 17, 1880, report, he says of Billy: "Indicted in 3rd District of U.S. Court for the murder of the Indian Agent. Came from Kansas here."

87. *LV Gazette*, Nov. 3, 1880; *LV Daily Optic*, March 3, 1881.

88. *SF New Mexican*, Oct. 31, 1880.

89. *SF New Mexican*, Oct. 31, 1880.

90. *LV Daily Gazette*, Nov. 11, 1880.

91. *LV Daily Gazette*, Nov. 11, 1880.

92. *LV Daily Gazette*, Nov. 19, 1880.

93. *LV Daily Gazette*, Nov. 11, 1880.

94. *LV Daily Gazette*, March 3, 1880.

95. *LV Daily Gazette*, March 3, 1880.

96. Miguel Antonio Otero, *My Life on the Frontier, 1864-1882*, (The Press of the Pioneers, 1935) p 197.

97. Otero, *My Life on the Frontier 1864-1882*, p 196.

98. Otero, *My Life on the Frontier 1864-1882*, p 196.

99. *LV Daily Gazette*, March 4, 1880.

100. *SF New Mexican*, Aug. 5, 1880.

101. *LV Daily Gazette*, Oct. 20, 1880.

102. *LV Daily Gazette*, May 14, 1880.

103. *LV Daily Gazette*, April 10, 1880.

104. *LV Daily Gazette*, April 10, 1880.

105. Otero, *My Life on the Frontier 1864-1882*, pp 205-206.

106. The first train arrived in Santa Fe February 16, 1880. The final spike was driven by Governor Lew Wallace; *SF Weekly New Mexican*, July 5, 1879; *LV Daily Gazette*, Nov. 11, 1880.

107. *LV Daily Gazette*, Aug. 11, 1880; *SF New Mexican*, Aug. 5, 1880; *LV Daily Gazette*, Aug. 6, 1880.

108. *LV Daily Gazette*, Nov. 16, 1880.

109. *Daily New Mexican*, Nov 13, 1880.

110. *LV Daily Gazette*, Nov. 13, 1880.

111. *LV Daily Gazette*, Nov. 13, 1880.

112. *LV Daily Gazette*, Nov. 16, 1880.

113. Otero, *My Life on the Frontier, 1864-1882*, p 199.

114. Otero, *My Life on the Frontier, 1864-1882*, p 199.

115. Bell's ranch occupies land granted to Pablo Montoya in 1824. Bought by John S. Watts in 1867. Bought by Wilson Waddingham in 1872. The brand was a bell, hence the name. Over 700,000 acres in size. David Remley, *Bell Ranch, Cattle Ranching in the Southwest*, 1824-1947, (Yucca Tree Press, 2000); Frank Clifford, *Deep Trails in the Old West* (University of Oklahoma Press, 2011), pp 70-71, 268-269.

116. *LV Daily Gazette*, Nov. 21, 1880.

117. *LV Daily Gazette*, Nov. 21, 1880.

118. *Dodge City Times*, Nov. 27, 1880.

119. *LV Daily Gazette*, Nov. 21, 1880.

120. Pat F. Garrett, *The Authentic Life of Billy the Kid*, Foreword by Jarvis P. Garrett (Horn & Wallace, 1964), p 88; this book is a new edition of Pat Garrett's *The Authentic Life of Billy the Kid, the Noted Desperado of the Southwest, Whose Deeds of Daring Have Made His Name a Terror in New Mexico, Arizona, and Northern Mexico* (New Mexican Publishing Co, 1882).

121. Garrett, *The Authentic Life of Billy the Kid*, p 89.

122. Garrett, *The Authentic Life of Billy the Kid*, p 89; *SF Daily New Mexican*, Dec. 8, 1880.

123. *Dodge City Globe*, Dec. 21, 1880.

124. Many accounts erroneously identify this place as belonging to James W. Bell, the Lincoln County deputy sheriff killed by Billy when he escaped from the courthouse jail in Lincoln. James W. Bell was, however, in the posse that went after Billy at Coyote Springs. Garrett, *The Authentic Life of Billy the Kid*, p 80.

125. Blake's saw mill was the first saw mill in White Oaks and the town was "almost entirely built of lumber sawed at his mill." Blake was the discoverer of the Vera Cruz mine in the Tuscon Mountains, NM. Garrett, *The Authentic Life of Billy the Kid*, p 80; *LV Daily Gazette*, Oct. 29, 1880; *LV Daily Gazette*, March 2, 1882; *Albuquerque Citizen*, Feb. 2, 1907.

126. *SF Weekly New Mexican*, Dec. 13, 1880; Otero, *The Real Billy the Kid*, pp 88-89.

127. Garrett, *The Authentic Life of Billy the Kid*, p 80.

128. *LV Daily Gazette*, Dec. 24, 1880.

129. Garrett, *The Authentic Life of Billy the Kid*, p 80-81.

130. *SF Weekly New Mexican*, Nov. 22, 1880; *SF New Mexican*, Dec. 3, 1880; *LV Daily Gazette*, Dec. 29, 1880.

131. Lamper was later released with no charges. Mose Dedrick was "placed under bonds to secure his appearance before the district court." He "skipped the country" and had his bond forfeited. Garrett, *The Authentic Life of Billy the Kid*, p80-82.

132. *LV Daily Gazette*, Dec. 24, 1880.

133. Garrett, *The Authentic Life of Billy the Kid*, p 80-81; William Bonney, letter to Lew Wallace, Dec. 12, 1880, published in *LV Gazette*, Dec. 22, 1880; Frederick W. Nolan, *The Lincoln County War*, Revised Edition (Sunstone Press, 2009), p 618; *LV Daily Gazette*, Nov. 30, 1880; *LV Gazette*, Dec. 24, 1880.

134. J. E. Sligh, "Billy-the-Kid," *Overland Monthly*, July, 1908, No 1, Vol. LII, p 50.

135. Garrett, *The Authentic Life of Billy the Kid*, p 81.

136. Special Agent Wild in his report of Nov. 30, 1880, said: that Billy's "gang" numbered 17 men. *LV Daily Gazette*, Dec. 24, 1880.

137. Otero, *My Life on the Frontier 1864-1882*, p 88; Garrett, *The Authentic Life of Billy the Kid*, pp 81, 88-89.

138. Garrett, *The Authentic Life of Billy the Kid*, pp 88-89; *LV Daily Gazette*, May 17, 1881.

139. No primary source says they walked to White Oaks, but since they had lost their horses, what alternative did they have? Several sources say they rode, but again, how is that possible since they had lost their horses? Once they obtained horses from Dedrick and West's livery stable, they were observed riding in White Oaks when one of them fired at Redman. Probably that sighting led to the assumption that they had rode in from Coyote Springs.

140. James J. Dolan, letter to William T. Thornton, June 30, 1896, Lewis A Ketring Papers, Archives and Special Collections, NMSU.

141. "The leading man of his gang is W. H. West who I will hereafter call 'No. 700.' He left before I came into this section of the country and is now at Topeka Kansas." Special Agent Wild in his report of October 28, 1880.

142. Garrett, *The Authentic Life of Billy the Kid*, p 82.

143. J. E. Sligh, "The Lincoln County War," Overland Monthly, September, 1908, No 3, Vol. LII, pp 168, 170.

144. Garrett, *The Authentic Life of Billy the Kid*, p 82.

145. Gladwell Richardson, "Whiskey Jim Greathouse," Real West Year Book, Spring, 1974, pp 58-63; Frank Collinson, "Jim Greathouse orWhiskey Jim," unpublished manuscript, Panhandle-Plains Historical Museum (PPHMRC), Canyon Texas.

146. A field excavation of the roadhouse site was conducted by a team led by George E. Scott in 2001. Among the period artifacts found were almost 100 spent cartridges and about 20 bullets. Kurt House and Roy B. Young, *Chasing Billy the Kid, Frank Stewart and the Untold Story of the Manhunt for William H. Bonney* (Three Rivers Publishing Co., 2022), pp 327-328; *LV Daily Gazette*, Dec. 24, 1880.

147. Joe Steck, "Reminiscences of White County and White Oaks," *Lincoln County Leader*, March, 1890, copy in Maurice G. Fulton Papers, Special Collections, UA.

148. Steck, "Reminiscences of White County and White Oaks."

149. Steck, "Reminiscences of White County and White Oaks."

150. Steck, "Reminiscences of White County and White Oaks."

151. Bonney, letter to Lew Wallace, Dec. 12, 1880, published in *LV Daily Gazette*, Dec. 22, 1880.

152. Bonney, letter to Lew Wallace, Dec. 12, 1880, published in *LV Daily Gazette*, Dec. 22, 1880.

153. Leon Claire Metz, *The Encylopedia of Lawmen, Outlaws, and Gunfighters* (Facts on File, Inc, 2003), p 20.

154. *LV Daily Gazette*, Dec. 24, 1880.

155. *LV Daily Optic*, Jan. 21, 1881.

156. *LV Daily Optic*, Jan. 21, 1881.

157. Bonney, letter to Lew Wallace, Dec. 12, 1880, published in *LV Daily Gazette*, Dec. 22, 1880.

158. Bonney, letter to Lew Wallace, Dec. 12, 1880, published in *LV Daily Gazette*, Dec. 22, 1880.

159. Garrett, *The Authentic Life of Billy the Kid*, p 84; *SF Weekly New Mexican*, Dec. 13, 1880.

160. Steck, "Reminiscences of White County and White Oaks."

161. This might be a coded reference to Secret Service Agent Azariah F. Wild, who was in the area investigating counterfeiting. In his report to his superiors in D.C, dated October 20, 1880, he writes: "I have organized secretly a Posse Constatus [Comitatus] of thirty men here to go and assist in making these arrests. Not only those who are wanted for passing counterfeit money but those who are wanted for murder, and robbing the U.S. Mail, and are indicted in U.S. Courts." The person who led the group that burned Greathouse's roadhouse was John Hurley.

162. Garrett, *The Authentic Life of Billy the Kid*, p 84.

163. *LV Daily Gazette*, Dec. 24, 1880; *LV Daily Gazette*, Dec. 11, 1880.

164. Charles A. Siringo, *A Texas Cowboy, or Fifteen Years on the Hurricane Deck of a Spanish Pony* (Siringo & Dobson, 1886), pp 213-214.

165. Siringo, *A Texas Cowboy, or Fifteen Years on the Hurricane Deck of a Spanish Pony*, pp 213-214.

166. *LV Daily Gazette*, Dec. 24, 1880.

167. Richardson, "Whiskey Jim Greathouse," Real West Year Book, Spring, 1974, pp 58-63.

168. Wild Report, Nov. 22, 1880.

169. Rudabaugh Indictment for Killing Carlyle, Aug. 8, 1881, Herman B. Weisner Papers, Archives and Special Collections, NMSU; *LV Daily Gazette*, March 23, 1881.

170. The Point of the Rocks is a "conspicuous cluster of rock outcrops" in the southern stretch of the Jornada del Muerto. Spanish explorer Diego de Vargas recorded his discovery of the landmark in 1692, calling it Las Peñuelas. Robert Julyan, *The Place Names Of New Mexico*, (The University of N.M. Press, 1996) p 199.

171. *SF New Mexican*, Dec. 20, 1881; Richardson, "Whiskey Jim Greathouse," Real West Year Book, Spring 1974, pp 58-63.

172. *SF New Mexican*, Dec. 20, 1881.

173. *SF New Mexican*, Dec. 20, 1881; Richardson, "Whiskey Jim Greathouse," Real West Year Book, Spring 1974, pp 58-63.

174. F. Stanley, *Notes on Joel Fowler*, March, 1963, pp 10-11.

175. *SF New Mexican*, Dec. 20, 1881; Richardson, "Whiskey Jim Greathouse," Real West Year Book, Spring 1974, pp 58-63.

176. *SF New Mexican Review*, Jan.31, 1884; *LV Daily Optic*, Jan. 23, 1884.

177. *LV Daily Gazette*, Jan. 24, 1884.

178. *Lincoln County Leader*, Jan. 24, 1884.

179. *LV Daily Gazette*, Jan. 24, 1884

180. Garrett, *The Authentic Life of Billy the Kid*, p 97.

181. Stewart never left an account of his actions in pursuing Billy. *Raton Range*, May 13, 1935; John L. McCarty, *Maverick Town, The Story of Old Tascosa* (University of Oklahoma Press, 1988), pp 82-83.

182. Mason had also been hired as a spy by Secret Service Agent Wild: "I this day agreed with Barney Mason to act as informer for such length of time as his services are actual necessary at the rate of $2.00 per day and actual necessary expenses and he to furnish his own saddle horse." Wild Report Nov 21, 1880.

183. Marriage Registry, Anton Chico Catholic Church. Copy in author's possession.

184. David G. Thomas, *Billy the Kid's Grave, A History of the Wild West's Most Famous Death Marker* (Doc45 Publishing, 2017), pp 8-9, 98; 1880 Fort Sumner Census Records, taken June, 1880.

185. Charles A. Siringo, *A Texas Cowboy, or Fifteen Years on the Hurricane Deck of a Spanish Pony* (Siringo & Dobson, 1886), p 198.

186. Clifford, *Deep Trails in the Old West*, p 86.

187. Garrett, *The Authentic Life of Billy The Kid*, pp 113-114; J. Evetts Haley, interview with James Henry East, Sept. 27, 1927, PPHMRC.

188. Garrett, *The Authentic Life of Billy the Kid*, p 100.

189. Garrett, *The Authentic Life of Billy the Kid*, p 101; *LV Gazette*, Dec. 22, 1880.

190. Ft Sumner history: In 1880, Fort Sumner was no longer a government fort. The fort and an adjoining million-acre reservation for Mescalero Apache and Navajo Native Americans had been authorized in October, 1862, during the second year of the Civil War. The fort was named after Major General Edwin Vose Sumner. The reservation was called Bosque Redondo (round woods), the Spanish name for the dense scrub-brush lining the Pecos River where the reservation and fort were established.

With the reservation abandoned, there was little purpose in maintaining Fort Sumner, so it was ordered sold by the Federal Government. On October, 17, 1870, Lucien Bonaparte Maxwell bought the grounds and buildings of the fort, less the cemetery burial ground, for $5,000. He had earlier offered $700 for the property, which was rejected.

An unidentified correspondent for the *Cincinnati Gazette*, writing from Fort Sumner on June 12, 1879, described place as follows:

"Probably no where [sic] on the frontier have so many changes occurred, in the last fifteen or twenty years, as at this little village on the Rio Pecos, 120 miles south of Las Vegas, New Mexico...."

"Fort Sumner has lost much of its former glory, but is still an attractive place. A broken flagstaff and a solitary cannon alone mark the parade ground... the Adjutant General's office is occupied as a storeroom and Postoffice by Messrs. Garrett & Smith the former an old buffalo hunter, and the latter the greatest beaver hunter of the Southwest, and widely known through this country and Texas as 'Old Beaver Smith.' His intimate friends claim that he has trapped more beaver than any two men who ever followed this business for a livelihood. The old man has entirely forsaken his favorite pursuit, but still loves to be called 'Old Beaver.' There is another store here kept by a Mexican who, in consequence of seldom keeping anything to sell, has but little patronage. The population of the place is probably 200 souls, the inhabitants, with few exceptions, being Mexicans. They all live in houses belonging to the Maxwell estate, and the only recompense they give for the use of them is an occasional coat of whitewash." Quoted in *The Saline County Journal* (Saline KS), Sept. 4, 1879.

191. Author and researcher Richard Weddle argues convincingly that light and shadow evidence within the tintype indicates that it was probably taken in the Fort Sumner dance hall instead of Beaver Smith's saloon. Richard Weddle, "Shooting Billy the Kid," Wild West, Aug. 2012, pp 59-62.

192. *The Saline County Journal* (Saline KS), Sept. 4, 1879.

193. Haley, Interview with East, Sept. 27, 1927, PPHMRC.

194. The 1880 Fort Sumner Census taken June, 1880, shows Charles and Manuela Bowdre, William Bonney, A. B. Bennet (Bennett), and Willis Pruitt living in one room of the hospital building. Garrett, *The Authentic Life of Billy The Kid*, p 115.

195. Google maps shows the Brazel-Wilcox ranch to be 10.2 miles east and slightly north of Fort Sumner. Garrett, *The Authentic Life of Billy The Kid*, p 116.

196. Garrett, *The Authentic Life of Billy The Kid*, pp 117-118.

197. Haley, Interview with East, Sept. 27, 1927, PPHMRC.

198. "The Life of C. W. Polk," *The Capture of Billy the Kid*, p 26.

199. Haley, Interview with East, Sept. 27, 1927, PPHMRC.

200. O'Folliard had been Billy's best friend and constant companion for three years. O'Folliard was with Billy in the McSween house when it was burned down during the Lincoln County War, and escaped when he, Billy, Jim French, Chavez y Chavez, Yginio Salazar, and Harvey Morris dashed from the building; Haley Interview with East, Sept. 27, 1927, PPHMRC.

201. "The Life of C. W. Polk," *The Capture of Billy the Kid*, p 26; "East-Letter-to-Siringo"- *The Capture of Billy the Kid*, p 83; *LV Optic*, Dec. 27, 1880.

202. Garrett, *The Authentic Life of Billy The Kid*, p 120.

203. Brazil was born June 12, 1850, in Rosais, Sao Jorge Island, then as now a Portuguese colony in the Azores Archipelago. The name Brazil is common on the island. He came to the United States about 1865, and to the Fort Sumner area about 1871. He began ranching at a spring that became known subsequently as Brazil Springs, and he soon formed a ranching partnership with Thomas Wilcox.

204. Garrett, *The Authentic Life of Billy The Kid*, pp 121-122.

205. Garrett, *The Authentic Life of Billy The Kid*, p 122.

206. Garrett, *The Authentic Life of Billy The Kid*, p 122; Haley, Interview with East, Sept. 27, 1927, PPHMRC; McCarty, *Maverick Town*; *LV Gazette*, Dec. 27, 1880.

207. Garrett, *The Authentic Life of Billy The Kid*, p 123.

208. Garrett, *The Authentic Life of Billy The Kid*, p 122.

209. "The Life of C. W. Polk," *The Capture of Billy the Kid*, pp 26-27.

210. Garrett, *The Authentic Life of Billy The Kid*, p 123.

211. Garrett, *The Authentic Life of Billy The Kid*, p 125.

212. "The Life of C. W. Polk," *The Capture of Billy the Kid*, p 28.

213. *LV Gazette*, Dec. 27, 1880.

214. "Reminiscences of Louis Bousman," *The Capture of Billy the Kid*, p 53.

215. Haley, Interview with East, Sept. 27, 1927, PPHMRC.

216. Garrett, *The Authentic Life of Billy The Kid*, p 125.

217. Garrett, *The Authentic Life of Billy The Kid*, p 125.

218. *SF New Mexican Review*, Jan. 11, 1884.

219. Haley, Interview with East, Sept. 27, 1927, PPHMRC.

220. "The Life of C. W. Polk," *The Capture of Billy the Kid*, p 31.

221. Garrett, *The Authentic Life of Billy The Kid*, p 127.

222. East says that Beaver Smith was present and protested when Billy gave him – not Polk – the Winchester: "'Billy, I think you ought to let me have that Winchester as you owe me about $40 for ammunition and whiskey....' Billy said, 'Oh, give the old bastard the gun.'" Haley, Interview with East, Sept. 27, 1927, PPHMRC; "The Life of C. W. Polk," *The Capture of Billy the Kid*, p 31.

223. *LV Gazette*, Dec. 27, 1880.

224. David G. Thomas, *Killing Pat Garrett, The Wild West's Most Famous Lawman – Murder of Self-Defense?* (Doc45 Publishing, 2019), pp 207-210.

225. Haley, Interview with East, Sept. 27, 1927, PPHMRC.

226. "The Life of C. W. Polk," *The Capture of Billy the Kid*, p 31.

227. Garrett, *The Authentic Life of Billy The Kid*, pp 127-128; *LV Gazette*, Dec. 27, 1880.

228. *LV Gazette*, Dec. 27, 1880.

229. *LV Gazette*, Dec. 27, 1880, quoted in *Billy the Kid, Las Vegas Newspaper Accounts of His Career, 1880-1881* (Morrison Books, 1958), p 5.

230. *SF New Mexican*, Dec. 28, 1880.

231. *Leadville Daily Herald*, Dec. 29, 1880;

232. *LV Gazette*, Dec. 28, 1880, quoted in *Billy the Kid, Las Vegas Newspaper Accounts of His Career, 1880-1881*, pp 12-14.

233. *LV Daily Optic*, Dec. 27, 1880.

234. *LV Gazette*, Oct. 20, 1880.

235. Garrett, *The Authentic Life of Billy The Kid*, p 129.

236. Albert E. Hyde, "The Old Regime in the Southwest," The Century Illustrated Monthly Magazine, Vol 63, March, 1902, p 699.

237. *LV Gazette*, Dec. 28, 1880.

238. *SF Daily New Mexican*, Dec. 29, 1880; *Arizona Weekly Citizen*, Jan. 1, 1881.

239. J. F. Morley, letter to James East, Nov. 29, 1922, James H. East Papers, 1882-1931, Dolph Briscoe Center, UT.

240. *SF Daily New Mexican*, Dec. 30, 1880.

241. *LV Daily Gazette*, Dec. 30, 1880; *SF Daily New Mexican*, Dec. 30, 1880.

242. *LV Daily Optic*, March 3, 1881.

243. *LV Daily Optic*, Feb. 14, 1881.

244. *SF New Mexican*, March 1, 1881.

245. *SF New Mexican*, May 9, 1881.

246. *SF New Mexican*, Jan. 6, 1881; *LV Gazette*, Feb. 1, 1881.

247. *LV Daily Gazette*, Feb. 13, 1881.

248. *SF New Mexican*, Feb. 12, 1881.

249. *LV Daily Gazette*, Feb. 27, 1881.

250. *SF New Mexican*, Feb. 13, 1881.

251. *LV Gazette*, Feb. 19, 1881.

252. *LV Gazette*, Feb. 19, 1881.

253. *LV Gazette*, Feb. 22, 1881.

254. *LV Gazette*, March 8, 1881.

255. *LV Daily Optic*, Feb. 25, 1881.

256. *LV Daily Optic*, Feb. 25, 1881.

257. *LV Daily Optic*, Feb. 25, 1881.

258. *LV Gazette*, March 8, 1881.

259. *SF New Mexican*, Feb. 27, 1881.

260. *SF New Mexican*, Feb. 27, 1881.

261. *LV Daily Optic*, March 7, 1881.

262. Morley Statement, Territory of New Mexico vs David Rudabaugh, Case No. 128, January, 1882, New Mexico State Records Center and Archives; *LV Daily Optic*, March 18, 1881.

263. Territory of New Mexico vs David Rudabaugh, Case No. 128, January, 1882, New Mexico State Records Center and Archives.

264. Morley Statement, Territory of New Mexico vs David Rudabaugh, Case No. 128, January, 1882, New Mexico State Records Center and Archives.

265. *SF New Mexican*, March 23, 1881.

266. Territory of New Mexico vs David Rudabaugh, NM Territorial Supreme Court

Notes ~ 169

Collection, No. 1982-135, Case No. 128, January, 1882, New Mexico State Records Center and Archives; 1880 Census, Santa Fe, New Mexico, ancestry.com, accessed Aug. 9, 2022.

267. *LV Daily Optic*, April 18, 1881.

268. Territory of New Mexico vs David Rudabaugh, NM Territorial Supreme Court Collection, New Mexico State Records Center and Archives.

269. *SF Daily New Mexican*, April 20, 1881.

270. Territory of New Mexico vs David Rudabaugh, NM Territorial Supreme Court Collection, New Mexico State Records Center and Archives.

271. The jury members were: H. F. Swope, Walter N. Hoyt, Manual Sandoval, A. M. Dettelbach, Benito Pacheco, R. M. Stephens, Jesus Torres, Bisente Garcia, Simon Tilgard, P. A. Bierwell, Juan Luis Gallegos, Facundo Duran. Territory of New Mexico vs David Rudabaugh, NM Territorial Supreme Court Collection, New Mexico State Records Center and Archives; *SF Daily New Mexican*, April 20, 1881.

272. *SF Daily New Mexican*, April 20, 1881.

273. *SF Daily New Mexican*, April 22, 1881.

274. Territory of New Mexico vs David Rudabaugh, Case No. 128, January, 1882, New Mexico State Records Center and Archives.

275. *SF Daily New Mexican*, April 4, 1881.

276. Prince, *The General Laws of New Mexico*, Chapter LVII, Section 23, p 289.

277. *LV Daily Optic*, April 22, 1881.

278. *LV Daily Optic*, April 22, 1881; *LV Gazette*, April 23, 1881.

279. L. Bradford Prince, ed., *The General Laws of New Mexico* (W. C. Little & Co., 1880), LVII, Section 30, p 290.

280. Territory of New Mexico vs David Rudabaugh, Case No. 128, January, 1882, New Mexico State Records Center and Archives.

281. *LV Daily Optic*, Sept. 19, 1881.

282. *LV Daily Optic*, Sept. 19, 1881.

283. *LV Daily Optic*, Sept. 19, 1881.

284. *LV Daily Gazette*, Sept. 20, 1881.

285. *LV Daily Gazette*, Sept. 20, 1881.

286. *LV Daily Optic*, Sept. 19, 1881.

287. *LV Daily Optic*, Sept. 19, 1881.

288. *LV Daily Gazette*, Sept. 20, 1881.

289. *LV Gazette*, Aug. 31, 1881.

290. *LV Daily Gazette*, Dec. 4, 1881.

291. *LV Daily Optic*, Dec. 3, 1881.

292. *LV Daily Gazette*, Dec. 4, 1881.

293. *LV Daily Gazette*, Dec. 4, 1881; *Report of the Secretary of State of the State of Texas for the Year 1881* (State Printing Office, 1882), p20.

294. *LV Daily Gazette*, Dec. 4, 1881.

295. Kelly was under a death sentence for Reardon's killing. His lawyer, Edgar Caypless, filed an appeal, and when that was denied, he waged an indefatigable campaign to get Kelly's death sentence commuted to life in prison. On the very day he was to be hanged, February 18, 1882, U.S. President Arthur commuted Kelly's sentence to life imprisonment. On September 10, 1893, Kelly was released from prison and granted a full pardon by then Territorial Governor Thornton; *SF Weekly New Mexican*, Oct. 18, 1880; Thomas, *The Trial of Billy the Kid*, p 133.

296. *LV Gazette*, Dec. 4, 1881.

297. *Mora County Pioneer* quoted in *LV Gazette*, Dec. 14, 1881.

298. *LV Daily Gazette*, Dec. 29, 1885.

299. *LV Gazette*, Jan. 4, 1873.

300. *LV Daily Gazette*, Dec. 29, 1885.

301. *LV Gazette*, Dec. 6, 1881.

302. *LV Gazette*, Dec. 7, 1881.

303. *LV Gazette*, Dec. 8, 1881; *LV Gazette*, Dec. 10, 1881; *LV Gazette*, Dec. 11, 1881.

304. *Dodge City Times*, April 20, 1882.

305. *LV Gazette*, March 26, 1884.

306. *LV Gazette*, March 26, 1884; *LV Gazette*, March 30, 1884.

307. *Ford County Globe* (Dodge City, KS), May 23, 1882.

308. Ramon F. Adams, *Burs Under the Saddle: A Second Look at Books and Histories of the West* (Univ. of Oklahoma, 1964), p 448.

309. *LV Gazette*, June 16, 1882.

310. *SF New Mexican*, Jan. 14, 1883, transcript in Donald Cline Collection, No.

1959-032, Box 10420, F 101, NM State Records Center and Archives.

311. *Daily Commonwealth* (Topeka KS), April 1, 1884.

312. *Boston Weekly Globe*, May 20, 1884.

313. *Wichita Daily Eagle* (Wichita, KS), Nov. 27, 1884.

314. *St Louis Republican* (St Louis), Aug. 7, 1876.

315. *Southwesterner* (Columbus NM), Aug. 1, 1962. Some sources say he was killed Feb. 19.

316. Full name José Luis Gonzaga Jesús Daniel Terrazas Fuentes. "Terrazas, Luis (1829–1923)," *Encyclopedia of Latin American History and Culture*, encyclopedia.com, accessed Aug. 2, 2022; Fred M. Mazzulla, "Don't Lose Your Head," *1964 Denver Westerners Brand Book* (Johnson Publishing 1965), p 263.

317. *Southwesterner* (Columbus NM), Aug. 1, 1962.

318. *LV Daily Optic*, Feb. 23, 1886.

319. *Southwesterner* (Columbus NM), Aug. 1, 1962.

320. *Southwesterner* (Columbus NM), Aug. 1, 1962; Fred M. Mazzulla, "Don't Lose Your Head," *1964 Denver Westerners Brand Book* (Johnson Publishing 1965), p 263.

321. *Southwesterner* (Columbus NM), Aug. 1, 1962.

322. *LV Daily Optic*, Feb. 23, 1886.

323. *Southwesterner* (Columbus NM), Aug. 1, 1962; Fred M. Mazzulla, "Don't Lose Your Head," *1964 Denver Westerners Brand Book* (Johnson Publishing 1965), p 263.

324. *Southwesterner* (Columbus NM), Aug. 1, 1962; Fred M. Mazzulla, "Don't Lose Your Head," *1964 Denver Westerners Brand Book* (Johnson Publishing 1965), p 263.

325. Daniel D. Arreola, *PostCards From the Sonora Border, Visualizing Place Through a Popular Lens, 1900s-1950s* (Univ. of Arizona Press, 2017), pp 36, 62.

326. *Southwesterner* (Columbus NM), Aug. 1, 1962; Fred M. Mazzulla, "Don't Lose Your Head," *1964 Denver Westerners Brand Book* (Johnson Publishing 1965), p 263.

327. Fred M. Mazzulla, "Headless in Parral," Fred M. Mazzulla collection, Stephen H. Hart Research Center at History Colorado, box 11, f. 714.

328. *Lincoln Star* (Lincoln NE), July 22, 1923.

329. *Arizona Daily Star* (Tucson AZ), Feb. 7, 1926.

330. The most commonly-named suspect for stealing Villa's head is Emil Lewis Holmdahl. Holmdahl was in Parral when the gristly vandalism occurred. He was arrested the next day and his hotel room searched by Mexican police, but no head was found. Holmdahl's guilt may have been confirmed in 1955 when Haldeen Braddy received a letter from a L. M. Shadbolt. Shadbolt claimed in the letter that he had met Holmdahl in El Paso in 1927 and that Holmdahl had shown him Villa's severed head. Holmdahl claimed that he had stolen the head for a buyer in the United States. Haldeen Braddy, *Cock of the Walk, Qui-Qui-Ri-Quí! The Legend of Pancho Villa* (Kennikat Press, 1970); William Douglas Lansford, *Pancho Villa* (Sherbourne Press Inc, 1965).

Appendix B – Billy Wilson's Counterfeiting Case

1. William E. Brockway, alias Col. E. W. Spencer (1822-1920), is considered one of the most accomplished counterfeiters of the late 1800s. He was arrested October 24, 1880, for printing the fake $100 notes that Billy Wilson unknowingly passed. On November 25, 1880, he made a deal with the government and was given his complete freedom in exchange for turning states evidence and surrendering his counterfeiting plates to the Treasury Department. He was later arrested and jailed for other counterfeiting offenses. *New York Times*, Oct. 24, 1880.

2. Donald R. Lavash, *Wilson and the Kid*, (Creative Publishing Company, 1990), pp 52-54, 98-100; Philip J. Rasch, *Trailing Billy the Kid* (University of Wyoming, 1995), p58.

3. Lavash, *Wilson and the Kid*, p 99-100. In his sworn testimony at Wilson's trial, Roberts said that Wilson told him the money was bad when he gave him the bill. *SF New Mexican*, Feb. 12, 1882.

4. Azariah F. Wild, Report, Oct. 3, 1880, Leon C. Metz Papers, C. L. Sonnichsen Special Collections, UTEP.

5. *SF New Mexican*, Feb. 12, 1882.

6. *SF New Mexican*, Sept. 15, 1882.

7. *SF New Mexican Review*, Jan. 11, 1884.

8. Philip J. Rasch, *Trailing Billy the Kid* (University of Wyoming, 1995), p 67.

9. Rasch, *Trailing Billy the Kid*, p 68.

10. Lewis A. Ketring Papers, Archives and Special Collections, NMSU.

11. Lewis A. Ketring Papers, Archives and Special Collections, NMSU.

12. Lewis A Ketring Papers, Archives and Special Collections, NMSU.

Appendix D – Cast of Characters

1. 1880 Census Santa Fe, New Mexico, June 9, 1880, ancestry.com, accessed Aug 5, 2022; *LV Daily Gazette*, March 4, 1880; *LV Daily Gazette*, Nov. 13, 1880.

2. *SF Daily New Mexican*, Nov. 13, 1880; *LV Daily Gazette*, Feb. 26, 1881; *LV Daily Optic*, Dec. 4, 1896.

3. *Golden Era*, May 5, 1881.

4. Garrett, *The Authentic Life of Billy The Kid*, p 125; "The Life of C. W. Polk," *The Capture of Billy the Kid*, p 28.

5. Rich Eastwood, *Nuestras Madres, A Story of Lincoln County New Mexico* (Creative Space Independent Publishing, no date), pp 89, 92.

6. Geoffrey L. Gomes,, "Manuel Brazil, A Portuguese Pioneer in New Mexico and Texas," Outlaw Gazette, Jan., 1995.

7. *Daily Out-Look* (Parsons, KS), Sept. 29, 1877; *Lexington Intelligencer* (Lexington Missouri), Nov. 27, 1910.

8. 1880 Census, White Oaks, New Mexico, Jun 23-26, 1880, ancestry.com, accessed Aug. 15, 2022; Dan L. Thrapp, *Encyclopedia of Frontier Biography A-F* (Univ. of Nebraska Press, 1988), pp 227-228; Garrett, *The Authentic Life of Billy the Kid*, p 84.

9. *SF Weekly New Mexican*, Jan. 31, 1880; *The National Police Gazette*, Feb. 7, 1880, p 3; *Galveston Daily News*, Feb. 20, 1880.

10. Garrett, *The Authentic Life of Billy the Kid*, pp 88-89.

11. *LV Gazette*, July 18, 1881, quoted in The *Daily Gazette* (Colorado Springs CO), July 22, 1881; *LV Daily Optic*, Feb. 9, 1887.

12. Mary Jo Walker, *The F. Stanley Story* (The Lightning Tree, 1985), pp 21-23.

13. Walker, *The F. Stanley Story*, p 30.

14. Walker, *The F. Stanley Story*, p 30.

15. 1870 Census, Platte,Missouri, July 27, 1870 and 1880 Census, Las Vegas, New Mexico, June 16, 1880, ancestry.com, accessed July 5, 2022; *LV Daily Gazette*, April 10, 1880.

16. 1880 Census, Las Vegas, New Mexico, June 16, 1880, ancestry.com, accessed Aug. 1, 2022; Garrett, *The Authentic Life of Billy the Kid*, p 88.

17. 1870 Census Eagle Township, Agle, Illinois, ancestry.com, access Aug. 5, 2022; *Dodge City Times* (KS), June 29, 1878.

18. *Rolla Herald* (Rolla MS), Oct. 31, 1878; *Saline County Journal* (Salina KS), Oct. 31, 1878.

19. *SF Weekly New Mexican*, Feb. 14, 1880.

20. *Douglas Daily Dispatch*, May 14, 1930.

21. 1880 Census Lincoln, New Mexico, June 9, 1880, ancestry.com, accessed Aug 12, 2022.

22. *LV Gazette*, May 17, 1881.

23. *LV Daily Gazette*, May 11, 1881; *LV Gazette*, May 17, 1881.

24. *SF New Mexican Review*, Jan.31, 1884; *LV Daily Optic*, Jan. 23, 1884.

25. *SF New Mexican*, Dec. 20, 1881; Richardson, "Whiskey Jim Greathouse," Real West Year Book, Spring 1974, pp 58-63.

26. *LV Daily Optic*, Sept. 25, 1884.

27. *LV Daily-Optic*, Sept. 25, 1884.

28. David G. Thomas, *Killing Pat Garrett, the Wild West's Most Famous Lawman – Murder or Self-Defense?* (Doc45 Publishing, 2019).

29. *Great Bend Weekly* (Great Bend, KS), Feb. 2, 1878; *Edwards County Leader* (Kinsley, KS), Feb. 3, 1879.

30. Philip J. Rasch, *Warriors of Lincoln County* (Univ. of Wyoming, 1998), pp 88-97.

31. *SF New Mexican*, Dec. 20, 1881.

32. *Dodge City Times*, March 23, 1878.

33. *Sumner County Press* (Wellington KS), June 27, 1878.

34. *Chicago Tribune*, Jan. 24, 1880; *SF Weekly New Mexican*, Feb. 14, 1880.

35. *Lincoln County Leader*, Jan. 10, 1885.

36. *Lincoln County Leader*, June 2, 1883; *Rio Grande Republican*, Feb. 9, 1884; Roberta Key Haldane, "William and John Hudgens: Double Trouble from Louisina," Southern New Mexico Historical Review, Dona Ana Historical Society, Jan. 2008, Vol. XV, pp 25-37.

37. *LV Daily Gazette*, March 5, 1880; *Dodge City Globe*, March 9, 1880; *LV Daily Gazette*, March 5, 1880.

38. 1940 Census Nogales, Arizona, undated, ancestry.com, accessed July 5, 2022; *Southwesterner* (Columbus NM), Aug. 1, 1962.

39. *Southwesterner* (Columbus NM), Aug. 1, 1962.

40. https://www.findagrave.com/memorial/103836524/albert-william-lohn, accessed July 5, 2022.

41. *LV Daily Gazette*, Feb. 27, 1881.

42. *Clovis News-Journal*, December 22, 1940; *SF New Mexican*, Feb. 27, 1890.

43. *Reno Gazette Journal*, Jan. 30, 1981.

44. Cline, *Antrim and Billy*, p 49.

45. Cline, *Antrim and Billy*, p 59.

46. *Mining Life*, Sept. 19, 1874.

47. *Arizona Republic* (Phoenix), Dec. 30, 1951.

48. Thomas, *The Trial of Billy the Kid*, (Doc45 Publishing, 2020), pp 172-178.

49. *LV Daily Gazette*, March 3, 1880.

50. *SF New Mexican*, Aug. 5, 1880.

51. *LV Gazette*, Jan. 23, 1880; LV Gazette, Jan. 16, 1881.

52. *LV Daily Gazette*, Aug. 6, 1880; LV Daily Gazette, Aug. 11, 1880.

53. *LV Daily Gazette*, Nov. 13, 1880.

54. Territory of New Mexico vs David Rudabaugh, Case No. 128, January, 1882, New Mexico State Records Center and Archives.

55. *LV Daily Gazette*, Aug. 11, 1880; *SF New Mexican*, Aug. 5, 1880; *LV Daily Gazette*, Aug. 6, 1880.

56. Thomas, *The Trial of Billy the Kid*, (Doc45 Publishing, 2020).

57. Don Cline, "Tom Pickett, Friend of Billy the Kid, True West," July, 1997, pp 40-49; *SF New Mexican Review*, Jan. 11, 1884; *Winslow Mail*, May 18, 1934.

58. Helen Haines, *History of New Mexico, 1530-1890* (New York Historical Publishing, Co, 1891), p 391.

59. *The National Police Gazette*, Feb. 7, 1880, p 3

60. *Dodge City Times* (KS), June 29, 1878.

61. *Atchison Daily Champion* (Atchison KS), Nov. 1, 1878.

62. *Weekly News Democrat* (Emporia KS), March 21, 1879.

63. 1880 Census, Las Vegas, New Mexico, June 9 and 10, ancestry, accessed July 5, 2022; *An Illustrated History of New Mexico* (The Lewis Publishing Co., 1895), pp 343-344; *LV Daily Optic*, July 21, 1903.

64. *SF Weekly New Mexican*, Feb. 14, 1880; *LV Daily Gazette*, March 5, 1880.

65. 1870 Census, Sanford, New York, Aug. 10, 1870, ancestry.com, accessed July 10, 2022; *LV Daily Gazette*, April 10, 1880.

66. *The Raton Range*, May 13, 1935.

67. *LV Daily Gazette*, Aug. 6, 1880; *LV Daily Gazette*, Aug. 11, 1880.

68. *LV Daily Gazette*, Aug. 6, 1880; *LV Daily Gazette*, Aug. 11, 1880; *Dallas Daily Herald*, May 11, 1881.

69. 1880 Census, Las Vegas, New Mexico, June 16 and 26, ancestry.com, accessed Aug. 1, 2022.

70. 1880 Census, Las Vegas, New Mexico, June 16 and 26, ancestry.com, accessed Aug. 1, 2022; *LV Daily Optic*, Feb. 25, 1881; *LV Daily Gazette*, March 5, 1880; Grand Jury True Bill, Territory of New Mexico vs John J. Webb, County of San Miguel, March 4, 1880, Case 1024, New Mexico State Records Center and Archives.

71. *Dodge City Times* (Dodge KS), April 20, 1882.

72. *Great Bend Weekly* (Great Bend KS), Feb. 2, 1878; *Hays City Sentinel* (Hays City, KS), Feb. 8, 1878; *Kinsley Graphic*, June 22, 1878, quoted in Kansas Historical Quarterly (Kansas Historical Society, Autumn, 1961); *Dodge City Globe*, Jan. 1, 1878.

73. *LV Daily Gazette*, Feb. 10, 1880.

74. *LV Daily Gazette*, Feb. 10, 1880.

75. 1910 Census, New Orleans, Louisiana, ancestry.com, accessed July 20, 2022; Nolan, *The Lincoln County War*, Revised Edition (Sunstone Press, 2009), pp 664-665.

76. Donald R. Lavash, *Wilson and the Kid*, (Creative Publishing Company, 1990); Rasch, *Trailing Billy the Kid*, pp 67-68.

Index

A

Allen, James 136-138, 147, 155-156,
Allen, John J. 2, 26-27, 30-33, 35, 67-71, 73, 75-78, 80-81, 83-85, 101, 105, 111-119, 121-124, 137, 139-140, 158, 143
Anderson, David L. (see Billy Wilson)
Anderson, George 11
Antrim, William H. 154
Apodaca, Desidero 33, 147, 155
Arámbula, José Doroteo Arango (see Pancho Villa)

B

Bacheco, Benito 99
Barney, J. W. 21, 23
Bell, James W. 36, 41, 140, 143
Bell, Jason B. 36, 138
Bennet, A. B. 48
Bennett, W. H. 24
Biersuth, R. A. 99
Bill, Curly (William Brocius) 91
Billy the Kid (William Henry McCarty) 3, 27-28, 35-39, 40-44, 46-47, 49-50, 53, 55-57, 60, 86, 95, 129-131, 137-140, 143-146, 149-150, 154, 156, 158, 160
Bishop, Tommy 88, 141
Blackington, C. F. 45
Blake, Fletcher A. 36
Blanchard, Judge 9, 21
Bodenhemn, James 89
Bostwick, John F., Judge 57
Bousman, Philip "The Animal" 46
Bowdre, Charles 47-48, 50-51, 138, 143, 156
Bowdre, Manuela Herrera 47-48, 144
Brady, William 3, 86, 140
Brazel, Jesse Wayne 150
Brazil, Manuel Silvestre 49-51, 145
Breeden, Marshal A. 61-64, 66-68, 70, 72-73, 75, 77, 99, 100-102, 104-106, 109, 111-113, 119-120, 123
Breeden, William 61, 70, 72, 99, 108, 115, 118
Brickley, William 20-21, 23-24, 136, 153
Bristol, Warren Henry, Judge 86
Brockway, William E. 127
Brown, Hoodoo (Hyman Graham Neill) 15-16, 20-21, 23-26, 35, 59, 137, 141, 145-146, 149, 151, 153, 157

C

Cale, James E. 46, 141, 150
Carlyle, James 36, 39, 40-44, 138, 145, 151
Carrolton, Dick 91
Carson, Joe W. 15-16, 19, 25, 32, 57, 136-137, 140, 145-146, 149, 151, 153, 155-159
Carson, Mrs. 25, 137, 146
Catron, Thomas B. 27
Cauldwell, J. C. 66-70, 81, 84, 111-115, 137, 111
Caypless, Edgar A. 60
Chambers, Lon 46
Chisum, John S. 44, 138, 146
Clancy, R. W. 125
Cleveland, Grover, President, 129
Clum, R. H. 90-91
Cody, William "Buffalo Bill" 91
Colborn, Edward P. 91, 141
Collum, Virgil 150
Cook, Joseph "Joe" 36-38, 138, 146
Corona, Maximiano 143
Cosgrove, Cornelius "Con" 28-29, 146
Cosgrove, Michael "Mike" 28, 35, 47, 55, 146-147
Crocchiola, Stanley Francis Louis (see F. Stanley)

D

Davidson, George 30, 32-33, 35, 137-138, 147, 155-156, 158
Davis, George 30, 33, 35-36, 138, 147, 155-156
Dawson, Jim (see Jim Dorsey)
Dedrick, Dan 36-37, 138, 147, 159
Dedrick, Mose 36-37
Dedrick, Sam 37, 39
Deering, Mollie 155
Dement, Dan 7-10, 13, 135, 136, 147, 149-151, 157, 159
Deolatere, Mrs. 28-29, 55, 137, 155
Dettelbach, A. M. 99
Detwiler, 24
Dolan, James J. 127, 129-131, 133, 137
Dominguez, Juan Antonio 16
Dominguez, Pablo 29
Dorsey, Jim "Loco" (Jim Dawson) 16-17, 19, 26, 136, 146, 149, 157
Duffy, Thomas 86-88, 141
Duran, Benedito 17, 63, 76, 80, 84
Duran, Fasmundo 99

E

Eaker, John P. 36, 41
Earp, Morgan 1, 5
Earp, Virgil 2, 91
Earp, Wyatt 1, 5, 91, 141
East, James 46-47, 50-51, 53, 55, 149
Easton, David 127
Echeverría, Luis 97

Edwards, Joseph Samuel Marion "Bob" 36-38, 140, 146, 148-149
Ellison, Samuel 56
Emory, Thomas "Poker Tom" 46, 53, 55
Evans, Frank 58, 83

F

Farris, John 153
Felgard, G. 99
Finley, Jim 44-45, 150
Fiske, Eugene A. 57
Foor, Charlie 48
Fountain, Albert J. 3, 150
Fowler, Harry A. "Joe or Joel" 44-46, 141, 149, 151
Fowler, Josie, 150
Frank Kearney, 141, 88
Fulkeson, Susan C. 149
Fuller, John 10, 13
Furlong, James 68

G

Gallegos, Juan Luis 99
Garcia, Bisente 99
Garcia, Dionicio 17
Garcia, Iginio 47
Gardner, 9
Garrett, Apolinaria Gutierrez 53, 136, 154
Garrett, Patrick Floyd Jarvis 3, 34-37, 39, 41, 43-44, 46-47, 49-51, 53, 55, 61, 89, 127, 129-130, 132-133, 136-141, 143, 145-147, 149-151, 154-156, 158-160
Gatlin, Bob 129
Gerhardt, John 35, 47, 53, 139
Goodlett, William L. 21, 23-24
Goodman, William 88-89, 141
Gott, Thomas 7-13, 135-136, 147, 150-151, 157, 159
Graham, Jesse 33
Greathouse, James "Whisky Jim" 39, 40-41, 43-45, 138, 141, 145, 150-151
Green, J. D. 7-13, 135-136, 147, 150-151, 157, 159
Green, John W. (see Frank Stewart)
Grzelachowski, Alexander 36, 53, 138-139

H

Hall, Lee 46, 50-51
Harmon, Judson 129, 131
Harrison, Hank 37
Harrison, William 151
Heard, Josie Nellie 32, 158
Henry, Tom "Dutch" 16-17, 136, 146, 151, 156-157, 159
Henry, Tom "Dutch" (Thomas Jefferson House) 17, 19, 26, 149
Herrera, José Fernando 143
Herrera, Manuela 143
Hill, Tom 135

Holliday, John Henry "Doc" 1, 5, 135
House, Thomas Jefferson (See Tom Henry)
Hoyh, Walter N. 99
Hudgens, John 36-37, 153
Hudgens, William Harrison 36, 38-39, 95-96, 138, 146, 151-153
Hurley, John 43, 138

I

Ike, Jim 44-45, 150

J

Jilson, Arthur 91
Johnson, L. 57
Jones, Charles 24
José, 2-3, 94, 141, 153

K

Kay, Jim 44-45, 150,
Kelliher, Michael 20-21, 23-25, 30, 35, 57, 59, 136, 143, 145, 153, 159
Kelly, Edward M. "Choctaw" 57, 88-89, 137, 140-141
Kersey, William 13, 136, 147, 149, 157
Kimbrell, George 35, 137
Kincaid, 8-9
King, Sam 159
Kozlowski, Martin 107
Kuch, Fred W. 39-40, 43, 44, 138

L

Lafeu, 11
Lamper, William J. 37
Lea, J. C. 146
Leonard, Ira Edwin 41, 127
Light, Evander 13, 136, 149, 157
Locke, F. D. 57
Lohn, Albert W. 2-3, 8, 92-94, 96, 142, 153-154
Longworth, Thomas "Pinto Tom" 36, 39, 138, 145
Lovell, Harry 10
Lowe, Anthony W. (see James West)
Lowe, Mary E. 19

M

Mackenzie, Ranald S. 44, 151
Madrid, Juana María 136, 154
Mares, Florenzo 86-87
Martin, Joseph "Joe" 15-16, 32, 57, 136-137, 140, 145, 153, 155, 158
Martin, María Juliana 143
Martin, Robert Levi 133
Martinez, Romulo 57
María, Juana 48
Mason, Barney 46, 48, 51, 53, 55, 136, 138-139, 146, 153, 160

Masterson, William Barclay 'Bat' 10-12, 25, 81, 96, 135-136, 150-151, 159
Mather, David Allen "Mysterious Dave" 15-16, 21, 23, 26, 146, 149, 151, 156, 159
Maxwell, Pete Menard 48,140
Mazzulla, Fred Milo 94, 96, 142, 153-154
McCarty, Catherine 154
McCause, Robert 10, 135
McDonald, Jonathon. 26
McGaw, William 94
McKinney, Thomas "Kip" 37, 140, 149
McSween, Alexander A. 136
Monjeau, Louis N. 152
Montaño, José 127, 131-132, 137
Moore, Bill 46
Morehead, James 30-31, 34, 136-137, 143, 155
Morley, J. F. 28-29, 55-56, 61, 140, 155
Morrison, Judge 30, 33, 35
Morton, William "Buck" 135
Mullen, William 15-16, 30, 32-34, 56, 71-73, 75, 78, 83, 85, 110, 115-121, 137-139, 155-156, 158
Murphy, 86-88
Murray, John 30, 32-33, 138, 155-156

N

Neil, George C. 36
Neill, Hyman Graham (see Hoodoo Brown)
Neis, Anthony "Tony" 57, 90, 140-141

O

O'Folliard, Thomas "Tom" 47-49, 139, 146, 156
Ochoa, Pablo Montes de 30, 33
Olinger, Robert Ameredith Maxwell "Bob" 140
Otero, Miguel Antonio 33-34

P

Patton, John 24
Perea, Alejandro 52
Pickett, Thomas "Tom" 3, 15, 28, 47, 51, 55-56, 67, 75, 81, 111-112, 114, 121, 127, 129, 137, 139, 146, 156
Polk, Calvin Warnell "Cal" 46, 50
Portillo, José 143
Posey, George G. 61, 62, 64-65, 69-71, 75-76, 99, 102-103, 106-110, 113-118, 120-123, 156
Prince, LeBaron Bradford, Judge 59-60-61, 77-78, 81, 85-86, 99, 125, 132-133
Pruitt, Wilis 48

Q

Quillan, Thomas 141, 88-89

R

Radenbaugh, A. (Anna) 5-6, 135
Radenbaugh, D. (David) See David Rudabaugh
Radenbaugh, I. (Ida) 5, 135

Radenbaugh, J. (John) 5, 135
Radenbaugh, Z. (Zeth or Zadek) 5, 135
Ramirez, José 64-65, 71, 76, 80, 84, 108, 105, 109-110
Randall, William "Tom" 16, 146, 156
Reardon, John 89, 137
Redenbaugh, James 5
Redman, James S. "Jim" (S. J. Woodland) 36, 39, 138
Reed, Lon 51-52
Reymond, Numa 129
Ritch, William G., Governor 57, 139
Roarke, Michael "Big Mike" 7, 8-11, 13, 15, 135-136, 140, 147, 149, 150-151, 157, 159
Roberts, William "Buckshot"140, 143
Roberts, William 127, 137
Robinson, A. A. 56
Rodenbaugh, James W. 5, 135
Roibal, José 156
Roibal, Juan 47
Romero, Benigno 157
Romero, Hilario 27, 33, 56, 60-62, 80, 84, 99, 136-137, 140, 100-103, 108, 157
Romero, Quinterio 21
Ross, Edmund G., Governor 154
Rudabaugh, David 1-3, 5, 7-8, 10-13, 15-16, 19-20, 26-28, 32, 36-39, 41, 44, 47, 49, 51, 55-57, 59-65, 67-73, 75-81, 83-91-97, 99, 101, 105, 107, 111-123, 125, 127, 135-141, 143, 145-147, 149-151, 153-159
Rudolph, Charles Frederick 47, 51
Ryan, Pat 8

S

Salsberry, James 143
Sandoval, Manuel 99
Schafer, George 154
Schroeder, S. 88, 141
Schunderberger, John "Dutchy" 16, 20-21, 24, 137, 157, 159
Scott, J. A. 90
Sebben, 24
Sena, Ignacio 27
Sheldon, Lionel A., Governor 89
Sherman, John 160
Slaughter, John 149
Smith, Henry A. "Beaver" 47-48
Spencer, Lon 43-44, 138
Stanley, F. (Stanley Francis Louis Crocchiola), 1, 3, 5, 96, 142, 146-147, 157
Starbird, Charles Nelson W. 32, 137, 147, 158
Steck, Joe 39, 40, 43, 138
Stephens, R. M. 99
Stern, Isidor 89
Stewart, Frank (John W. Green) 46, 51, 53, 55, 61, 139-140, 158
Stokes, Joseph 15-16, 56, 120, 122, 137, 139, 155, 158

Stokes, William 15-16, 32, 56, 120, 122, 137, 139, 155, 158
Stone, J. J. 14
Stone, William 36
Swape, H. F. 99

T

Tafoya, Jesus Maria 62-65, 76-77, 80, 84, 103-108, 123, 158
Terrazas, Luis 94
Thatcher, 13
Thornton, Charles 26
Thornton, William T., Governor 129-131, 133, 141
Tilghman, William 11, 135, 11
Tillman, William 13, 136, 147, 157
Torres, Jesus 99
Truelove, 155
Tunstall, John Henry 33, 135

V

Valdez, Antonio Lino 2, 17, 26-27, 55, 59-61, 64, 68, 70-71, 73, 76-77, 80-81, 83, 85, 99, 137, 101, 108-109, 123-124, 139-140, 143, 155-156, 158
Valdez, José 47, 156
Valentine, Ed "Red" 129, 160
Villa, Pancho (Arámbula, José Doroteo Arango) 97, 141

W

Wallace, Lewis "Lew," Governor 40-41, 43, 57-59, 89, 136, 138-139, 159
Webb, John Joshua 2, 11, 15-16, 20-21-26, 30, 33-36, 57-59, 63, 67, 71-72, 75-78, 83-85, 87-91, 111, 113, 116-118, 120-123, 135, 137-141, 143, 145, 153, 155-156, 158-159
West, Edgar J. 7-10, 12-13, 20, 135, 147, 150-151, 157, 159
West, Edgar J.'s father, 12
West, James (Anthony W. Lowe) 16-17, 19, 26, 136, 146
West, William H. 39, 127, 129, 137
Weston, Fred 28-29, 55, 137, 155
Whitelaw, W. M. 60
Wilcox, Thomas 53, 145
Wild, Azariah F. 44, 127, 137-139, 154, 160
Willard, 24
Williams, Robert "Tenderfoot Bob" 46
Wilson, Billy (David L Anderson) 3, 28, 36-37, 39, 41, 44, 47, 49, 51, 55-57, 60, 87, 127-129, 130-133, 137-139, 141, 145-146, 149, 154, 156, 158, 160
Wilson, George 47
Wilson, H. S. 86, 88
Woodland, S. J. (see James S. Redman)

Z

Zimmerman, 8

Doc45 Publications

Killing Pat Garrett, The Wild West's Most Famous Lawman - Murder or Self-Defense?

Pat Garrett, the Wild West's most famous lawman – the man who killed Billy the Kid – was himself killed on leap day, February 29, 1908, on a barren stretch of road between his Home Ranch and Las Cruces, New Mexico.

- Who killed him?
- Was it murder?
- Was it self-defense?

No biographer of Garrett has been able to answer these questions. All have expressed opinions. None have presented evidence that would stand up in a court of law. Here, for the first time, drawing on newly discovered information, is the definitive answer to the Wild West's most famous unsolved killing.

Supplementing the text are 102 images, including six of Garrett and his family which have never been published before. It has been 50 years since a new photo of Garrett was published, and no photos of his children have ever been published.

Garrett's life has been extensively researched. Yet, the author was able to uncover an enormous amount of new information. He had access to over 80 letters that Garrett wrote to his wife. He discovered a multitude of new documents and details concerning Garrett's killing, the events surrounding it, and the personal life of the man who was placed on trial for killing Garrett.

- The true actions of "Deacon Jim" Miller, a professional killer, who was in Las Cruces the day Garrett was killed.
- The place on the now abandoned old road to Las Cruces where Garrett was killed.
- The coroner's jury report on Garrett's death, lost for over 100 years.
- Garrett's original burial location.
- The sworn courtroom testimony of the only witness to Garrett's killing.
- The policeman who provided the decisive evidence in the trial of the man accused of murdering Garrett.
- The location of Garrett's Rock House and Home Ranches.
- New family details: Garrett had a four-month-old daughter the day he killed Billy the Kid. She died tragically at 15. Another daughter was blinded by a well-intended eye treatment; a son was paralyzed by childhood polio; and Pat Garrett, Jr., named after his father, lost his right leg to amputation at age 12.

Garrett's life was a remarkable adventure. He met two United States presidents: President William McKinley, Jr. and President Theodore Roosevelt. President Roosevelt he met five times, three times in the White House. He brought the law to hardened gunmen. He oversaw hangings. His national fame was so extensive the day he died that newspapers from the East to the West Coast only had to write "Pat Garrett" for readers to know to whom they were referring.

2020 Will Rogers Medallion Award Finalist for Excellence in Western Media
2020 Independent Press Award Distinguished Favorite, Historical Biography
2019 Best Book Awards Finalist, United States History
2019 Best Indie Book Notable 100 Award Winner.

Doc45 Publications

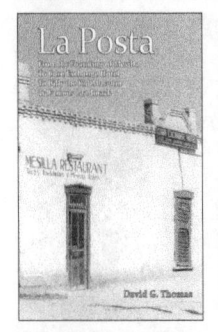

La Posta – From the Founding of Mesilla, to Corn Exchange Hotel, to Billy the Kid Museum, to Famous Landmark, David G. Thomas, paperback, 118 pages, 59 photos, e-book available.

"For someone who grew up in the area of Mesilla, it's nice to have a well-researched book about the area – and the giant photographs don't hurt either.... And the thing I was most excited to see is a photo of the hotel registry where the name of "William Bonney" is scrawled on the page.... There is some debate as to whether or not Billy the Kid really signed the book, which the author goes into, but what would Billy the Kid history be without a little controversy?" –Billy the Kid Outlaw Gang Newsletter, Winter, 2013.

Giovanni Maria de Agostini, Wonder of The Century – The Astonishing World Traveler Who Was A Hermit, David G. Thomas, paperback, 208 pages, 59 photos, 19 maps, e-book available.

"David G. Thomas has finally pulled back the veil of obscurity that long shrouded one of the most enduring mysteries in New Mexico's long history to reveal the true story of the Hermit, Giovanni Maria de Agostini. ...Thomas has once again proven himself a master history detective. Of particular interest is the information about the Hermit's life in Brazil, which closely parallels his remarkable experience in New Mexico, and required extensive research in Portuguese sources. Thomas's efforts make it possible to understand this deeply religious man." – Rick Hendricks, New Mexico State Historian

Screen With A Voice - A History of Moving Pictures in Las Cruces, New Mexico, David G. Thomas, paperback, 194 pages, 102 photos, e-book available.

The first projected moving pictures were shown in Las Cruces 110 years ago. Who exhibited those movies? What movies were shown? Since projected moving pictures were invented in 1896, why did it take ten years for the first movie exhibition to reach Las Cruces? Who opened the first theater in town? Where was it located? These questions began the history of moving pictures in Las Cruces, and they are answered in this book. But so are the events and stories that follow.

There have been 21 movie theaters in Las Cruces – all but three or four are forgotten. They are unremembered no longer. And one, especially, the Airdome Theater which opened in 1914, deserves to be known by all movie historians – it was an automobile drive-in theater, the invention of the concept, two decades before movie history declares the drive-in was invented.

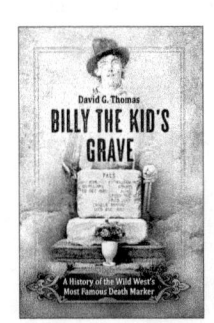

Billy the Kid's Grave – A History of the Wild West's Most Famous Death Marker, David G. Thomas, paperback, 154 pages, 65 photos.

"Quien es?"

The answer to this incautious question – "Who is it?" – was a bullet to the heart.

That bullet – fired by Lincoln County Sheriff Patrick F. Garrett from a .40-44 caliber single action Colt pistol – ended the life of Billy the Kid, real name William Henry McCarty.

But death – ordinarily so final – only fueled the public's fascination with Billy the Kid. What events led to Billy's killing? Was it inevitable? Was a woman involved? If so, who was she? Why has Billy's gravestone become the most famous – and most visited – Western death marker? Is Billy really buried in his grave? Is the grave in the right location?

These questions – and many others – are answered in this book.

Doc45 Publications

The Stolen Pinkerton Reports of the Colonel Albert J. Fountain Murder Investigation, David G. Thomas, editor, paperback, 194 pages, 28 photos.

The abduction and apparent murder of Colonel Albert J. and Henry Fountain on February 1, 1896, shocked and outraged the citizens of New Mexico. It was not the killing of Colonel Fountain, a Union Civil War veteran and a prominent New Mexico attorney, which roused the physical disgust of the citizenry - after all, it was not unknown for distinguished men to be killed. It was the cold-blooded murder of his eight-year-old son which provoked the public outcry and revulsion.

The evidence indicated that although Colonel Albert J. Fountain was killed during the ambush, his son was taken alive, and only killed the next day.

The public was left without answers to the questions:

- Who ambushed and killed Colonel Fountain?
- Who was willing to kill his young son in cold-blood after holding him captive for 24 hours?

The case was never solved. Two men were eventually tried for and acquitted of the crime.

The case file for the crime contains almost no information. There are no trial transcripts or witness testimonies. The only reports that exist today of the investigation of the case are these Pinkerton Reports, which were commissioned by the Territorial Governor, and then stolen from his office four months after the murders. These Reports, now recovered, are published here.

These Reports are important historical documents, not only for what they reveal about the Fountain murders, but also as a fascinating window into how the most famous professional detective agency in the United States in the 1890s - the Pinkerton Detective Agency - went about investigating a murder, at a time when scientific forensic evidence was virtually non-existent.

Paperback, 196 Pages, ISBN 978-0-9828709-6-9

Torpedo Squadron Four – A Cockpit View of World War II, Gerald W. Thomas, paperback, 280 pages, 209 photos, e-book available.

"This book contains more first-person accounts than I have seen in several years. ...we can feel the emotion... tempered by the daily losses that characterized this final stage of the war in the Pacific. All in all, one of the best books on the Pacific War I have seen lately." – Naval Aviation News, Fall 2011.

When New Mexico Was Young, Harry H. Bailey, paperback, 186 pages, 10 photos.

The autobiography of Harry H. Bailey (1868-1954) Mr. Bailey was a pioneer New Mexican who took a major role in the development of the Mesilla Valley. In 1900, he built the "Natatorium," the first public swimming pool in El Paso, Texas. Three years later, he built the Angelus Hotel. In 1906, part of the Angelus Hotel building became the Crawford Theatre. After leaving El Paso and returning to New Mexico, he helped develop Radium Springs as a health resort and built the hotel and baths there.

His autobiography contains many stories about the early-day Mesilla Valley settlers who were his companions. Among the individuals he knew were Sheriff Pat Garrett, Colonel Albert J. Fountain, Attorney Albert B. Fall, Oliver Milton Lee, Sheriff Mariano Barela, Demetrio Chavez, Humbolt Casad, and George Griggs. He was a close friend of Western author Eugene Manlove Rhodes. For almost a year, he lived in the courthouse building in Mesilla where Billy the Kid was sentenced to hang.

Paperback, 186 Pages, ISBN 978-1-952580-0-17

Doc45 Publications

The Trial of Billy the Kid

This book is about Billy the Kid's trial for murder, and the events leading to that trial. The result of Billy's trial sealed his fate. And yet Billy's trial is the least written about, and until this book, the least known event of Billy's adult life.

Prior biographies have provided extensive — and fascinating — details on Billy's life, but they supply only a few paragraphs on Billy's trial. Just the bare facts: time, place, names, result.

Billy's trial the most important event in Billy's life. You may respond that his death is more important — it is in anyone's life! That is true, in an existential sense, but the events that lead to one's death at a particular place and time, the cause of one's death, override the importance of one's actual death. Those events are determinative. Without those events, one does not die then and there. If Billy had escaped death on July 14, 1881, and went on to live out more of his life, that escape and not his trial would probably be the most important event of Billy's life.

The information presented here has been unknown until now. This book makes it possible to answer these previously unanswerable questions:

- What were the governing Territorial laws?
- What were the charges against Billy?
- Was there a trial transcript and what happened to it?
- What kind of defense did Billy present?
- Did Billy testify in his own defense?
- Did Billy have witnesses standing for him?
- Who testified against him for the prosecution?
- What was the jury like?
- What action by the trial judge virtually guaranteed his conviction?
- What legal grounds did he have to appeal his verdict?
- Was the trial fair?

Supplementing the text are 132 photos, including many photos never published before.

Available in both paperback and hardcover.

Paperback, 254 Pages, ISBN 978-1-952580024
Hardcover, 254 Pages, ISBN 978-1-952580048

2022 Will Rogers Medallion Award Finalist for Excellence in Western Media
2022 Pasajero Del Camino Real Award Winner.

Doc45 Publications

The Frank W. Angel Report on the Death of John H. Tunstall

"In the matter of the cause and circumstances of the death of John H. Tunstall...."

So begins the single most important contemporary document recounting the origins of the Lincoln County War. That document is the "Report of Special Agent Frank Warner Angel on the Death of John Henry Tunstall," known today to historians as the "Angel Report."

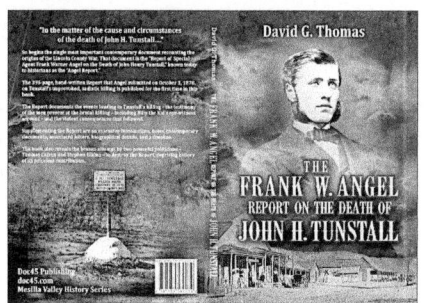

The 395-page, hand-written Report that Angel submitted on October 3, 1878, on Tunstall's unprovoked, sadistic murder is published for the first time in this book.

The Report documents the events leading to Tunstall's murder – the testimony of the men present at the brutal killing – including Billy the Kid's eye-witness account – and the violent consequences that followed.

It includes sworn accounts by William "Frank" Baker, Robert W. Beckwith, Henry N. Brown, James J. Dolan, William Dowlin, Pantaleón Gallegos, Godfrey Gauss, Florencio Gonzales, John Hurley, Jacob B. Mathews, Alexander A. McSween, John Middleton, Lawrence G. Murphy, John Wallace Olinger, Juan B. Patron, George W. Peppin, David P. Shield, Robert A. Widenmann, and 18 others.

Supplementing the Report are an extensive introduction, notes, contemporary documents, associated letters, biographical details, and a timeline.

The book also reveals the brazen attempt by two powerful politicians – Thomas Catron and Stephen Elkins – to destroy the Report, depriving history of its priceless contribution.

Forty three images, many never published before.

Available in both paperback and hardcover.

Paperback, 254 Pages, ISBN 978-1-952580079
Hardcover, 254 pages, ISBN 978-1-952580055

Doc45 Publications

Water in a Thirsty Land
by Ruth R. Ealy
David G. Thomas, Editor

"Water in a Thirsty Land" is a chronicle of Dr. Taylor Filmore Ealy's 1874 to 1881 sojourn as a medical missionary in Indian Territory (Oklahoma) and New Mexico Territory, compiled by his daughter Ruth R. Ealy.

Dr. Ealy's first assignment was Fort Arbuckle, Chickasaw Reservation, Oklahoma Territory. His second was Lincoln, New Mexico Territory. His final assignment was Zuni Pueblo, New Mexico.

Dr. Ealy's faithful accounts of his struggles and challenges at these — at the time — exotic locations make for fascinating reading. His daily records of eye-witnessed events in Lincoln are of exceptional historical value. He arrived in Lincoln on February 19, 1878, the day after John Henry Tunstall was murdered. The unprovoked, sadistic murder of Tunstall kicked off the bloody Lincoln County War. Dr. Ealy was present at Tunstall's funeral, the killing of Lincoln County Sheriff Brady and Deputy Hindman, and the five-day shootout that ended with the firing of Alexander McSween's home, and the heinous slaughtering of McSween and four others as they frantically fled the blazing conflagration.

There are many details about the Lincoln County War in Dr. Ealy's account not recorded in other sources. Here are examples:

- Tunstall's funeral was held at 3 pm. His bullet-holed, bloody clothes were lying on the dirty ground in McSween's back yard during the service.
- The book provides many details about Tunstall's store: *"The floors were good ones and the windows were large."* One room was *"12 feet high, 18 feet long, and 18 feet wide, with a huge window and a door with a large glass in it."* That room was *"large enough to hold three hundred people."* The store lot was five acres in size and fully fenced.
- When the McSween house was fired during that 5-day shootout, one of Elizabeth Shield's children stepped in the coal oil used to ignite the fire.
- Among the items in McSween's house destroyed by the fire were an elegant piano, a Brussels carpet, costly furniture, rich curtains, and fine paintings.
- After Taylor testified at the Dudley Court of Inquiry, he was warned by anonymous note that he would be killed before he got back to his home in Zuni (a "coffin note").

From Lincoln, Dr. Ealy went to Zuni Pueblo. His keen observations are one of the primary, early sources of halcyon life in Zuni in 1878.

The Editor has added an extensive introduction, contextual notes, footnotes, appendices, and an index to the text of this extremely rare book.

Paperback, 208 Pages, ISBN 978-1952580-10-9
Hardcover, 208 Pages, ISBN 978-1952580-11-6

Doc45 Publications

Incident at Ple Tonan, An Imperial Japanese War Crime and the Fate of U.S. Navy Airmen in French Indochina

This book began 33 years ago, in early 1990, with a question posed to the author by his father. The author's father was just completing his memoir of his World War II military experiences and he was greatly troubled by not knowing the fate of two of his fellow fliers in his USS ESSEX based air squadron, Torpedo Four (VT-4). The two men whose fate still haunted the author's father 45 years after the fact were shot down in an air raid on Japanese-occupied French Indochina.

The answer to this question would have remained hidden but for an Imperial Japanese war crimes trial. In this book, you will find the events, investigations, statements, related documents, and stories of the men that led to that trial – and the riveting testimony of the trial itself.

Not surprisingly, uncovering the stories of the two missing squadron members' fates also uncovered the stories of other men. Many of these others, as disclosed in this book, paid the ultimate price – some for heroism, and some for acts later judged war crimes.

A courtroom criminal trial is unlike any other human institution. It is combat without physical weapons. And as in combat, the stakes can be as high as death.

Here you will find the statements and interrogations that led to the belief that multiple war crimes were committed at Ple Tonan in French Indochina on April 27, 1945. You will find the pre-trial statements of witnesses. You will find the charges presented against the defendants. You will find the daily transcripts of the 13 day trial. You will find the closing arguments and sentencing. You will find the decisions of the appellate authority.

You will find the pleas for clemency submitted for each defendant. You will find their last letters home to their families. You will find the details of their punishments.

A courtroom criminal trial can reveal a defendant's inner being in a way no other human institution can. A defendant that appears on the stand must try to explain and justify the actions for which the person is being tried. And that person must do so in an adversarial setting in which every assertion is open to challenge and refutation.

The men who appeared in the trial presented in this book all appeared on the stand in their own defense. This book is no cold reporting. With their trial testimony, each defendant got to explain and justify his actions. This book, based on the way in which it is presented, puts you in the position of, first, an investigator trying to determine whether a war crime was committed, and, second, a jury member who must decide the guilt or innocence of a defendant after hearing the evidence against the defendant.

59 images, many never published before.

Paperback, 320 Pages, ISBN 978-1-952580-14-7